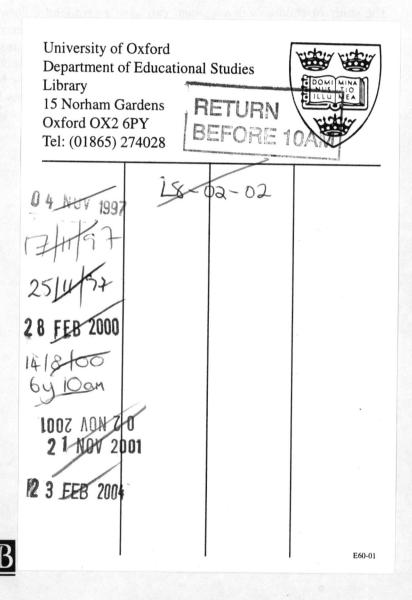

Understanding Children's Worlds
General Editor Judy Dunn

The study of children's development can have a profound influence on how children are brought up, cared for, and educated. The central aim of this series is to encourage developmental psychologists to set out the findings and the implications of their research for others – teachers, doctors, social workers, students – who are responsible for caring for and teaching children and their families. It aims not to offer simple prescriptive advice to other professionals, but to make important innovative research accessible to them.

How Children Think and Learn
David Wood

Children and Emotion
Paul L. Harris

Making Decisions about Children
Psychological Questions and Answers
H. Rudolph Schaffer

Bullying at School
What We Know and What We Can Do
Dan Olweus

Children and Political Violence
Ed Cairns

Children Doing Mathematics
Terezinha Nunes and Peter Bryant

Children Doing Mathematics

*Terezinha Nunes
and Peter Bryant*

BLACKWELL
Publishers

The right of Terezinha Nunes and Peter Bryant to be identified as authors of this work has been asserted in accordance with the Copyright, Designs and Patents Act 1988.

First published 1996

2 4 6 8 10 9 7 5 3 1

Blackwell Publishers Ltd.
108 Cowley Road
Oxford OX4 1JF
UK

Blackwell Publishers Inc.
238 Main Street
Cambridge, Massachusetts 02142,
USA

British Library Cataloguing in Publication Data

A CIP catalogue record for this book is available from the British Library.

Library of Congress Catalogue-in-Publication Data
Nunes, Terezinha.
    Children doing mathematics / Terezinha Nunes and Peter Bryant.
        p.   cm. – (Understanding children's worlds)
    Includes bibliographical references and index.
    ISBN 0–631–18471–6 (hbk.:alk. paper). – ISBN 0–631–18472–4
(pbk.:alk. paper)
    1. Mathematics – Study and teaching (Elementary) – Psychological
aspects.   2. Cognition in children.   I. Bryant, Peter, 1937–
II. Title.   III. Series.
QA135.5.N855 1996
372.7'01'9–dc20   95–42700
                                                                    CIP

Typeset in 11 on 13 pt Sabon
by CentraCet, Linton, Cambridgeshire
Printed in Great Britain by
T.J. Press Ltd., Padstow, Cornwall

This book is printed on acid-free paper

Contents

List of Tables   ix
List of Figures   x
Series Editor's Preface   xiii
Preface   xv
Acknowledgements   xii

1 **Explaining Numeracy**   1

  1 To be numerate, children need to be logical   4
  2 To be numerate, children need to learn conventional
    systems   11
  3 To be numerate, children need to use their mathematical
    thinking meaningfully and appropriately in situations   17
  4 Conclusions   19
  5 Plan of the book   20

2 **Beginning with Counting**   21

  1 Learning to count properly   22
  2 Children's use of counting   30
    2.1 Producing sets with equal numbers   30
    2.2 Comparing two sets   35
    2.3 Inferring number from that of an equivalent set   41
  3 Conclusions   42

3 **Understanding Numeration Systems**   44

  1 Invariants of numeration systems with a base: the
    concepts of unit and additive composition   47

1.1 Counting and mastering the properties of the
numeration system   48
1.2 Addition and mastering the properties of the
numeration system   52
1.3 Linguistic cues and children's understanding of
additive composition   60
2 Understanding written numbers   66
3 Conclusions   74

4 **Measurement Systems**   76

1 Logic and measurement   78
2 Units of measurement   79
2.1 Making inferences about relative size   80
2.2 What does a ruler look like?   86
2.3 Measuring with a broken ruler   91
3 Conclusions   94

5 **Mathematics under Different Names**   96

1 Are you good at maths?   97
2 Mathematics as a socially defined activity   100
2.1 When the new mathematics was brought to an old
culture   101
3 Street mathematics and school mathematics   104
4 Practical and theoretical maths and the ownership of
knowledge   108
5 Conclusions   112

6 **Giving Meaning to Addition and Subtraction**   114

1 Situations, representations and invariants in the
concepts of addition and subtraction   115
2 What might numbers refer to in addition and subtraction
situations? A detailed analysis of number meanings   122
2.1 Numbers as static measures   124
2.2 Numbers that measure transformations   124
2.3 Numbers that measure static relations   129
3 Conclusions   140

7   **The Progress to Multiplication and Division**   142

1 Multiplication, division, and new number meanings   144
1.1 The one-to-many correspondence situations   145
1.2 Situations that involve relationships between
variables – that is, co-variation   146
1.3 Situations that involve sharing and successive splits 149
1.4 Overview   153
2 Children's understanding of multiplicative situations   154
2.1 One-to-many correspondence situations   154
2.2 Co-variation of variables and the understanding of
functions   168
3 Systems of signs and the development of multiplicative
reasoning   191
3.1 The effect of systems of signs on understanding
multiplicative problems   192
3.2 Getting to grips with the discontinuity between
addition and multiplication in a computer
environment   195
4 Conclusions   199

8   **Understanding Rational Numbers**   202

1 Understanding division and simple *n*-splits   206
1.1 Dividing sets   206
1.2 Dividing continuous quantities   208
1.3 Inverting splits   210
1.4 The beginnings of quantification   212
2 Coordinating extensive and intensive aspects of rational
number: the understanding of equivalences in successive
splits   221
3 Connecting rational numbers with their representation:
knowledge of rational numbers developed in and out of
school   227
4 Conclusions   232

9   **Conclusions**   234

1 Starting with the beginning   236
2 Logical invariants   240

3 Using logic in different situations: the acquisition of new
number meanings   243
4 Logic and conventional systems   244
5 Children's concepts of mathematics   246
6 Final comments   248

References   249
Index   261

Tables

3.1 Learning to count in Japanese   45

3.2 Inter-correlations within and across the two groups of tasks, soluble and not-soluble by counting ones   57

3.3 Number of children passing/failing additive composition and addition with an invisible addend   58

6.1 Children's rate of success in different kinds of addition and subtraction tasks   129

7.1 The onion soup problem   174

Figures

1.1   A problem that can be solved by measurement   12

2.1   The percentage of children who succeeded in constructing sets with the correct number   34

3.1   Children's success in reading and writing numbers   56

3.2   Examples of one-to-one correspondence between numbers and words in children's written numbers   70

3.3   Different types of error in writing numbers   72

3.4   Writing numbers: percentages of concatenations and refusals   73

4.1   Children's responses to items where either different or the same units were used   84

4.2   Children's responses to items with centimetres and inches and same/different number of units   85

4.3   Numbers written on a ruler by 5- and 6-year-old children   88

4.4   Children's correct responses to working out line length with a ruler   93

5.1   Darts board showing the doubles and trebles rings   97

5.2   Suggested best ways to finish a game of darts   99

6.1   Children's rate of success in different kinds of addition and subtraction tasks   120

6.2   Children's responses for problems in different conditions with very small and small numbers   123

6.3   The material used in Hudson's children and balloons task   132

6.4   Children's responses in different types of comparison problems   136

6.5   Children's responses in pre- and post-tests for
      comparison problems   139
7.1   One-to-many correspondence   147
7.2   Number meanings in co-variation situations   149
7.3   Successive splits and divisions   152
7.4   Sharing 'singles' and 'doubles' to two recipients   159
7.5   Children's success with one-to-many correspondence
      and Cartesian product problems   165
7.6   Exercise of enlarging a house predesigned using a
      LOGO procedure   197
8.1   Sample items from the equivalence questions   203
8.2   Examples of the items used to study children's
      understanding of fractions   204
8.3   Correct responses in the partitive and quotative tasks   214
8.4   The material used to test the importance of the half-
      boundary in children's judgements about proportions   217
8.5   The material used to study part–part and part–whole
      judgements   219
8.6   The material used to study division of continuous
      quantity   223

Series Editor's Preface

This book is about how children think about mathematical problems, and the significance of the development of this reasoning for their everyday lives. Its focus is, then, much broader than the issue of how children cope with mathematics in the classroom. Rather, the themes explored include both *how children learn mathematics and what mathematics learning can do for their thinking*. Terezinha Nunes and Peter Bryant present us with a framework for organizing and understanding children's growing mathematical knowledge and its development, an account that has three overall themes. One is that children's understanding of mathematics changes time and time again in the early years of childhood, in a generative manner. Nunes and Bryant alert us to the very early starting points of children's grasp of concepts, such as addition, multiplication and division, and take us step by step through the progressive elaboration of children's understanding. They argue convincingly that if teachers and parents are aware of these early starting points they can most effectively support the growth of knowledge. A second theme is that the development of mathematical knowledge and understanding involves three aspects: learning about logical invariants, learning to master and use conventional mathematical systems, and learning to see the mathematical demands of different situations. Each of these is vividly illustrated with examples from the authors' own studies and those of others.

The third theme is that mathematics is an activity that is socially defined. How children approach mathematical problems depends crucially on how they define and respond to the social situation in which these are presented. It is a theme that is powerfully illustrated by the authors' own work showing that Brazilian children who were street-vendors solved arithmetical problems on the streets with good sense and logical agility, yet failed the same logical problems when these were presented as maths problems in school. The challenge, Nunes and Bryant argue, is then to help children form a view of mathematics that will enable the children to bring their understanding from everyday life into the classroom. This challenge and the argument of the book illustrate particularly powerfully the theme of the series *Understanding Children's Worlds* in which the book appears – the importance of linking what psychologists have discovered about children's development with the everyday experiences of children within their own worlds.

JUDY DUNN

Preface

We wish to begin with a brief statement about the purpose and the contents of our book. Our aim is to give an account of children's mathematical reasoning. We want to show how children think about mathematical problems and what mathematics means to them.

It is our view that children set about building their mathematical knowledge with remarkable ingenuity and persistence. Sometimes these qualities do not filter through at all well to the classroom, and sometimes they are not recognized by the children's teachers or parents or even by the children themselves. But the solutions which even quite young children offer for various mathematical problems are hardly ever vacuous, even when they are quite wrong; and they usually contain elements of genuine and intelligent thought, which deserve to be respected and ought to be encouraged.

People must pay attention, therefore, not just to the ultimate goal of children getting mathematical concepts completely right, but also to the many steps that they take along the road to the full understanding of different aspects of mathematics; and one must remember that even when they are not far down that road they have perfectly respectable solutions for some problems, though others defeat them for a while. Even when they are only just beginning to add or to multiply or divide, there are some kinds of addition or multiplication or division problems which they readily understand and solve without any difficulty at all. We believe – and this is a belief that will permeate our book – that teachers and parents who are trying to help their pupils and their children should always bear these starting-points in mind and build on them. They should think of the starting-points as well as the end-points, and that means respecting what children can do and can understand as well as thinking about what they cannot do and do not understand.

We will show that the ways in which children reason about mathematics change time and again and continue to change right through childhood. Why is this so? The answer is that children have a lot to learn. In this book we shall emphasize three facets of mathematical concepts which, we think, lie at the heart of all mathematical learning. Children have to pick up a great deal of knowledge about logical relations (a controversial claim on our part, but one which we shall document profusely); they must master, and then put to good effect, a whole set of conventional mathematical systems; and they have to learn that certain mathematical relations which they originally regard as tied to very specific situations have much wider uses. On top of all this, they have to coordinate these three quite different kinds of learning. It is a packed agenda, and one that we adults urgently need to know about and to understand.

We hope that our book will help teachers and parents as well as psychologists by telling them something new about children's mathematical ideas. But we should like, at the same time, to warn everyone that this is not an educational book in the traditional sense. We are not going to write much about educational methods and we have few direct recommendations to make for new ways of teaching mathematics. We are psychologists who are interested in children's reasoning, and that is the subject of this book. But we do think that what we write will be useful to parents and teachers, because we believe that, when it comes to mathematics, they should begin where we ourselves are beginning – with children's own mathematical ideas.

Our theory about these ideas is based on a programme of research that we have been carrying out with colleagues and students over the last five years or so, and we shall spend an appreciable amount of the book describing this work. But the ideas and research of many other people have of course contributed enormously to our work, and we will write about research on mathematical development generally. Generally but not exhaustively: we will stick to aspects of mathematics which are relevant to our own theory, and even with these we will not describe all the research because we want to keep our account a fairly simple one.

So, our book is an attempt to provide a clear theory about

children's mathematical reasoning. We hope that it succeeds and we hope that it helps.

T. Nunes
P. Bryant

Acknowledgements

It took us about ten years in all to plan and eventually to write this book, and the prospect of writing it prompted us to do quite a lot of new research. We found that we needed answers to some of the questions that we wanted to present to our readers. During this time we have had the good fortune to be able to rely on the generous support of the institutions that we worked in and of our colleagues and friends.

The Federal University of Pernambuco in Brazil, the Institute of Education in the University of London, the Open University and the University of Oxford between them, and in rather different ways, provided the insititutional framework that we needed: it was essential to us and it worked.

We enjoyed working with Luisa Morgado of the University of Coimbra in Portugal, John Mason of the Open University, Paul Light of the University of Southampton, Mauricio Lima, George Falcao and Alina Spinillo of the University of Pernmabuco, and Olivier Frydman of the University of Mons in Belgium. All of them collaborated in one or more of the main studies on which the argument that we present in this book is based. We are very grateful to them and also to the many graduate students who worked with us in Brazil and in the UK and whose energy and lively ideas about children's mathematics always encouraged us.

Ita Raz collected some interesting data for us; John Elliott of the National University of Singapore provided us with many acute comments on the manuscript: Anna Brett and Fay Luteijn helped us greatly with the proofs.

The financial support for various parts of our work on mathematics came from Brazilian and British sources. In Brazil we were helped by CNPQ, by CAPES (SPEC) and by the Fundacao Vitae; the ESRC, the Nuffield Foundation and the British Council supported our research in the UK.

The patient and good-humoured teachers and children in the schools where we did our research were astonishingly generous to us. Our best hope is that our work will help them as much as they helped us.

1
Explaining Numeracy

There are many ways to begin a book on children's mathematical knowledge, but for us the first and the most important point to make is that children need to learn about mathematics in order to understand the world around them. Mathematics is a school subject but, as far as children are concerned, it is also an important part of their everyday lives: without mathematics they will be ill at ease not only at school but in a great many of their everyday activities. When they share valuables with their friends, when they plan to spend their pocket money, when they argue about speed and distance, when they travel and have to deal in different currencies, and when eventually they have to begin to understand the world of money, of buying and selling, mortgages and insurance policies, they need mathematical skills. These are activities that are not usually seen as 'mathematics', but to carry them out one has to respect mathematical principles and often to use the mathematical techniques learned at school or at home.

This need for mathematical knowledge has always been there, but the details of the picture change with time. In some ways mathematics is easier now for children as well as for adults. Calculators and computers have taken away a lot of the drudgery which previous generations found so unattractive. Yet at the same time the significance of mathematical skills and the demand for them have both changed quite strikingly. In many societies people express considerable worries about the mathematical skills of the population at large, and when they do so their thoughts usually turn to schoolchildren and their teachers. What can be done, the question usually becomes, to make sure that in future children leave school with much more in the way of mathematical ability and knowledge than they do at the moment?

The question is a fair one, but it immediately leads us to another set of concerns. If we want to teach mathematics to children in a way that makes *all* children numerate in today's (and even tomorrow's) world, we have to know much more about *how children learn mathematics* and *what mathematics learning can do for their thinking*. As societies change, the concept of what it is to be numerate and literate also changes.

Concepts of literacy have clearly changed with time. A definition of literacy offered by Gray (1956), which served as a basis for that later proposed by UNESCO for use in surveys of literacy, has this flexibility of the concept built in from the outset: 'A person is functionally literate when he has acquired the knowledge and skills in reading and writing which enable him to engage effectively in all those activities in which literacy is normally assumed in his culture or group' (p. 19). This functional criterion implies flexible specific concepts of literacy both across countries and over time. Resnick and Resnick (1977) point out such a historical change for the United States, for example, where they verified that the percentage of illiteracy did not change much over time up to the Second World War but the criteria for illiteracy did.

The same may be said with respect to being numerate. It may have been enough to master arithmetic and percentages (the five operations, as they were called) to be considered numerate 100 years ago, but requirements for numeracy in today's world seem rather different (see, for example, Willis, 1990). It is important for practically everyone to be able to do more than simple calculations in order, for example, to read critically a newspaper clipping that contains even very simple numerical information, and our school systems may not be succeeding in preparing even our teachers to do that. An interesting example can be quoted from Streefland (1990a). A test was given to 312 future primary school teachers in the Netherlands and they were asked to comment on a newspaper clipping, which we present here in an abbreviated form (1990a, p. 36).

Since it requires some arithmetic, let us restrict ourselves to The Netherlands. The country has about 14 million inhabitants, versus the 3 billions of the US, that is two hundred times as much. The area of The Netherlands is, say, 40,000 square metres, versus the 33,000 square kilometres of the US, that is a thousand times as much. This weighed against each other yields for The Netherlands a population coefficient one fifth of that of the US.

'Distressing' is how Streefland described the results of this test. The issue here is, of course, that the starting-point – the size given for the Netherlands – is absurd. How could the Netherlands be the same size as a square 200 metres by 200 metres? The figure for the United States is just as implausible. Yet Streefland found that only 18 of the 312 future teachers discussed this newspaper clipping appropriately by pointing out its gross inaccuracies right from the start. About one third of the future teachers made no comments at all about the newspaper clipping.

Being numerate, we see, is not the same as knowing how to calculate, even if employers may sometimes think so (see, for example, Foyster, 1990). It is being able to think about and discuss numerical and spatial relations using the conventions (that is, numeration and measurement systems, terminology such as area and volume, tools such as calculators and protractors etc.) of one's own culture. To quote from the definition proposed in the Cockcroft Report, which has been a significant landmark in redefining the goals of mathematics education (Cockcroft, 1982, para. 34):

> We would wish the word 'numerate' to imply the possession of two attributes. The first is an 'at-homeness' with numbers and an ability to make use of mathematical skills which enable an individual to cope with the practical mathematical demands of his everyday life. The second is an ability to have some appreciation and understanding of information which is presented in mathematical terms, for instance in graphs, charts or tables or by references to percentage increase or decrease. Taken together, these imply that a numerate person should be expected to be able to appreciate and understand some of the ways in which mathematics can be used as a means of communication.

This view clearly reaches beyond learning the arithmetic operations (although it obviously does not exclude this learning) and, consequently, we see, does not fit at all well with any 'back to basics' movement in the teaching of numerary.

Numerary is involved in different learning contexts in school but mathematical concepts are not always clearly identified as such because they are presented as ideas, not as numbers. Chapman et al. (1990) have pointed out that concepts used in geography and social studies, for example, involve mathematical ideas but people may remain unaware of this. 'Fertility' and 'mortality', 'inflation' and 'acceleration of growth', for example, are expressions which involve the idea of ratio, a basic mathematical concept which may go unrecognised as such in the context of other disciplines. These authors claim that every teacher in the primary or the secondary school should see himself/herself as involved in the teaching of numerary, in the same way that it has already been recognized that children are taught literacy in the context of all the school subjects.

Numeracy is also involved in everyday life and on the job (see, for example, Nunes, Schliemann, and Carraher, 1993; Harris, 1990) but often also goes unrecognized as mathematical knowledge. In these contexts, Foyster (1990) argues, computation is often a much less important aspect of mathematical knowledge than more advanced concepts.

How then do we teach children to be numerate in the full sense of the word? How do we create school environments in which they not only learn about numbers and arithmetic but also think in mathematical ways? When it comes to *teaching mathematics*, it is clear then that we must consider both how children learn about numbers and arithmetic operations and also how they come to think mathematically in ways that are progressively more complex.

It is the main purpose of this book to present our own synthesis of how children's thinking becomes progressively more complex, although we will not go beyond the first four to six years of children's learning of mathematics. We will consider different aspects of becoming numerate – that is, of thinking with mathematical concepts – but will concentrate in this book only on number concepts. The exclusion of other aspects of mathematical knowledge, like geometry, is necessary in order to accomplish greater coherence across the topics and paint a more integrated picture of development.

Some of the aspects discussed in this work have been widely acknowledged and are not at all controversial but others in our view need more attention than they have had up till now. The framework we use below is inspired by the work of the French psychologist, Gerard Vergnaud, and his definition of mathematical concepts.

1   To Be Numerate, Children Need to Be Logical

To say that mathematics depends on logic does not make it in any way unique among school subjects. The same is true of physics and biology, of history and geography. No one can get far in any of these subjects by violating the rules of logic. But the relation between logic and mathematics is particularly strong and clear.

It is easy to see that even the most basic mathematical tasks can only be properly understood and solved by someone who explicitly recognizes logical rules, and this is true from the start. Let us take the simple example of learning to count. In order to understand what they are doing when they count a set of objects, children have to obey many logical principles. For one thing they must understand the ordinal nature of number – that numbers are arranged in an ascending order of magnitude. This means more than just remembering the order of the number words: it means understanding that this order obeys the rule that if 3 is more than 2 and 2 more than 1, then because of that 3 is necessarily more than 1. It is surely quite a reasonable suggestion that children who do not understand this system of relations (A > B, B > C, thus A > C) will have a terribly incomplete understanding of number even if they say the number words in a perfect sequence.

But this is not all. Children also have to understand the significance of what they are doing whenever they count a set of objects (the number of buses going by the window, the number of stairs to climb to the bathroom), and this too involves a set of rules firmly based on logic. Each object must be counted once and only once and, although the number words must be kept in a fixed order, the order in which the objects are counted (left to right, right to left, middle outwards) makes no difference at all. The final number (called the cardinal number) is the number of objects in the set. This is the number which relates this set of objects to other sets. If there are six objects in the set then it has the same number as any other set with six objects: whatever the physical arrangement of these sets they are the same in number as the set which the child has just counted.

These simple and basic rules about ordinal and cardinal numbers are logical rules *par excellence*, and it is easy to see that every child has to understand all of them in order to grasp what counting means. Logic is essential even for counting, which is usually the first conventional aspect of numerary conquered by children. The point about the central importance of logic in children's mathematics is, of course, an extremely familiar one and we owe this insight mainly to Jean Piaget (see, for example, Piaget, 1965). The relation between logic and mathematics had been studied by mathematicians and logicians for a long time, but Piaget first drew the world's attention to the possibility that the basic logic needed for mathematics might actually cause young children considerable difficulty.

Piaget has become a controversial figure. Many of his specific claims about children's logic and their mathematics are hotly disputed at the moment, to the extent that some authors even argue that his theories should be discarded. We will be dealing with some of these controversies later, but for the moment we would like to make the point that there are really two parts to his theory about the links between children's logic and children's mathematics, one of which is controversial and the other not at all.

The controversial aspect of his theory is that he suggested that it takes children a long time to rely on the same logical principles as we do. Even by the time that they begin school and for several years after, they usually do not grasp some of the most basic logical principles that are needed to learn mathematics. So, according to him, teachers often try to teach children mathematical concepts for which they are quite unprepared. Whether it is true or not that young schoolchildren only grasp some aspects of logic is a question on which there is still very great disagreement.

But there is no disagreement at all, so far as we know, about the other aspect of Piaget's theory, that *children must grasp certain logical principles in order to understand mathematics*. This goes almost without saying, and the only alterations that other researchers have tried to make recently have taken the form of additions to Piaget's list of logical requirements. Now let us see what these requirements are.

The most famous item on this list of logico-mathematical principles was conservation. To understand conservation is to know that the number of a set of objects can only be changed by addition or subtraction: all other changes are irrelevant. If you take six oranges out of a bag and spread them out on a table there are still six oranges there, even though their spatial arrangement has changed drastically.

We are dealing here with an essential form of understanding. One only has to imagine the difficulties of a child who does not understand conservation to see that. Suppose that such a child counts a bowl of oranges and decides that there are six there, and then someone spreads the oranges out into an extended row. If the child thinks that there are more oranges than before, it follows, and this was one of Piaget's main concerns about counting, that the child does not know what the word 'six' really means. The child can count all right in the sense that the right numbers are produced in the right order, but the child will not understand the significance of these numbers until he/she has grasped conservation.

Furthermore children who have not grasped conservation will have no inkling at all of cardinal number. If they think that a change in the spatial arrangement of a set of objects is tantamount to a change in its quantity, they cannot know that one set of six objects is the same in number as any other set of six. Their ideas of number are too capricious for that: alter the appearance of one set of six and, to children who do not understand conservation, it immediately becomes a different quantity from other sets of six. They will not be able to see how important the number of each set is.

All the controversy mentioned earlier concerns the age when children do grasp this principle. This is an empirical question: people try to find out what children understand about the conservation of number by giving them various tasks, and there is a great deal of argument about the meaning of children's reactions to these various tasks. For the moment we will avoid these arguments, and simply stick to Piaget's first point which is that logic here is the strongest criterion in defining children's understanding of number. Children must understand conservation in order to know what they are doing when they count. Otherwise they will simply be parroting the number words. Here is a clear example of a logical requirement. We have already pointed out that one cannot simply rely on transmitting a mathematical convention devised by the culture – which in this case is the numeration system. We also have to be sure that the child has grasped the logical principles on which the system is based, that is, the meanings that come with the conventions.

Another example which plays a crucial part in Piaget's system involves logical inferences. All quantities (number, size, weight, temperature) can be arranged in a certain order from smaller to larger. In order to understand the nature of this order one has to grasp a basic logical rule which is called transitivity. If one quantity, A, is greater than another, B, and B itself is greater than a third quantity, C, then it follows that A must also be greater than C. It is easy to see that children who do not grasp this rule will have an incomplete idea of the relations between different numbers. They may be able to remember their order. They may indeed know something about the relationship between neighbouring numbers – that 3 is more than 2 and 2 more than 1 – but they will not be able to work out anything about the connection between numbers which they cannot directly compare. Their knowledge of ordinal number will be completely fragmented.

Again, for the moment, we are concerned with only one claim here. This is Piaget's idea that the understanding of transitivity is a requirement for true understanding of number. Children simply will not understand the significance of the order of numbers, however well they can reproduce this order when they count, unless they understand this basic logical rule. This argument seems indisputable to us. There is little point in being able to count unless the child knows about transitivity.

Of course this claim too raises the empirical question of the age at which children are able to make transitive inferences, and here again there is much disagreement, which we shall come to later. But no one disputes the essential need for children to be able to make and to understand transitive inferences.

In a sense we have not gone far along the road of children's mathematical learning with these two examples. For the two logical rules mentioned here are requirements for the most basic mathematical activity of all, which is counting. But Piaget's list of logical requirements goes further than this: he argues that all mathematical procedures from the simplest to the most complex make their own logical demands. Addition and subtraction provide another example.

We have already seen that children have to understand which changes will alter a quantity and which will not. But it is not enough just to know that adding increases and subtracting decreases a quantity. Children must also understand that these changes have inverse effects: one cancels the other out: so $5 + 2 - 2 = 5$. There are several reasons why the understanding of this rule is important, and one of them concerns what is called the additive composition of number. It is one thing to find out that adding 2 oranges to a group of 5 means that there are now 7 of them, but it is quite another to be able to work out from that, that if one were to take 2 oranges away from the 7, 5 oranges would be left. A child who cannot do so may not realize that the group of 7 oranges can be said to consist of a subgroup of 5 and a subgroup of 2 oranges (or 4 and 3, or 6 and 1). Nor would that child be likely to understand that $4 + 3$ must be the same as $3 + 4$.

Not to understand these things would mean not grasping the logic of addition and subtraction. Children may learn how to carry out simple additions and subtractions with great ease but, according to Piaget, they cannot understand what they are doing unless they also grasp the relations between addition and subtraction and the additive composition of number.

The principles that we have discussed so far are very basic ones, but logic is at least as important with more complex mathematical reasoning. One example is any problem about relationships between two different types of quantities. For example, two children may help out a neighbour in the garden and receive a certain amount of money to share between them. If they worked for the same length of time, sharing will be a simple problem. Fair sharing means giving each of them the same amount. However, they may have worked for different lengths of time. Perhaps one put in three and the other five hours of work. Fair sharing now means giving different amounts of money to the children, but keeping the constant relationship between time worked and pay. If they were given a total of £24, one will get £9 and the other £15. In spite of the difference in the total amount, this way of sharing is fair. In fact, each one is getting £3 per hour.

The actual arithmetic operations involved in solving the second sharing problem, where the amounts received are different but the pay for the number of hours of work is fair, are not significantly different from those involved in sharing equally. All that you need to do is to multiply and divide. However, Piaget suggested, the reasoning called for in sharing proportionally to time is more complex. It involves two variables, time and money, and keeping the relationship between them constant. Piaget suggested that establishing a relation between two amounts is a complex intellectual operation: to use this relation in order to solve a problem is in his terms to perform a *second order operation*, an operation on an intellectual operation. Second order operations, according to him, are only mastered relatively late in the life of a school youngster, around the age of 11–13 years.

As with other parts of Piagetian theory, some aspects of this analysis are controversial and others are not. The contribution of this theory in pointing out the difficulty of proportion problems in contrast to simple multiplication and division problems is widely recognized. However, there is controversy about when children come to understand proportionality, how they get there, and what this acquisition means. Piaget attributed much importance to the development of what he called the scheme of proportionality. He saw this development as an indication that the youngsters could now think in terms of mathematical functions, proportionality being only one possible functional relationship between two variables. This aspect of his theory has received relatively little attention but certainly is of significance if we want to think of what kinds of reasoning a numerate person should be capable of. Confrey (1994) has recently made the argument that many of the difficulties people face in understanding biological phenomena, for example, where relationships are often not linear, have to do with the fact that very little time is spent in school in teaching children about other sorts of relationships between variables.

The logical principles that we have described so far are only some of those that we will be discussing in the rest of this book. These particular examples simply make the point that there are logical requirements that must be respected in thinking mathematically. We will refer to such logical requirements as *invariants*, following Piaget (1965) and Gerard Vergnaud (1985), a French psychologist who studied with Piaget and who has made significant contributions to the study of children's understanding of mathematical concepts.

The term *invariants* covers more than the logical principles studied by Piaget. It also includes relationships which are introduced in mathematics by conventions but, once introduced, must be kept constant. A very simple example can be given at this point, although many more will be discussed throughout the book. This example concerns measurement systems. Units of measurement are arbitrary. There is no particular reason why a centimetre should be the size it is or why it should be equal to 10 millimetres and 1/100 metre. In fact, other measurement systems exist with other units (for example, inches and feet) and with different relationships between the units. However, once these relationships are specified, then they must be kept constant – that is, invariant.

The curious thing about mathematical thinking is that it involves a mixture of a general logic which seems to appeal to anyone anywhere, irrespective of language spoken or culture, and another form of logic which is equally appealing once you have reached some agreement about the starting-point – that is, once you have agreed on certain initial assumptions (axioms, conventions, primitives of the system). Once the conventions have been established, for example, about the relationships between different units in a measurement system, these particular relations become logically compelling to the users. They find it difficult to think of measuring in different ways. It is to this second aspect of mathematical concepts that we turn now.

2 To Be Numerate, Children Need to Learn Conventional Systems

So compelling is the argument about logic that it is often quite hard to remember that learning mathematics may involve more than merely mastering logical rules. But one only has to think of measurement, long division, fractions, trigonometry and graphs to see that a child who understands all the logical rules needed for these mathematical procedures still has to be taught conventions and also some procedures. The reason for this is simple.

Mathematical techniques obey the rules of logic, but they go further than this. There is also a set of conventions, which were devised by our ancestors and have been transmitted from generation to generation in the culture that the child happens to be in. These conventions are needed for the mastery of mathematical techniques. They provide ways of representing concepts that allow people to think and talk about them. For example, the numeration systems used in different cultures are conventional ways of referring to and thinking about the number of objects in a set. The logical rules that regulate the counting activity, such as the need to keep the order of counting words constant, are embedded in the logic of the specific number system that the child learns. But the way in which the conventional system was set up in order to make it easier for the users to respect the principle of fixed order may vary from one numeration system to another.

In English we use a base-ten system of counting. The number labels are reorganized when we reach ten, ten tens and so on. Up to nine, we count only units. From the number ten on, we count tens and units. This is not so apparent in the number words from eleven to nineteen but becomes more apparent in the number words from twenty on. When we say 'twenty-one', this word indicates two tens and one unit. From the number one hundred (that is, ten tens) on, we count hundreds, tens, and units. The phrase 'three hundred and forty-five' indicates three hundreds, four tens, and five ones. Our system thus helps us maintain the order of labels fixed through the understanding of these conventions of regrouping counting units on a base-ten fashion.

Of course this system is not the only possible one. Other counting systems use different numbers of units for regrouping (base twenty, for example) and some systems do not use regrouping at all. Among

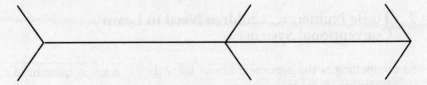

Figure 1.1   A problem that can be solved by measurement: two horizontal lines that are the same in length, even though one looks longer than the other.

the Oksapmin of Papua New Guinea, for example, the counting system uses the names of body parts as number words. This allows the Oksapmin to maintain the labels in a fixed order because all they have to do is be systematic about which body-part names are used and follow strictly the order in which the labels are taken (for further information, see Lancy, 1983, and Saxe, 1981). Thus different systems have the principle of fixed order embedded in their organization but the way in which the principle is part of the system may vary. This variation means that each system has in some sense its own logic, and this particular logic influences the ways in which problems can be solved.

Forms of measurement offer another example of variation in the way in which the general logic is embedded in particular systems. In order to compare the length of two objects through measurement, we need to use logic. As Piaget pointed out, the minimum requirement for understanding how to use a ruler is the ability to make the following transitive inference: if A = B and B = C, then A = C. B, in this case, may be the length of two lines measured by a ruler, like the two horizontal lines in the drawings in figure 1.1. If we look at the two lines, they *do not look the same length* but if you were to measure them, you would find that they *are* the same length. The value that you read on the ruler is the quantity 'B' in the logic of transitive inferences and it should convince you of the equality of the two lines.

This logic is quite fundamental, but children have to know a great deal more than transitivity in order to be numerate about measurement in their own environments. Measurement involves arbitrary units (inches, centimetres, pounds in weight, degrees of temperature, litres) which play an important part in our lives. These units are standards which we use all the time, about which we talk to other people, and they are quite arbitrary. We measure lengths with rulers and tape measures. The Oksapmin in Papua New Guinea use body parts (e.g. arm lengths) as units of measurement. However, once the units have been chosen, they are organized in a system with its own logic. This logic makes its own intellectual demands.

For example, measurement scales may have units of different sizes – inches and centimetres are both used to measure length and are of different sizes. Furthermore, the relationship between different units in the same system may also vary – '12 inches make 1 foot; 3 feet make 1 yard' are relationships very different from '100 centimetres make 1 metre; 1,000 metres make 1 kilometre'. It is clear that children using inches, feet and yards need to rely on rules for converting one unit into another that differ from the rules used by children who grow up in cultures where the metric system is standard. Once again, the logic underlying the different measurement systems is the same: children need to understand transitive inferences and the logic of units, but the way in which the logic of units is embedded in the particular systems may vary. In order to be numerate about measurement, it is necessary to understand both the logic and the conventions of measurement.

Another quite arbitrary aspect of measurement is the way in which the numbers within the same scale are related to each other. For example, the numbers used in the measurement of length are additive – that means that the absolute difference between 1 and 2 inches is the same as that between 2 and 3 inches. In contrast, the numbers used in the measurement of the intensity of sound are multiplicative – that means that the absolute difference between 1 and 2 decibels is much smaller than the difference between 2 and 3 because the sound doubles with each step in the scale: 2 decibels is twice the intensity of 1 decibel, and 3 is twice the intensity of 2.

It goes without saying that these aspects of measurement all have to be learned by children. In fact anything in mathematics which could be called a 'cultural invention' can only be understood by some form of cultural transmission. But learning to use these cultural tools is not as simple as it may seem at first glance. Although the way we use such systems of representation seems obvious to us, the same may not be true of children. One very simple example involving the use of rulers can illustrate this point. When we take a ruler and place it against something that we are measuring, we are actually finding out how many times a certain unit of length (centimetre, inch) fits against the length of the object. If we understand this logical aspect of measurement, we have no difficulty in measuring even if the ruler is smaller than the object. We mark the end of the ruler on the object in some way and repeat the measuring operation from this point, adding the result of the two readings in some way. However, Heraud (1989) has shown that this simple idea may not occur to children aged about 5 or 6.

Another difficulty for some children at this age is to decide where to measure from, from 0 or from 1 (Nunes, Light, and Mason, 1993). There is a sense in which this question reveals an incomplete grasp of what measuring with a ruler means. If we were to start from 1, the actual number of centimetres that fits against the object measured would be 1 less than the number read from the ruler. Children need to learn the conventions in the system and also to understand the logic embedded in the system.

The picture that we have painted so far is actually quite a familiar one. Most people would accept that in mathematics learning there are logical principles and there are cultural inventions, and that children have to master both aspects. The actual dividing line between the two is often quite hard to draw, and the extent to which children's difficulties are logical ones or result from the need to learn particular conventions is often not completely clear. But there is wide agreement that children must learn about both things. However, the next step in our argument is a much less familiar one. We wish to put forward the idea that learning about these cultural inventions may actually increase children's ability to respect logical principles. In other words it may not just be a question of children acquiring the correct logic and applying it to the learning of new mathematical techniques. The children's intellectual power in using their logical ability may improve quite radically as a result of learning culturally devised systems.

The simplest and yet the most compelling example of how this might work is our counting system. It is a cultural invention, with its own characteristics which are quite different from those of other systems in other cultures. The most important characteristic of our system, as we have already noted, is the decimal structure. It is such a commonplace in our lives that ten units make a decade, that ten decades make a hundred, and so on that we easily forget that this is an arbitrary system. There is, of course, nothing especial about base ten (some other base would be just as valid); it is the idea of a base system itself that represents a considerable human invention. It is not an inevitable feature of counting systems, and yet the systems which have a base structure are much more powerful than those which do not.

One has only to think of the task that children face when they try to remember and reproduce number words in the right order to see the advantages of a base system. If the children simply try to remember as many number words as they can in a fixed order, there will be a strict limit to how many words they can commit to memory. But if they take advantage of the base system, they do not have to remember all the words in a rote fashion. Children certainly have to remember all the numbers from 0 to 10 since these are the basic words for the units, and they must also commit to memory all the teen words because some of these (eleven, twelve, thirteen, fifteen) are hard to derive from the system. They will have to remember the decade words because again some of them (twenty, thirty, fifty) are hard to derive from the structure. They will have to learn the words for units of a new size (hundred, thousand, million) – but that is all. With these 35 or so number words and a knowledge of how the system works the children could, if they had the time and the patience, count to a million and beyond.

What happens when a counting system has no base structure, as the Oksapmin system we mentioned earlier? Their number words are the names of parts of the body taken in a particular order. The word for one is also the word for right thumb, the word for two is right index finger, three is right middle-finger, and so the numbers continue around the right hand, up the right arm, around the face on the left and then down the left side of the face and on until they reach the last finger of the left hand.

Even though this system has no base structure it does nevertheless contain an *aide-mémoire* for the order of the number words, as pointed out earlier. The child simply has to think of the next part of the body to remember the next number word. But the system has a big disadvantage: the lack of a base structure means that no one using the system can generate numbers into the hundreds and thousands.

The contrast between our numeration system and that of the Oksapmin helps us to make two general points about the decade structure and other cultural inventions in mathematics. Our argument here is that two things happen to children as a result of learning and understanding the structure of our numeration system. One is that they gain a powerful way of counting. With the decade structure, or any other base system, they can generate numbers; without it, they would either have to remember a long sequence of numbers, which would be very hard indeed to do, or would soon meet a point from which they could count no further. That much is indisputable. Our second argument is that the system will become a *thinking tool*, a means to solve problems which could not be solved without a numeration system.

This can be illustrated by problems, some of them quite simple ones, which we would find difficult without the support of a numeration system. For example, if we have to compare the number of jelly beans in two jars and this number is between 15 and 20 in both jars, it is unlikely that we would be able to make the comparison without counting. We also use the numeration system to compute sums. If we have to figure out the sum of two sets of marbles, for example, we use the numeration system to do so. Just understanding that the sum is where we get to when we put the two sets together is not enough: we need a numeration system to calculate with.

Thus, once children have learned a numeration system, they have as a result a tool for thought. In our culture, numeration systems come in two forms, oral and written. These have some characteristics in common and also some that are quite distinct. A common feature is that they are both base-ten systems. A distinctive feature is that the oral numeration system uses distinct expressions to indicate units, tens, hundreds etc. (five, fifty, five hundred) whereas the written system uses position from right to left (the value of the digit 5 in 50 and 500 is different although the digit itself is the same).

The fact that we have different ways of representing numbers has two interesting consequences. One is that, because the two systems embed the same logic, we have more than one source of experiences for learning about those logical principles. When the same logic is embedded in different cultural systems – and this happens often in mathematics – it may be the case that it is easier to grasp the embedded logic by exploring one system than the other. This has serious implications for mathematics instruction because it makes sense to start with the system that is easier to master and learn the more difficult one later.

Another consequence is that the particular characteristics of each kind of representation are likely to affect the way we use the system. We have seen that users of a counting system based on the names of body parts have a different power when it comes to counting from that of users of a system that has a base. With a base system, one can count indefinitely on, whereas without a base this is not possible. In much the same way, the same person may manage much better when solving problems using one system than another system. For example, if we have to add a long list of numbers, it might be better to use written than oral numbers.

3   To Be Numerate, Children Need to Use Their Mathematical Thinking Meaningfully and Appropriately in Situations

We have considered two different aspects of mathematical concepts so far. The first one was what we called the invariants, the logic of the concept. The second aspect was the conventions used in mathematics, that is, the systems of signs that we use to talk and think about mathematics. We now want to turn to a third aspect: the situations in which mathematics is used.

One of the complaints of mathematics teachers is that pupils often do not know which mathematical technique to use in a new situation. An 8-year-old child may use subtraction in a problem that should have been solved by division. A 9-year-old may add the values of the sides in a rectangle when trying to figure out the area of the rectangle. An 11-year-old may calculate 12 divided by 4 to solve a certain problem when the appropriate calculation would have been 4 divided by 12. A 13-year-old may subtract one number from the other when these should have been added in a problem that involves negative numbers. A 15-year-old may multiply the probability of two events when they should have been added. A college student may calculate the mean when the median would have been a better option. In all of these examples, there is no question of lack of knowledge of the mathematical procedures. Each one of these children could very well have carried out the appropriate operation if only they knew what the appropriate operation was.

One of the difficulties of using mathematical techniques as thinking tools stems from the relationship between the mastery of general procedures and their use in specific situations. Mastering a general procedure often does not tell us when the procedure is a good choice for solving a problem. *We have to understand the problem situation in order to think mathematically about it.*

No one would want to have to invent a new procedure for solving every new problem. Knowledge of general procedures is a most economical way of approaching new problems. But it is clearly not sufficient.

The difference between learning general procedures and understanding particular situations is a central issue in mathematics. The meaning of mathematical symbols (or of any symbols, for that matter) comes from the fact that they can be used in certain situations but not in others. For example, the number 3 can be used to refer to some problems but not to others. We can use addition to solve some problem but not others. In order to use mathematical techniques and tools appropriately we have to know whether the invariants related to them are the same invariants in the situation at hand. It is the connection between the invariants in the problem situation and those in the mathematical tool that defines whether it will be a good tool for that situation.

This may seem much too complicated but it is basically quite simple. We can start from a simple example. Suppose a 5-year-old is asked to solve the following problem: 'Mary had seven sweets. She ate two of them. How many does she have left?' Now this child may not know the 'subtraction facts' and may not be able to answer immediately. That does not mean that the child will not solve the problem. The child may hold up seven fingers, then cover two of them and count those that remain. The answer will be correct for a very important reason: whatever happens in the addition and subtraction of fingers also happens in the addition and subtraction of sweets. The relations between fingers are used by the 5-year-old as a model for the relations between sweets. If the model is appropriate, the procedures applied to fingers will give the right answer about sweets.

Although a very simple example, this is not radically different from other uses of mathematics. The correct mathematics for a situation involves a concept that has the same invariants as the situation. It is the understanding of situations that gives meaning to general mathematical procedures because it allows us to know what it means to keep something invariant. We can learn procedures without understanding them but this learning is rather inconsequential for our thinking. We can only think mathematically with concepts that mean something to us. If systems of representations and procedures to manipulate these symbols are going to influence our thinking, they must have meaning – that is, they must be connected with some situations in which they can be used.

4 Conclusions

In summary, being numerate involves thinking mathematically about situations. To think mathematically, we need to know *mathematical systems of representation* that we will use as tools. These systems must have meaning, that is, must *be related to situations* where they can be used. And we need to be able to understand the logic of these situations, *the invariants*, so that we can choose the appropriate forms of mathematics. Thus it is not enough to learn procedures; it is necessary to make these procedures into thinking tools.

The question still remains about which tools we may need in order to be numerate in today's world. Undoubtedly we need numeration systems. But we actually need much more to work in many contexts that have become part of everyday life. We need to think proportionally in order to understand about 'best buys'. We probably need to think algebraically in order to use certain types of computer software like spreadsheets. We may need to think in terms of functions to understand certain graphs, and graphs are such a widely used form of data display. In order to compare the efficiency of different treatments, be they medical or agricultural, we need to think in statistical terms.

It is clearly not a simple task to make a list of the particular types of mathematics that are necessary for being numerate in contemporary societies. On the other hand, a list of topics may not be what we need. Perhaps we need to think about mathematics teaching differently. In the design of a curriculum that will make our youngsters numerate for today's world, we may have to remind ourselves continuously that the mathematics that children learn must give them access to new ways of thinking and must increase their power to think mathematically.

This is why the study of how children think is so fundamental to mathematics teaching. There are occasions when giving children access to new ways of thinking will be a matter of learning new conventional systems of representation. They may need to learn to use a protractor, to count money, or to input commands into a computer program. On other occasions they may need to connect their old knowledge with new situations. The significance of old procedures will be changed by their use to solve new problems. There will also be occasions when children's thinking will be expanded through their attempts to come to grips with new sorts of invariants.

In this case, instruction may involve them in using their own symbols and resources for some time before they are asked to use conventional forms of representation.

Conceptual development in mathematics is thus not equivalent to the mastery of a list of procedures, as some approaches to curriculum development in the past have assumed. Progress can come from understanding new invariants, learning new forms of mathematical representation, and connecting old forms to new situations that will enrich them with meaning.

5 Plan of the Book

In the following chapters we will look at children's growing understanding of invariants in different types of situations. The chapters are organized from simpler to more complex forms of mathematics. In chapter 2 we discuss the logic of counting and the understanding of number. Chapter 3 deals with the invariants of numeration systems that have a base, and other situations that involve the same invariants. Chapter 4 considers the understanding of measurement. Chapter 5 picks up once again on more general themes, considering how the same logical moves may be embedded in different systems of signs and the importance of analysing the underlying logic when trying to understand conceptual development. Chapters 6 and 7, respectively, discuss children's understanding of additive and multiplicative reasoning. Chapter 8 concentrates on the understanding of fractions. Finally, in chapter 9 we present an overview of the main ideas in the book and how they fit with the evidence presented throughout.

2
Beginning with Counting

It is quite difficult to say exactly when children start to learn about mathematics. In a formal sense, of course, their mathematical career usually begins at school, but it would be absurd to say that these are the first mathematical experiences that children ever have or that they understand nothing about mathematics until they are taught about it by a teacher. It is perfectly obvious to most parents that their children learn something about mathematical principles long before they go to school, and to most teachers that they already know quite a lot when they get there.

If one searches for the first genuine mathematical experiences in a child's life, then one probably has to go back a very long way indeed. Some experimental psychologists have claimed that human babies are able to distinguish sets of objects with between one and three objects in each purely on the basis of the numbers of objects in each set (for example, Starkey and Cooper, 1980; Starkey et al. 1983; Starkey et al., 1990), and that they realize that the number of objects in sets changes when one object is added or taken away from it (Wynn, 1992). All these achievements, it is claimed, can be demonstrated easily and reliably in babies under a year in age. However, the significance of these findings is still unclear because there is no evidence connecting these reactions of the infants to perceptual displays and their later understanding of number.

We still have a lot to learn about what children understand of quantities before they learn to speak. We do, on the other hand, have a great deal of information about a significant development which is quite clearly relevant to mathematics and which takes place very often before children go to school: learning to count. Counting, therefore, will be our starting-point in our exploration of the growth of children's mathematical knowledge.

When children begin to count they have to learn about a system which is partly an expression of universal laws about number and partly a bundle of convenient but arbitrary inventions, as we have discussed in chapter 1. In this chapter we shall concentrate on the universal, logically necessary, features of counting, and in chapter 3 we shall deal more with the conventional, culturally-determined aspects of counting systems.

When children begin to count things they have to wrestle with the activity of counting itself. They have to remember the number words; they have to count each object in a set, if they are counting a set, once and once only; they have to understand that the number of objects in the set is represented by the last number that they produce when they count the set. In other words, they have to learn to do it properly.

But that is not all. They also have to learn what counting is for. Counting is a way, and sometimes the only way, to solve certain problems – whether there are enough chairs for the people coming to the birthday party or how to make sure that everyone there is given the same amount of sweets. They have, therefore, to understand how to determine numbers by counting as well as to understand the uses of number.

We shall deal with these two questions separately, starting with how they learn to count.

1   Learning to Count Properly

The universal principles that we have already mentioned distinguish counting from all other activities. You have to respect a set of principles when you count and, if you do not do so, you are not counting or, at any rate, not counting properly. These principles are simple and extremely familiar to all of us, but they need to be recognized explicitly.

Let us begin with the child counting a single set of objects. This is not the only context in which children count. They also take part in abstract counting, which is counting but not counting anything in particular; and when they are older they count two or more sets in order to make comparisons between them. But one of the simplest and most direct ways of studying children's counting is to give them a set of visible and tangible objects and ask them how many there are.

The most useful account of the principles which children have to respect when they count was made some time ago by Gelman and Gallistel (1978). They argued that there are three 'how-to-count' principles, but one must add here that it would be more accurate to call these 'how-to-count-a-single-set-of-objects' principles. Gelman and Gallistel's analysis and their subsequent research is entirely about the child counting a group of visible objects.

One of their principles, which we have already mentioned, is the one-to-one correspondence principle. When you count, you must count all the objects and count each of them once and only once. If we were to count one object twice, skip one object, or count in the spaces between the objects in the collection, we would come up with the wrong total.

The second principle is about constant order. Whenever we count we must produce number words in the same order each time. If we were to change the order of the numbers (1, 2, 3, 4, 5, 6 on one occasion and 1, 3, 6, 5, 2, 4 on another) we could actually come up with different totals for the same set of objects at different times.

Their third how-to-count principle is about how to decide the actual quantity of the set of objects being counted – that is, the total of objects corresponds to the last number word in our counting. Gelman and Gallistel referred to this requirement as the 'cardinality principle'. This principle, in the sense that Gelman and Gallistel use it, simply means that if we use labels in counting, say, up to 'five' (1–2–3–4–5), then there must be five objects altogether in the set that we have been counting.

These three requirements are indisputable. A child who does not respect them is definitely not counting properly, and any child who does respect them consistently is doing well. One could not say that this latter child understands what he or she is doing, but that is a question that we will deal with later. For the moment we are concerned with how well children count objects when they are asked to do so.

Gelman and Gallistel's own research on children counting objects paints an optimistic picture. In their original work they asked children whose ages ranged from 2 to 6 years to count single sets of objects. These sets which were always arranged in straight rows varied in size from 2 to 19 objects. Gelman and Gallistel observed the children counting these sets and recorded whether they counted each object once, whether they counted always in the same order (1 before 2, 2 before 3), and also whether they seemed to recognize that the last number counted signified the number of objects in the set. In a later set of experiments Gelman and Meck (1983) also asked children to make judgements about a puppet which they saw counting. This puppet occasionally violated the one-to-one principle and the cardinal principle, and the aim of these experiments was to see whether the children could spot these violations.

By and large the children did rather well, particularly when they were counting small sets. When they counted, they usually did count each object once and only once (the one-to-one principle), and they were quick to judge that the puppet had counted wrongly when he failed to count one of the objects or when he counted a particular member of the set more than once.

The children's respect for the stable order principle seemed as strong: they tended to produce the same number words in the same sequence over different occasions, even though the actual order of the words, and sometimes the words themselves, were not always correct. Gelman and Gallistel rightly claim that the important point here is the child's consistency: a child who produces the same order of number words over time is respecting the stable order principle even if the words (or their order) are not the conventional ones.

The children also seemed to obey the third principle, the cardinality principle, well. The puppet studies produced the strongest evidence that they respect this principle. If the puppet counted up to 6, for example, and then said that there were 5 objects in the set, the children usually spotted that he had made a bad mistake. When counting sets with more than four objects, however, children under 5 years of age made a considerable number of mistakes in the coordinated use of the three principles and only about half of the children succeeded in the counting task.

The conclusion that Gelman and Gallistel reached from all this is neatly captured in the name that they gave to their own hypothesis. They called it the 'principle before skills' model, and by that they meant that, although young children may fumble occasionally, their respect for the three how-to-count principles is strong from the start. Children make many mistakes when they begin to count, but, according to this model, they do not ever have to be taught the rules. They know these already.

This is a striking claim, and it is not surprising that it is also a controversial one. One objection is that it is based entirely on studies which involved counting objects in a particular arrangement – in straight lines and at regular intervals from each other. This may mean that the demands of the tasks that Gelman and her colleagues gave to the children were not stringent enough. We don't only count straight rows. The argument for looking at children counting objects in other arrangements is compelling, and it led to some further research.

The most notable example is a study by Karen Fuson (1988). She asked children whose ages ranged from 3½ to 6 years to count sets of blocks, and these were arranged in rows or in circles or they were simply spread randomly about the table. Like Gelman and Gallistel, she also varied the numbers of objects that she gave to the children on different occasions: with each child she started with four or five blocks but increased the number in the displays as the children counted on several trials.

The main result in this study was Fuson's discovery that children do indeed make more mistakes with other arrangements. Even with straight rows the children in her study seemed not to do so well as Gelman and Gallistel would have predicted: the youngest children (3½ to 4 years) showed little sign of respecting the one-to-one principle when they had to count objects arranged in straight rows. They usually did not even conform to the one-to-one principle with quantities in the smallest sets – four and five objects. The oldest children, in contrast, usually kept to the one-to-one principle with sets as large as 40 in number.

However, with other spatial arrangements, and particularly with objects spread out randomly round the table, the children at all age levels found it much harder to respect the one-to-one principle. How are we to explain this difference between counting a straight row and counting a randomly arranged set?

There are two possible views. One (principles before skills) is that the children try to respect the one-to-one principle but lose track with the random displays. They forget which objects they have counted already and which they have not counted and make errors of omission and commission much more easily than they do with straight rows in which the starting-point and the end-point are clearly defined and there is no problem about the path between the two. So their relative success with the straight rows shows their respect for the one-to-one principle, and their failure with the random displays is simply a trivial matter of not keeping an effective running account of the objects that they have already counted.

The alternative explanation (failure in principles) is harder on the children. The successes that children have with the regularly spaced straight rows might be spurious. They might simply treat counting as a regular, rhythmic activity which has something to do with repetitive actions. So when young children count each regularly spaced stair as they go up or count each regularly spaced dot that they point at, they might have no idea that they have to count every object only once. They might just count that way because the arrangement of regularly spaced steps or dots matches well the rhythm of their repetitive actions. Random arrangements would not provoke this sort of fortuitous association. According to this account, random displays are a much better test of the one-to-one principle than straight rows.

It is actually impossible to say, on the evidence that we have discussed so far, which of these two accounts is the more plausible one. But the introduction of random arrangements into these studies does provide us with another intriguing observation, which concerns the possibility of moving objects. One extremely effective way of ensuring that you are respecting the one-to-one principle when counting movable objects is to move to one side those that you have counted already. If children do adopt this strategy spontaneously they definitely do understand the need for the one-to-one principle. Fuson herself, and Herscovics et al. (1986) working with French-speaking children in Canada, observed that only about half of the children under the age of about 5 or 5½ used the trustworthy method of moving objects as they were counted even when the blocks could clearly be moved. In contrast, Fuson noted that most of the older children (5½ to 6 years) in her study spontaneously moved the blocks into a group of already-counted objects and made no more errors counting objects which had been spread about on the table than those displayed in a row.

The fact that the younger children do not use the more efficient strategy of moving objects when counting is puzzling. Do they fail to use it simply because they did not think of it or because they do not realize the need to rely on a method that will guarantee one-to-one correspondence? A look at the age patterns suggests that the latter hypothesis may be correct. The children who use one-to-one correspondence well when counting in rows are in the age group that consistently uses the strategy of moving objects spread about on a table in order to count them. Young children under 5 years of age, make many mistakes when counting rows and do not seem to recognize the need to look for an efficient strategy when counting movable objects in a scattered display.

Fuson also observed young children counting dots on a card with the dots organized in a circle. Because these were not movable objects, the children had to remember the point at which they started counting in order to respect the one-to-one correspondence principle. Remembering where to stop counting when the objects are in a circle can, of course, be much easier if we use something to mark off the starting-point. Fuson investigated whether children discovered this efficient memory-supporting strategy easily. Even the older children (5- and 6-year-olds) seemed very bad at using observable marks in this situation: only one 5-year-old (out of sixteen 5/6-year-olds) consistently used an external mark to make sure that the stopping point would be correctly identified. Due to this lack of a good strategy, most children were wrong in their counting by one or two dots, either counting the same dots twice (39 per cent of the trials) or stopping short of the last dot (13 per cent). Correct performance was observed on only 22 per cent of the trials; the remaining 25 per cent involved errors larger than two dots.

Fuson suggested that the children may simply have trusted their memories too much in this situation because the spatial location of the dots may have been taken as a strong cue for where to stop. She then attempted to improve children's performance in this task in two ways. First, she used a red dot as the starting-point when all other dots were green. This procedure was rather efficient in improving the performance of even very young children: more than half of the 3-year-old children (11 out of 19) consistently used the red dot (over three trials) to stop counting just where they should – that is, right before the red dot. The second procedure Fuson used was to show the same children that they could use the red dot as a marker of the point where they should stop counting. This demonstration had a marked effect on the children's performance, since 86 per cent of the trials were now correct. However, the number of children who performed consistently well and stopped counting just where they should did not increase significantly: only 12 out of 19 children counted correctly in all three trials.

The difficulty that many 3-year-old children had in employing this apparently simple strategy of starting and stopping at the red dot, even after being taught, fits well with the idea that children of this age do not recognize the need to respect the one-to-one correspondence principle when counting. But, of course, Gelman and her colleagues could always plead that the children were perfectly aware of the importance of one-to-one counting but did not understand that the strategy that they had been taught would help them to stick to the principle.

In fact Gelman's most telling evidence for the idea that even very young children do respect this principle comes from one of her puppet studies which we have briefly mentioned already and will now describe in more detail. This method was adopted by two groups of investigators, Gelman and Meck (1983) and Briars and Siegler (1984). Both studies were done with 4- and 5-year-olds. In both studies there were trials in which the puppet counted in the usual sort of way from left to right without making any mistakes and other trials in which it blatantly flouted the one-to-one principle. Both studies, too, had trials in which the puppet counted each object once and thus respected the one-to-one principle, but actually counted in an unusual way. In Gelman and Meck's study the puppet started in the middle and worked its way outwards, and in the Briars and Siegler study the puppet counted all the objects of one colour first and of another colour second. In both studies, the children had no trouble in judging as 'correct' the trials in which the puppet counted in the usual sort of way and made no mistakes about it. In both studies, too, the 4-year-olds did have some difficulty in judging the puppet as wrong when he made one-to-one errors, but nevertheless the vast majority of their judgements was right: most of the time they said that the puppet was wrong.

However, the studies diverge strongly with respect to children's ability to judge the correctness of counting in the other trials. Briars and Siegler reported rates of success much more modest than those registered by Gelman and Meck (1983). The rates of success obtained by Briars and Siegler for the trials in which the puppet first counted the red and then the blue tokens were equal to 35, 65 and 53 per cent, respectively, for the 3-, 4-, and 5-year-olds whereas Gelman and Meck (1983) reported 95 and 96 per cent correct responses, respectively, for 3- and 4-year-olds.

How can this discrepancy be understood? Gelman and Meck (1986), having acknowledged the need to examine this discrepancy, examined their own and Briars and Siegler's method in greater detail. They concluded that they had engaged the children in much more discussion about what was right and what was wrong in counting than Briars and Siegler had done. They also gave their children the opportunity of trying the item again if they felt that the children had not given their best response. Thus they repeated the study using their own method once again but recording this time the children's first and best response. Comparing the first with the best response generated no discrepancy in the success rates for trials in which the puppet had counted correctly or for those in which an error had been made. However, a clear discrepancy in the rates of success of 4-year-olds was obtained for the trials in which the puppet counted all the tokens only once but did so in a non-conventional way (started from the middle of the row and counted to the end, and then returned to the beginning of the row and counted to the middle): while approximately 80 per cent of the 'best responses' were correct, only about 60 per cent of the first responses were correct.

The contrast between the 'best' and the first response must be looked at with caution. In this situation, there were only two possible responses: either children judged that the puppet had counted right or they thought the puppet had counted wrongly. There is much research evidence (Rose and Blank, 1974; Samuel and Bryant, 1984) that shows that if the same question is put to a child twice in a row, the child tends to change the answer. Thus the improvement between the first and the best response may be an artefact of the situation: children may have interpreted the fact that the same question was being asked again as an indication that they should change their answer. By doing so, they would change to the only other possible alternative, the correct one. Since there were several trials in the Gelman and Meck study, this risk may be smaller than in others where fewer trials are used and children can more easily recognize the repetition. We will take here the approach of accepting their results as indicating that there is often a difference between children's first and best response.

This series of studies based on Gelman and Meck's method of having children judge a puppet's performance in counting rather than do the counting themselves is rather instructive. First, the studies clearly show that children's performance is influenced by the situation. If an adult engages the child in a discussion about what is right and wrong in counting, the child is more likely to reflect about the counting principles and probably also observe the puppet more closely when the puppet does the counting afterwards. Children can perform significantly better with the support of an adult even if the adult does not give further clues to the solution of a task than directing the child's attention to an appropriate analysis of the situation. Second, children's first response in the judgement tasks and their counting ability appear to point to the same level of unaided performance for each age level: 4-year-olds show a shaky knowledge of the counting principles both when they count arrays and when they judge the performance of a puppet, while 5-year-olds consistently show a good level of performance regardless of whether they count objects in rows, spread around a table, or whether they have to make judgements about other people's counting. It seems safe to conclude that 4-year-olds can count relatively well with help but their counting may or may not come out right when they carry it out without help. In contrast, most 5-year-olds seem to have a good command of the counting principles and we can reasonably expect them to tell us the right number of objects in arrays up to perhaps 20/40. They have (within the limits of their knowledge of number words) acquired a powerful cultural tool. But how do they use this tool, and when? This is the core of our discussion in the next section.

2 Children's Use of Counting

We have reached a conclusion about children's counting which answers one of our two questions and reminds us about the other. The question that it answers is about counting properly. We know now that by the age of about 5 years children usually do count properly in the sense that they appear to respect the basic, universal, principles of counting when they count a single set of objects.

Our second question is whether children know what counting is for. Do they understand when counting will help them to solve a problem, and when it will not? We need the answer to this question because we cannot be sure that children understand the counting system unless they know how to use it properly. It is perfectly possible, as Piaget often pointed out, that a child could count properly and still not understand the nature of the numbers whose names he has learned so proficiently. But if that child sees that counting is a way of working out a solution to a particular problem, we can be reasonably sure that he has shown an understanding of the system which has helped him.

2.1 *Producing sets with equal numbers*

Piaget and his collaborators (Piaget, 1965) were the first to point out that, when children learn to count, they still have a long way to go in their route to understanding number. His evidence for this view came from the many demonstrations which he produced that children around the age of 5 years, though able to count reasonably well, often fail to use counting as a tool when they could profit from this use.

In some of the tasks that Piaget devised, the children were given a succession of arrays of counters and were asked to take from a pile of counters the same number as there were in the array on the table. These arrays were of three different types: (1) unstructured arrays, in which the tokens were simply spread about on the table; (2) structured arrays with undetermined numbers, like rows, circles and right angles, which are figures that may be built with different numbers of tokens; and (3) structured arrays with determined numbers, like a square or a cross or a triangle, where the number of tokens is related to the shape.

Piaget observed that young children, 4- and 5-year-olds, although able to count, did not use counting in order to get the right number of tokens when the arrays could easily be made with different numbers and thus did not succeed with these arrays. However, they were much better at producing the right number of counters when copying the structured arrays with determined numbers. Piaget concluded that these young children attempted to reproduce the global shape of the displays rather than to obtain the same number of tokens.

For example, Hug, aged 5, faced with an unstructured array, said that he could not find the right number of tokens. When stimulated by the interviewer to try, he spread some tokens on the table and said he had the same number. But when asked how many tokens there were, he did not know, although he maintained that there were just as many on the table as he had himself taken because he had looked twice (Piaget, 1965, p. 67).

Confronted with structured arrays that could be made with different numbers of tokens, young children reproduced the shape – row, circle, right angle – and attempted to get the size of the array correctly but did not count the tokens in order to get the same number. Slightly older children were more careful in the reproduction of the array, looking carefully at the model and trying to put down one token in their figure for each token in the model. This one-to-one correspondence was, of course, difficult to maintain when larger numbers (15, for example) had been used to build the models.

Piaget also observed that when some of the children were told to count the tokens in the unstructured array and then asked whether they had taken the correct number of tokens from the pile, they did not necessarily base their judgement on the number obtained from counting. Gis, aged $5\frac{1}{2}$, was asked whether there were just as many in two unstructured arrays and encouraged to count. She counted 19 in one array and 21 in the other but ended up concluding that there were more counters in the array with 19 (1965, p. 72). Thus Piaget concluded that young children who know how to count may not use counting either when trying to construct a set with the same number of items as another one or when evaluating whether two sets have the same number of items.

Only the older children ($5\frac{1}{2}$ to 6 years of age) relied on counting to obtain the correct number of tokens. Even if these children started out by copying the array, they would soon realize that they had to count the tokens and conclude by adjusting the number (e.g. 'I need three more' or 'I've put too many') in their final production.

Piaget does not describe his results in terms of percentages and age levels, as the previously cited researchers did. However, Fuson (1988) obtained quantitative data on children's ability to construct equivalent sets. She gave the children two types of task. In one, she asked the children to give her a specific number of counters without showing any model set. In the second task she showed them rows of red counters and asked them to give her as many blue counters as there were red ones – a task similar to Piaget's. The comparison between children's success in these two tasks is instructive. We know from the earlier studies that 5- and 6-year-olds can count sets displayed to them rather well. But can they build sets of desired numerosities? Children's failure in Piaget's task could result either from the fact that they cannot construct sets with a desired numerosity or from their failure to realize that counting can be used as a measure of set size when a set equivalent to a model must be constructed. We will compare the results of Fuson's two tasks in order to choose between these two possibilities.

The children were in the age range of $3\frac{1}{2}$ to 6 years. Their performance in producing a set of a desired numerosity was rather good except for that of children under 4 years of age, most of whom did not count the tokens as they produced the sets. Most or all of the children in the other age ranges counted the tokens and all successful solutions were obtained through counting. Thus, children's difficulties with the task of producing an equivalent set cannot be attributed to their inability to produce a set of a desired numerosity.

In the second task, Fuson looked both at the children's success in creating a set equivalent to the model and at the strategy that they had used. The percentages of children in each age level succeeding in her tasks (for the two trials in which numbers in the sets were smaller than 10) are presented in figure 2.1. Performance clearly improved sharply between 3½ and 4½ years in both types of task. Still, about one quarter of the 6-year-olds, who had counted rather well in other tasks, was unable to construct a set equivalent to one displayed by the interviewer. The figure also shows rather clearly that children of all age levels were more proficient in producing a set with a specified numerosity than they were in creating an equivalent set.

These results strongly support Piaget's contention that when children first learn to count they do not at first realize the usefulness of counting as a tool for producing equivalent sets. Fuson's analysis of children's strategies further supports the Piagetian thesis. Most children (73 per cent) used matching procedures in attempting to obtain the same number of tokens and only 25 per cent ever counted. If these overall results are split by age level, it becomes clear that even 5- and 6-year-olds, who were proficient counters in her study, still do not use counting systematically in producing an equivalent set. Only 42 per cent of the 5-year-olds and 25 per cent of the 6-year-olds relied on counting on every trial.

Recently another study has confirmed Piaget's results with 4-year-olds. Geoffrey Saxe, et al. (1987) asked 4-year-old children to solve several simple arithmetic tasks, including counting arrays and producing sets of equivalent size. The task was presented embedded in a meaningful context, in which children were asked to give the same number of pennies to one puppet as the experimenter had given to another one. The children were asked to reproduce two arrays, one with three and the other with nine elements. These sizes of array were well within the children's knowledge of number, which was assessed previously. Failure in the task could not be explained as a function of lack of knowledge of numbers. Despite their good knowledge of number words, children were not very successful with either size of array. Although more successful in the one with three pennies, the success was still very modest considering that arrays of that size could easily be reproduced even through a matching strategy. The percentages of children producing the correct size arrays was 60 and 10 per cent, respectively, for the three- and nine-element arrays. Saxe and his colleagues also examined children's strategies for the array with nine elements (it was not possible to judge strategies

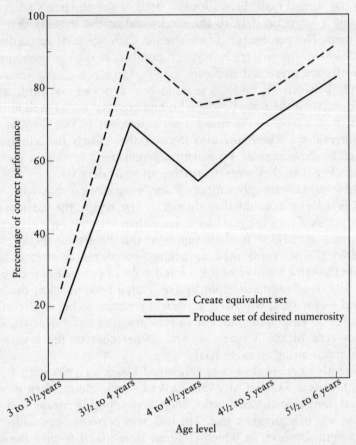

Figure 2.1   The percentage of children who succeeded in constructing sets with the correct number
SOURCE: Fuson (1988)

reliably for the array with three elements) and observed that the number of children who counted was the same as the number who correctly produced the equivalent set (10 per cent).

Thus, despite the fact that other methods are not reliable and that children know how to count rather well at the age of 5 and 6, they still do not realize that counting is their best tool for the construction of equivalent sets. It is likely that they do not realize that counting is a measure of set size although they can count and tell how many objects there are in the set.

2.2 Comparing two sets

We can look at children's use of counting to obtain a measure of set size in another way. We can show children two sets and ask them whether they have the same number of elements. If the sets are arranged in rows with the elements in one-to-one correspondence, children won't have to rely on counting to compare the sets. But if they are presented in different ways, such as in rows but not in correspondence, or spread around the table, or inside a box, counting becomes necessary. In this section we will look at childrents judgements about set sizes and examine their ability to use counting as a tool in comparing sets.

Piaget (1965) and his colleagues were the first researchers to point out that children who know how to count may not use counting to compare sets with respect to number. They designed an experiment, now widely known as the 'conservation test'. In the first phase children are initially asked to produce a set equivalent to one presented by the experimenter in which the elements are organized in a row. As we saw earlier, young children often try to produce equivalent sets by matching rather than counting. In the second phase, the experimenter changes the spatial arrangement of the elements in one row by spreading them out, bringing them together, or organizing them in a tower. The children are then asked whether the arrays still have the same quantity.

Piaget reported that young children did not rely on counting to decide whether the sets comprised the same quantity. The younger children (about 4 or 5 years-old) tended to rely on length cues rather than counting, and answer that the longer row contained more elements than the shorter one although they had just constructed the rows and judged them as equivalent. Occasionally the children focused on the density of the elements and judged the shorter row as containing more elements. Interestingly enough, slightly older children (about 5½- or 6-years-old), who were able to understand that the equivalence of the sets was conserved despite the change of their spatial disposition, did not seem to rely on counting either. Rather, they often argued on logical grounds for the equivalence of the sets. They knew that the numbers in the sets were the same before and that the sets had been merely re-arranged. They did not need to count the elements once again. Below is one example from Piaget (1965, p. 82), in which the objects in the row were coins and the child had to decide whether the owners of the rows were just as rich as each other:

FET (*5 years and 5 months*): 'Take the same number of pennies as there are there (6).' He made a row of 6 under the model, but put his much closer together so that there was no spatial correspondence between the rows. Both ends of the model extended beyond those of the copy. 'Have you got the same number? – Yes. – Are you and that boy just as rich as one another? – Yes. – (The pennies of the model were then closed up and his were spaced out.) – And now? – The same. – Exactly? – Yes. – Why are they the same? – Because you've put them closer together.'

In contrast to the children who succeeded in the task without having to count the elements in the rows a second time, the younger children might not succeed even if asked to count the elements in both rows. It is not unusual for the younger children to recognize that the number is the same but still maintain that the sets have different quantities, with the longer row having more. Thus Piaget concluded that counting was not seen as a measure of set size by young children, who basically used length cues in comparing rows.

Piaget's studies of children's understanding of conservation involve two different types of knowledge: the use of counting versus other cues in order to compare two sets, and logical inferences about the quantity in one set knowing what the quantity was before a transformation was carried out. Both aspects have inspired a lot of further research. In this section, we will consider only those studies which looked at children's use of counting or other cues to compare sets.

Several researchers have followed up Piaget's work and asked young children to make comparisons between two sets. We will review only some of these studies here since there are too many to cover them all. We will look at more than one study, though, in order to check whether results obtained by one researcher were independently replicated at least once.

Karen Fuson (1988) asked children of 4 and 5 years of age to make judgements about the numerosity of two rows of objects. She simply presented the rows and asked the children whether the number was larger in one row, in the other, or whether the rows had the same number of objects. She gave the children three tasks with three trials each, always in the same order. In all comparisons the number of objects in the two sets was the same.

In the first task, the objects were pictures on strips of cardboard and could not be moved. In all three trials, the length of the rows differed. Thus, if children did not count but judged quantity from the length cue, they would make a wrong judgement. However, they could still get the answer right without counting because there was a colour-correspondence between objects across sets. The leftmost picture on each strip was coloured the same, the next picture was also the same colour across sets but different from all the others in each set and so on. In the second task, the objects were small toys and could be moved. They were presented either in side-by-side rows, not in correspondence, or spread around the table, but always without a misleading cue. This task was used to encourage the children to count. If they made their judgement and gave no indication of counting (neither pointing, nor moving lips, nor saying how many objects were in each set), they were asked to 'do something' to show whether the quantities were really the same or different. The third task was similar to the first one, involving drawings of objects in rows with misleading length cues and colour-correspondence across sets, but children were initially told that they could be misled into thinking that there were more objects in one row when the rows actually had the same number. The children were then asked two questions: (1) which row looked like it had more elements and (2) whether it really had more elements or whether the number was the same or the other row had more.

The interpretation of children's response to the first task is rather simple. It indicates how children spontaneously compared sets, whether they relied on length, counting, or salient colour cues when making their judgements. The other two tasks were intended to lead children to use other than perceptual strategies. It is more difficult to interpret the results of the latter tasks for two reasons. First, all comparisons involved arrays with the same number. This lack of variation confounds the results because children may have realized that the sets were always the same. Since the order of tasks was always the same, children could do better in tasks two and three on this basis alone. Second, children only made one judgement in each trial on task one but were asked to revise their answers on tasks two and three ('do something to show me' and 'are they really . . .?'), a procedure which could influence the correctness of responses in unclear ways.

In task one, Fuson observed both among 4- and 5-year-olds a tendency to rely on the misleading length cues (70 and 60 per cent, respectively, of the children did so) and a low level of accuracy (33 and 37 per cent, respectively) despite the salient matched-colour cues. Thus she confirmed the Piagetian observation that young children do not reliably use counting as a tool when comparing the number of elements in two sets. She also confirmed previous findings by Cowan (1987), Greco (1962) and Schonfeld (1986) who observed that children in this age range compare set sizes on the basis of misleading length cues even when they can obtain information from counting. However, when asked to 'do something' to show that they were correct, a substantial number of children turned to counting: 70 per cent of the 4-year-olds and 80 per cent of the 5-year-olds counted in this condition and based their second response to task two on counting. Further, when told that sometimes quantities looked different but they may not be different, children also turned to counting rather frequently: 63 per cent of 4-year-olds and 60 per cent of 5-year-olds did so.

In short, although young children may not spontaneously use counting in order to compare two sets, they can be stimulated to do so. An important question to ask at this point is whether they will continue to do so without prompting from the experimenter or whether they will revert to their previous strategy of relying on length cues.

Fuson's experiment does not allow us to answer this question but a recent study by Cowan et al. (1993) does. They worked with older children, approximately $5\frac{1}{2}$ to $7\frac{1}{2}$ years, attending primary school in Sanaa, in the Yemen. The children were given a pre-test, in which the researchers verified their ability to count and whether or not they used counting in making comparisons between sets arranged in rows with misleading length cues. Those children who could count but did not use counting in comparing sets were then randomly assigned to participate in one of four different conditions. Two of these were experimental ones set up in order to show children that counting to compare sets is a good strategy. In one condition, which they called 'agreement between strategies', children were shown two ways of comparing the sets, one immediately after the other: establishing one-to-one correspondence and counting. They were encouraged to realize that the two ways of solving the task led to the same conclusion. In the second condition, which the researchers called 'feedback condition', children were presented with the arrays, asked to count the elements in each one, and only then asked to make the comparison judgement. Since comparison judgements based on counting were correct, children then received positive feedback for their counting-based judgement. In both of these groups, children had the opportunity of verifying that counting led to correct judgements, either by comparing it with another strategy or by receiving positive feedback for their counting-based judgements.

In the control conditions, children had the same amount of experience in judging arrays and were also encouraged to count, but they neither verified their counting response against another strategy nor received feedback about their performance. Thus, although being told to count during the experiment, they had no experience that indicated to them that counting was a good tool for making comparisons between sets.

Following this phase, children were given a post-test and again asked to make comparisons between two sets. This time, as in the pre-test, they did not receive any instruction on what to do in order to make their judgements.

Children in all groups became better at comparing sets in the post-test. However, Cowan and his colleagues observed that children in the experimental groups, who had the opportunity of finding out that counting was a good basis for their judgement, improved their performance much more than those children in the control groups, who had been asked to count but did not have the opportunity to find out that counting is a good strategy in comparing sets. More than half of the children in the experimental groups (32 out of 56) counted in order to compare the sets on every trial in the post-test while only 32 per cent (18 out of 56) in the control groups did so. Children in both age levels improved with the experience provided in the experimental groups but the older children ($6\frac{1}{2}$ to $7\frac{1}{2}$ years) performed better when they counted than the younger ones ($5\frac{1}{2}$ to $6\frac{1}{2}$ years), presumably because they could count better. For the children who did not count, there was no difference between the age levels.

This experiment shows a relatively good result in encouraging children to count. Fuson (1988) had observed that slightly less than 40 per cent of the 5-year-olds spontaneously relied on counting to compare sets. Cowan and his colleagues succeeded in bringing slightly more than half of the non-counters to rely on counting on every comparison given after training. Encouraged by this success, they decided to work with a younger group of children. This time they carried out the work with children approximately $3\frac{1}{2}$ to $4\frac{1}{2}$ years in a nursery school in London. The same design was used with children taking part in a pre-test, which verified whether they could count but did not do so when asked to compare sets, followed by either an experimental or a control condition, which was then followed by a post-test. Conditions were the same as those in the previous experiment. Cowan and his colleagues observed two interesting results in this experiment. First, they obtained some success in bringing children even as young as these to count in order to compare two sets but this success was not as strong as that observed with the older children. Slightly less than half (10 out of 24) of the 3½- to 4½-year-olds counted on every trial after taking part in the experimental conditions, compared to 12.5 per cent (3 out of 24) in the control conditions. Second, there was a statistically significant association between counting and making correct judgements about the sets. However, counting did not turn out to be a foolproof method. Almost half of the children (6 out of 13) who counted on every trial never made a correct judgement. As a group, they did better than the non-counters, since 20 of the 28 non-counters never made a correct judgement in six trials. Although Cowan and his colleagues do not report what type of error these young children made, we do know that they had been pre-tested and had succeeded in a counting task. They presumably counted the objects in the arrays but made judgements which went against the information they had from counting. If this is the case, Cowan's results strongly support the Piagetian thesis that children may learn to count without understanding that counting is a measure of set size. Even when successfully encouraged to count, many of the young children still did not base their comparisons between two sets on counting.

A final experiment in comparing sets will be reported because it relies on a different strategy but still produces results which converge with those reported so far. Catherine Sophian (1988), instead of asking children to compare sets, asked them to judge whether a puppet was doing the right thing when asked to compare sets. Her subjects were 3- and 4-year-old children. The puppet's task was sometimes to say whether two arrays had the same number and sometimes to say how many tokens there were altogether in the two arrays. In order to succeed, of course, the puppet would have to use different ways of counting when carrying out these two different tasks and the puppet did use different counting strategies. However, sometimes he used the right one for the task and sometimes the wrong one. The children were rather unsuccessful in deciding when the counting had been done correctly and when it had been done wrongly if the task was to compare the arrays. The children clearly did not have the idea that in order to compare arrays the right way was to count the tokens in each array separately, starting again from one when counting the tokens in the second array.

In short, in spite of differences in methods, the results of these studies seem to converge in indicating that it is one thing to be able to count and answer the question 'how many?' but quite another to understand the significance of the number uttered at the end of counting as a measure of set size. This sort of result was the reason for Piaget's emphasis on the need to consider children's understandings of the invariants of number in describing their mathematical reasoning and not only their knowledge of culturally transmitted number conventions, such as their knowledge of counting.

2.3 *Inferring number from that of an equivalent set*

In the previous sections we have looked at children's use of counting to construct equivalent sets and to compare two sets. These studies investigate whether children use numbers to measure sets. In this section we will look at the converse question: given that children know that two sets are equivalent, do they deduce the number of elements in one set if they count the number in the other one?

This question was analysed by Olivier Frydman and Peter Bryant (1988), who asked 4-year-old children to share some pretend-sweets (unifix blocks) between two puppets so that the puppets would receive the same amount. All children were successful in carrying out this fair sharing and proceeded in a one-for-you one-for-me fashion. When the sharing was completed the experimenter counted out loud the number of sweets that one puppet had and then asked the children how many sweets the other one had. Although they had meticulously shared the sweets, none of these 4-year-old children straightaway made the correct inference that the other puppet had the same number. Instead all of them tried to count the second lot of sweets. The experimenters stopped them and asked the question again but less than half of the children made the correct inference and said that the number of sweets was the same. Thus we see a new demonstration that young children (in this case 4-year-olds) may learn how to count but not realize the significance of counting as a measure of set size and may not use transitive inferences in determining the size of one set if they know the size of another that has the same amount.

3   Conclusions

In this chapter we have looked at two aspects of children's counting: their understanding of the counting principles and their use of counting. The counting principles represent the invariants of the activity of counting. It seems that young children (aged 4 years) may learn some number words and say them in a sequence but have difficulty in respecting the logic of counting. Their ability to respect the counting principles can be described as 'shaky'. Children aged 5 and 6 are significantly better at respecting the counting principles. In a sense, they can be said to master the counting activity. However, the evidence we have reviewed indicates that their counting ability is restricted to situations where they are trying to ascertain the number of objects. They do very well if we ask them the question 'how many?'. However, they do not seem to have connected their ability to say 'how many in a set' after counting with other aspects of the logic of number.

Although able to count well, these young children do not realize the significance of counting in order to compare sets or to produce equivalent sets. They rely on other strategies or other cues from the situation, such as the length of rows, rather than on counting. This is an example of knowing how to but not knowing when to do something. The children know how to count but do not know when counting is a good problem-solving strategy. They do not realize the significance of counting because they have not connected counting with situations that make it meaningful besides trying to find out 'how many?'. In other words, they learned a procedure that has potential for being used in a wide range of situations but they attribute limited meaning to it. For these children who know how to count but do not realize the significance of counting, conceptual development will involve learning about new situations in which counting is a good strategy. As we have seen, Fuson and Cowan and his colleagues have independently shown that children can be helped to see the significance of counting for comparing sets. Although not all 5-year-old children in their studies profited from instruction in their experimental conditions, it is clear that the instruction was not a waste of time.

We have also seen that 4-year-old children fail to connect their uses of counting with other aspects of the logic of number, such as transitivity. They may know that two sets are the same, they may know how many elements are in one set, but they will not necessarily realize that they could then tell how many are in the other set. Thus they have mastered the principles of counting but not all the invariants of number.

Teaching activities for children in this age level clearly need to involve the children in a variety of situations where counting is a good strategy for solving problems and where they can make inferences on the basis of counting. Their use of this general strategy in meaningful situations is expected to make number more meaningful to them. In other words, teaching at this age level may have the aim of making counting into a thinking tool.

3

Understanding Numeration Systems

In chapter 2 we considered the essential and inevitable aspects of counting. There are other aspects of our number system, however, which are not inevitable, which took some time to be invented and which are not universal. The base structure is the best example. We mentioned briefly that the Oksapmin of Papua New Guinea used until recently only a numeration system which was not a base system; they used the names of body parts to signify numbers. A number system such as this might be looked on as a curious oddity, and nothing much to do with the decimal base structure which has taken over most of the rest of the world. But the Oksapmin's way of counting is a useful reminder that the base-ten system is an invention which cannot be taken for granted and which has to be passed on from generation to generation. There is no logical reason why we should carve up our numbers into tens rather than into threes or eights or sixteens, and there is nothing to force us to use a base system at all, although it has proved very useful to do so.

Even among the numeration systems which use a base ten, there are considerable variations in the way that the structure is represented in different languages. In some, like Japanese, the relation between the words for numbers in different denominations is entirely transparent. The word for the number 12, as table 3.1 shows, is the equivalent of 'ten-two'. Once you know the Japanese words for 2 and 3 and 10 you can work out the words for 12, for 20, for 23 and for 32. This is not always true of English or of French. Where the Japanese say the equivalent of 'ten-two' for 12 we say 'twelve' and the French say 'douze'. The Japanese words for 20 and 30 are the equivalent of 'two-ten' and 'three-ten'; the English words for these

Table 3.1 Learning to count in Japanese

	10 **ju**	20 **niju**	30 **sanju**
1 *ichi*	11 ju*ichi*	21 niju*ichi*	31 sanju*ichi*
2 *ni*	12 ju*ni*	22 niju*ni*	
3 *san*	13 ju*san*	23 niju*san*	
4 shi			
5 go			
6 roku			
7 sichi			
8 hachi			
9 ku			

numbers are 'twenty' and 'thirty', and the French 'vingt' and 'trente'. The Japanese construct numbers above 10 using combinations of the words for tens and for ones. We, and the French, do so in many cases but not always.

Why has the invention of numeration systems with a base been so successful? The answer is that the advantages of a base structure, and therefore of our own decade system, are very great indeed. For one thing the structure makes it possible for the learner to generate number names, rather than memorizing them all by rote. We only have to remember a few number words. The rest we can generate for ourselves. Consider what it means to count, say, 1,000 objects. It means that you should be able to say 1,000 words, always in the same order. This would be a trying task for human memory if, throughout the course of history, cultures had not developed solutions for this memory problem. Most counting systems are organized in such a way that saying the number words in a fixed order becomes a relatively simple task. *When we understand the logic of a number system, we can generate numbers which we have not heard before.* This is particularly true of the transparently regular systems like Japanese, but once you have mastered the irregular teen words and decade words in English it is just as true of our system.

You can easily verify this for yourself if you are someone who does not know how to count in Japanese. In table 3.1 there are some numbers in Japanese, it shows 19 number words. If you study them carefully, you will understand how the number words are put together in Japanese and from these 19 examples you will be able to generate all the number words up to 99.

A second advantage is that a base structure can also be used to organize a notation system. When we use place value to write numbers, the digit on the right represents units, the digit just to the left of it representing tens, and so on. In other words, the same structure used in counting becomes the source of organization for the writing of numbers.

A third advantage is that computations based on the notation then become both economic and efficient. Just consider the difference between adding, for example, numbers written in the Hindu-Arabic notation that we use and carrying out the same operation when the numbers are written in Roman numerals. When we arrange the numbers in place-value notation into columns, we can just operate on each column sequentially. This helps relieve memory demands – or, as Hatano (forthcoming) says, helps 'off-load' some of the computation effort on to the written signs. We get no such support from the Roman notation.

$$263 \qquad\qquad CCLXIII$$
$$+\ \ 35 \qquad\quad +\quad XXXV$$

But in order to take advantage of the system, it is necessary to understand its structure. You must be able to see how larger numbers can be created by combining smaller ones. Any number n can be decomposed into two others that come before it in the ordinal list of numbers in such a way that these two add up exactly to n. This property or invariant of numbers is known as the *additive composition of number*.

The additive composition of number is an essential property of numeration systems with a base. The number words even in our irregular system make this additive composition rather explicit. For example, understanding a base system involves realizing that 23 can be decomposed into two tens plus three ones, and the words used with 'twenty' and 'three' highlight this particular way of breaking up this number.

Additive composition is also an important property of the idea of order in numbers. 'Six' is not simply the first word label after 'five'. The counting sequence means that 6 is greater than 5 and that 5 is a possible subset of 6 but 6 is not a possible subset of 5. Therefore when we wish to explore children's understanding of the numeration system we need to know much more than whether children can say number words in a fixed order.

It would be interesting to know whether children who can count well and know that 6 comes after 5 actually understand that 6 can be decomposed into 5 plus 1. This seems quite obvious to an adult and we might imagine that it is so also for children. After all, when children count objects and move them from a group of not-yet-counted to a group of already-counted objects, there is a moment when they have five objects in the already-counted group and add one object to it while saying 'six'. However, as we have seen in chapter 2, children may count without fully understanding the significance of their action. In this chapter, we will explore children's understanding of numeration systems, both oral and written, and some basic aspects of children's understanding of units.

1 Invariants of Numeration Systems with a Base: The Concepts of Unit and Additive Composition

A numeration system with a base involves *counting units of different sizes*. In our numeration system, for example, we count in ones, tens, hundreds, etc. These are units of different sizes (also referred to as orders) which can be counted within different classes – the class of ones, the class of thousands, the class of millions, etc. Because we use a base-ten system, when we have ten units of any size we regroup these into units of the next size. For example, we count ones up to ten. Ten ones make up one ten and then we combine tens and ones until we have nine tens and nine ones. Ten tens make up one hundred and then we combine hundreds, tens, and ones until we have nine hundreds, nine tens and nine ones. A new class of units, the class of thousands, is then introduced and we can repeat the same reasoning indefinitely.

This base structure of the number system is only partially reflected in English number words. When we count hundreds, for example, we clearly say a count word and the name of the unit that we are counting: one *hundred*, two *hundred*, three *hundred* etc. However, when we count tens we don't say a count word for the number of tens and then the word 'ten'; tens are counted with different names like ten, twenty, thirty etc.

We have seen that the Japanese counting system (table 3.1) shows much more clearly the fact that we are counting different units when we use decade labels. However, the English numeration system is not totally opaque. When we say a decade plus a unit – for example, twenty-one, twenty-two etc. – the system offers cues to the additive composition of number. These labels suggest that we are counting decades and ones separately. These cues, however, are not as clear as they are in Japanese or in Chinese.

Counting units of different sizes is not particular to the counting of objects. Measurement systems pose the same problem of sizes of units. Money, for example, is the measurement of how much we can buy. Coins and notes are units of different value – 1p, 2p, 5p, 10p etc. have different values. When we count how much money we have, we must take into account the value of the coins and notes. Similarly, measuring length involves us in the same issue of size of units. Centimetres and metres are units of different sizes. When we say something like 'one metre and twenty centimetres', we are also counting units of different sizes.

To understand a measurement system fully, we need to understand the equivalences within the system. If we have one 50p coin we can buy as much as our friend who has two 20p and one 10p coins. If something is 1 metre and 20 centimetres long, it could be covered by three pieces of tape, two 50 centimetres plus one 20 centimetres long.

Size of units is important both in counting and in ordering amounts. For example, if Kathy has ten 1p coins and Lisa has ten 10p coins, although they have the same number of coins, they have different amounts of money. Another example of the same principle is that if we measure a certain amount of sugar with tablespoons and then measure it with teaspoons, we get different numbers of spoonfuls; the larger the spoon, the smaller the number of spoons.

In this chapter we will look at studies which investigated children's understanding of units and of additive composition counting discrete quantities. Issues related to the measurement of continuous quantities will be discussed in chapter 4.

1.1   *Counting and mastering the properties of the numeration system*

The relationships that we have just outlined are a basic part of the numeration system. No one could understand our decimal system without also appreciating these facts. Mathematics teachers have for a long time realized that it is important for children to master the structure of the decimal system in order to use it in calculation. However psychologists did not for a long time research the origins of the concepts involved in mastering this structure. Although some work was carried out on the teaching of the structure and its consequence for children's ability to add and subtract multidigit numbers (see, for example, Resnick, 1982; Hall et al., 1985), little was known about the beginnings of this understanding. Now several studies have explored children's understanding of units and additive composition in the context of dealing with money. We will describe a series of studies which began with an investigation by Terezinha Nunes (T. N. Carraher, 1982; 1985) with preschool children and unschooled adults in Brazil.

Brazilian children, like English children, need to learn a numeration system with a base ten. Counting in Portuguese is roughly like counting in English: the decimal structure of the system is not clearly revealed in the values for the teens (for example, 11 = onze; 12 = doze) nor in the decade names (10 = dez; 20 = vinte; 30 = trinta; 40 = quarenta, and all other decades end in -enta). However, the combination of decades and units is spelled out in the number words (21 = vinte e um; 22 = vinte e dois etc.). Thus in the Portuguese oral numeration system the cues about units of different values and about additive composition are not completely clear.

The aim of the first study was to see whether children need formal teaching about decades before they understand the system. Alexander Luria (1969), a Russian psychologist, suggested that people only come to understand the base-ten structure when they are taught to write numbers. He argued that people could say the sequence of numbers without understanding their meaning but that the spatial arrangement of written numbers is a powerful, and a much needed, cue to what they mean. In the written numeration system, each digit represents a unit of a different size – for example, in the number 675 the 6 indicates the number of hundreds, the 7 the number of tens and the 5 the number of ones. Thus he expected that the written system would be the key to understanding the meaning of the numeration system.

Luria's evidence for the importance of the written system was based on his observation that patients with brain damage, who could not write numbers above 100, also had difficulty in recombining units in addition and subtraction. For example, when adding 38 and 57 we need to put the ones together into a new ten: Luria's patients had particular difficulty with such problems. This led him to suggest that we come to understand the structure of the numeration system through learning to write numbers.

Luria's observation is clearly important, but his conclusion about the two connected difficulties, writing numbers and combining units of different sizes, is not the only possible interpretation for his findings. The patients concerned may not have been able to write numbers as a direct result of their not being able to combine units of different size, rather than the other way round. The link between the two difficulties is interesting, but it is not yet clear which is the cause and which the effect.

Another way to look at this connection is to study young children and unschooled adults who have not been taught to read or write numbers. This is what Terezinha Nunes did in the first study of the base-ten structure that we shall describe (T. N. Carraher, 1985).

Nunes worked with 72 preschool children whose ages ranged from 5 years to almost 7 years (which is the age for entering primary school in Brazil) and 20 adults from a poor background who, as a consequence of their socio-economic circumstances, had never attended school. The children did not know how to write multidigit numbers but some of the adults did.

In order to investigate their understanding of the concept of unit and additive composition in the context of money, two tasks were used, but different presentations of the same questions were required in the work with children and adults.

In the first task, the subjects had to use the concept of units in order to compare the total value of sets composed by coins or notes of different denominations. In each comparison task, the children were shown two arrays with tokens that were pretend-coins of different values – for example, four 1c (c = *cruzeiro*, the Brazilian currency at the time) coins and four 10c coins. The children were interviewed individually and were asked to imagine that they were going to take the coins from one of the arrays to a shop to buy sweets and that the experimenter was going to take the other coins. The question that they had to answer was whether they would be able to buy the same amount of sweets or whether one of them could buy more sweets than the other.

The adults were just asked to imagine that they had the same number and value of coins used in the task with the children but no materials were presented. They were then asked to compare the two amounts.

Sixty per cent of the children succeeded in this task. Among them were some who could not even count the total amount of money in the arrays but were able to recognize that four 10c coins buy more sweets than four 1c coins. The unschooled adults made no mistakes at all in this task. We can conclude that children and adults can attain an understanding of the concept of units of different size in the context of money without going to school and also without knowing how to write multidigit numbers.

The second task, which was called the shop task, was about additive composition and the decade (i.e. base-ten) structure. Its purpose was to measure the children's ability to combine different denominations (tens and ones) in order to reach a particular number. The children were asked to play a game, in which they would buy objects and had to pay the exact price to the experimenter, who played the shop owner. They were given pretend-coins of different values: either 1c and 5c or 1c and 10c. They always had enough money to pay the amounts requested by the experimenter but they needed to consider the value of the coins when counting out the money. For example, the children might be given two 5c and four 1c coins and asked to pay 7c for a toy in the shop. In this case, they would have to use one 5c and two 1c coins. Or they might be given four 10c and four 1c coins and be asked to pay 13c. Although they only have eight coins, if they take into account the relative value of the coins they will realize that they have enough money. The amounts of money that the children were asked to pay were always within their counting range (that is, these values were lower than the largest number that they could count up to when asked to count out loud).

This additive composition task was much more difficult than the previous task, but it was not entirely impossible: only 39 per cent of the children succeeded in the shop task. However, their rate of success, even if modest, indicates clearly that it is not necessary for children to learn to write numbers in order to understand additive composition.

The parallel task given to adults did not involve any manipulable materials. They were not required to count money, which would have been a routine task for them: instead they were asked how many notes of 100c, 10c and 1c they would need if they had to pay, for example, 365 *cruzeiros* using the smallest number of notes possible. This was not a routine task for them but it was still very easy for all the adults irrespective of whether they did or did not know how to write numbers. Approximately 70 per cent of the adults answered all three items correctly and not one of them answered all three incorrectly.

These two studies led to the following conclusions:

1 *Knowing how to count and understanding the relative value of counting units and their additive composition are not one*

and the same thing. Children who know how to count may still not be able to understand the relative value of units and compose totals with different-value units in the context of dealing with money.

2   *Neither schooling nor the ability to write numbers is crucial for the understanding of these aspects of number*. They can be mastered from the use of the oral numeration system at least in coordination with familiarity with monetary systems.

1.2   *Addition and mastering the properties of the numeration system*

What then is the basis for mastering the decade system? We have decided that one does not have to learn to read and write numbers in order to understand the decade structure, and this seems to leave us with two other quite plausible alternatives. One is that practice in counting, and particularly in one-to-one correspondence, is the crucial experience that leads to this understanding. Children may come to realize that any number can be seen as the sum of its antecedent plus one (for example, that six is five plus one) and may then generalize this property to any other additive compositions simply as a result of frequent practice in counting objects. In that case their ability to count objects and to maintain one-to-one correspondence should correlate with their understanding of additive composition.

There is, however, another possibility. Children's encounters with addition might be the necessary experience for understanding the additive composition that underlies the decade system. There is a well-established change in young children's approach to adding which, on the face of it, could be the spur for understanding the base-ten system. This is the transition from counting-all to counting-on.

Suppose that children of 5 or 6 years have in front of them a number of tokens and are told a story about a boy who is given five sweets by his mother and three by his father. The children's task is to work out how many sweets this makes in all. Not yet knowing the 'number fact' $5 + 3 = 8$, the children use the tokens to help work out the answer, and either adopt a strategy called 'counting-all' or one called 'counting-on'.

The child who counts-all sets out a group of five counters and another of three, and then counts them all together, starting with one set and finishing with the other. The child who counts-on simply forms one set of three and begins counting it from 6: in other words he/she uses the total number of the first set as a starting-point and realizes that it is not necessary to count it all over again. It is easy to see that this is the more economic strategy of the two and it comes as no surprise that there is a developmental progression here. Younger children tend to count-all, older and more experienced children to count-on.

This developmental change could well be relevant to the understanding of the decade structure. The child who sees that she does not laboriously have to re-count the larger set may have realized that this set can be treated as a larger unit which can be combined with a smaller one. This child might therefore be in a better position to understand that one can form the number 23 by combining two units of one denomination (two tens) with three of another (three ones).

Our own view is that the second possibility – addition, rather than counting as the basis for understanding the decade structure – is the more plausible of the two. We expected that progress in understanding addition, particularly from counting-all to counting-on, rather than proficiency in one-to-one correspondence would be strongly related to the ability to solve additive composition of money in the shop task.

We carried out a study of the relative importance of counting and addition (Nunes et al., forthcoming) in which we interviewed a group of British 5- and 6-year-old children in Oxford. Many of the tasks that we gave them in this new study will by now be familiar. We gave them a version of the relative values task in which they had to judge the relative value of two quantities of money and the two quantities were either made out of units of the same value or of different values. We also put them through a version of the Shop Task that we have just described: again in this task the children had either to pay for items in a single denomination (pennies) or in combinations of two denominations (either of 10p and 1p or of 20p and 1p).

Because these tasks involved combinations of units of different sizes, they gave us a measure of the children's understanding of additive composition. The tasks that involved simply 1p coins gave us a good measure of the children's counting abilities. We also needed a measure of their ability to add, and particularly to use the more economic strategy of counting-on. In our addition tasks we asked the children to solve simple addition problems with the support of tokens, which were used as pretend-sweets. The problems were very simple (for example, Mary had 8 sweets and her Granny gave her 5 sweets. How many sweets does she have now?). The children had enough tokens on the table to represent both addends (i.e. quantities that have to be added) in the problem and then count all the tokens together. When we interviewed the children we recorded whether they got the answer right or wrong and also the method by which they obtained the answer, by counting-all, by counting-on, or by memory. No other strategies were observed.

We reasoned that the count-all strategy simply represented children's ability to use tokens as pretend-sweets (and pretend play is rather simple for 5-year-old children) and to count in a one-to-one correspondence fashion. In contrast, the count-on strategy would reflect a level of understanding of addition that goes beyond simple counting. Thus we expected: (1) to find a significant correlation between the children's ability to use the count-on strategy and their performance in the shop task; and (2) no significant relationship between the number of correct addition problems solved irrespective of strategy and performance on additive composition because the counting-all strategy, which relies on simple one-to-one correspondence, can lead to success. Our aim then was to see whether the total number of correct solutions to the addition problems correlated significantly with children's understanding of the numeration system or whether only the number of solutions obtained by other methods than the counting-all strategy (that is, count-on or memory) would correlate with the understanding of the numeration system.

These problems were not too difficult *per se* for the children. However, the average frequency of solutions by counting-on or memory was considerably lower than the rate of success: only 10 per cent of the solutions by 5-year-olds and 57 per cent of those by 6-year-olds were obtained by counting-on/memory.

The children's reactions to the problems in which they had to judge the relative values of two quantities and also to the shop task problems were much the same as in the earlier study. The children had little difficulty with items that simply required counting the number of coins in order to compare the arrays. However, it was much more difficult for them, especially for the 5-year-olds, to take the relative value of units into account. The statistical analysis showed that: (1) the 5-year-old children performed significantly better when the items did not require taking the relative value of the units into account; and (2) the children's performance in the two types of item was not correlated.

In the shop task the children were close to perfect when they were asked to pay for items in a single denomination (1p only). The other type of problem (where they had to use either 1p and 10p or 1p and 20p coins in combination) was significantly more difficult both for 5- and 6-year-old children.

We also compared their success *within the additive-composition items* when they involved combinations of 1p and 10p versus combinations of 1p and 20p. We reasoned that perhaps English-speaking children would find the combinations of 20p and 1p easier than combinations of 10p and 1p because in the first type of item the children can use linguistic cues but in the latter type they cannot. In other words, analysing 23 into 20 and 3 may be easier than analysing 13 into 10 and 3 because the children can use the verbal label (twenty-three) and its correspondence to the coins (20p and three 1p) as a guide. The results supported the hypothesis that the children can use the verbal cues as a support. The items with combinations of 20p and 1p were significantly easier than those with combinations of 10p and 1p for both 5- and 6-year-old children although the linguistic cues seemed to be more important for 5- than for 6-year-old children (see figure 3.1). It is important to point out that the additive-composition items involving 20p and 1p coins were still significantly more difficult for the children than those involving only 1p coins. That means that, although the linguistic cues may help, they are not sufficient for children to achieve the understanding of additive composition. It is interesting to note that the children's performance in the two types of items involving combinations of coins with different values was significantly correlated. Thus, in spite of the support that linguistic cues offer in the items with 20p and 1p combination, the sort of understanding involved in the two types of item is still basically the same.

These are interesting results because they demonstrate that we need to draw a distinction between children's counting skill and their understanding of the decimal structure of the numeration system in England just as strongly as we must do in Brazil. But the question relating to the origin of the understanding of the decimal structure requires further analysis. A major aim of this study was to compare the importance of counting and addition in the development of the understanding of the decimal structure of the system.

To start looking for answers, we examined the correlations

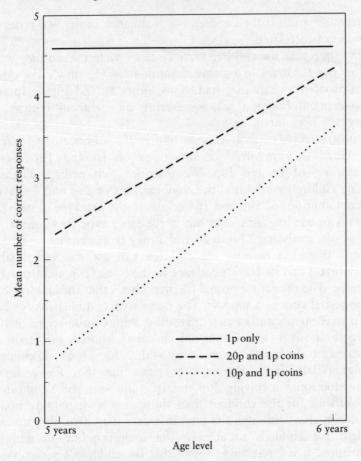

Figure 3.1   Children's success in reading and writing numbers
SOURCE: Nunes et al. (forthcoming)

between counting skill and additive composition, on the one hand, and solving addition problems and additive composition, on the other hand. The correlation between the children's success in the singles-only items and in the additive-composition items was not significant. Two scores were used for the addition tasks, one based on the number of correct responses and a second based on the number of items in which a count-on or memory strategy was used. Whereas the first score did not show a correlation with the additive composition items, the relationship between the number of items in which the count-on/memory strategy was used and performance in the additive composition items was significant.

Table 3.2 Inter-correlations within and across the two groups of tasks, soluble and not-soluble by counting ones

Soluble by counting ones

		CS	CN	CAN	RU	AD	AC
Counting-singles	CS	1.0	.47[a]	.19	.23	.20	.26
Comparing number of coins	CN		1.0	.15	.21	.33	.27
Count-all addition	CAN			1.0	−.05	−.02	.01

Not-soluble by counting ones

Relative value of units	(RU)				1.0	.67[b]	.52[b]
Additive composition	(AD)					1.0	.70[b]
Addition by count-on	(AC)						1.0

[a] Indicates correlations that are significant at the .05 level.
[b] Indicates correlations that are significant at the .001 level.
All other results are not significant.

A summary of the relationships across items in the tasks is presented in table 3.2. The items are organized in two groups, those where solutions depend simply on counting ones and those which require going beyond simple counting (that is, taking into account the relative value of units, using additive composition, or using the count-on strategy). It is clear that there are significant relationships in the children's performance within each group of tasks but little relationship across the two groups. These correlations suggest that it is unlikely that children come to understand the properties of the numeration system from more and more practice in one-to-one correspondence counting. It is much more likely that their progress in understanding addition provides a basis for understanding the properties of number systems with a base.

This conclusion has been bolstered by the results of another study carried out in Greece by Ekaterina Kornilaki (1994) with preschool children in the age range from 5½ to 6 years. She investigated the relationship between addition and additive composition by using an addition task in which she attempted to block the use of the count-all strategy.

In this task, the children were shown a wallet and told that a girl had, for example, 8d (*drachmas*, the Greek currency) in her wallet and that she had been given 7d more, which were put on the table in

Table 3.3 Number of children passing/failing additive composition and addition with an invisible addend

		Additive composition	
		Pass	Fail
	Pass		
Addition with an		12	21
invisible addend			
	Fail	0	17

front of the child. The question that they had to answer was how much money the girl had now. The point of using the wallet was to block the count-all strategy by making sure that the children had a visual representation for the second addend (7 coins on the table) but not for the first (the 8 coins inside the wallet). To solve this problem, known as addition with an invisible addend, the children need to count-on from 8 using the coins outside the wallet to figure out the total.

It turns out that this is not such a simple task for 5/6-year-olds. Only 66 per cent were able to come up with the correct answer. Knowing how to count and using the counting system to solve this problem are not exactly the same thing.

The number of children failing/passing additive composition and the addition task with an invisible addend is presented in table 3.3. It is noteworthy that all the children who passed additive composition also passed the addition task with an invisible addend but the reverse is not true. This relationship between the two variables is highly significant. It means that it is possible that passing the addition with an invisible addend task involves a necessary but not sufficient ability for understanding additive composition.

Kornilaki observed the children's strategies for solving the addition tasks with an invisible addend in great detail. Her observations revealed that the strategies described by Steffe et al. (1982) in the United States were also adequate descriptions of the behaviour of Greek children. The children who were not successful only counted what was visible. Thus they either gave as an answer to the problem the value of the second addend (that is, they counted the 7 visible drachmas and answered 'seven') or they counted the wallet as one and added the visible drachmas on to that (that is, their answer would be 'eight' for the problem above).

The children who succeeded consistently used one of a variety of possible strategies in the different problems. Some children (23 per cent) represented the first addend using their fingers. They then counted their fingers, starting from one, and went on to count the visible drachmas. Another strategy, used by 37 per cent, consisted of pointing at the wallet (either with the fingers or through head movements) while counting from one up to the value of the first addend and then going on to count the visible drachmas. These children seemed to represent the drachmas inside the wallet through movements. Thus, these two strategies involved a representation of the invisible drachmas through some gesture produced by the children plus counting.

Two other strategies that were also successful did not involve an overt, gestural representation of the invisible drachmas plus counting: the invisible drachmas were represented only by words. In the first of these, used by 21 per cent of the children, they simply said the number words from one up to the value of the first addend quite quickly and then went on to count the visible drachmas. Thus each invisible drachma was represented by the count word only. In the second strategy, the children (18 per cent) simply said the cardinal for the first addend and went on to count the visible drachmas. In this case, the cardinal was considered a sufficient representation for the whole set of invisible drachmas.

Kornilaki then investigated whether the type of strategy the children had used to solve the addition problems with an invisible addend made a difference for how successful they were in the additive composition task. The results of this analysis indicate that children who did not use an overt representation for the invisible addend associated with verbal counting were more likely to succeed in the additive composition task. All the children who just used the cardinal value of the set of invisible drachmas were successful and five out of seven who used the count words without pointing or counting fingers also succeeded in the additive composition task. These children comprise 11 of the 12 successful children in the additive composition task.

Thus Kornilaki's results strongly support the idea that one-to-one correspondence is not the basis of the understanding of additive composition. Children need to go beyond this form of reasoning about numbers to understand the cardinal value as a sufficient representation of the set and to be able to add on to it in order to master additive composition.

Educational implications   The results of these studies have clear educational implications. They indicate that children can be stimulated to further their understanding of the numeration system by being involved in solving simple addition problems as early as the age of 5. A sequence in the way these problems could be introduced is also indicated through the overall analysis of these results. It may be useful for 5-year-olds initially to have the option of representing both addends in an addition problem with tokens but progress in understanding addition is likely to be stimulated by their need to solve problems with invisible addends. The results indicate that there are intermediary strategies that children can use in the construction of their understanding of the cardinal as a sufficient representation for the number of objects in a set. We have seen that some children use their fingers and others use counting gestures to overcome the difficulty of dealing with an invisible addend before they can rely only on words.

Teachers can set their pupils problems with invisible addends and let them solve the problems together so that they can try to figure out what to do about representing an invisible addend in order to solve the problem. Other studies of children solving addition problems (Groen and Resnick, 1977) indicate that they tend to work towards more efficient strategies when given the opportunity to solve a variety of problems. Thus they may discover on their own the possibility of abandoning the fingers or gestures for the representation of one of the addends.

1.3   *Linguistic cues and children's understanding of additive composition*

So far we have concluded that neither counting *per se* nor learning to read and write numbers are crucial experiences for learning about the base-ten structure, and we have argued that what children learn about addition is far more important. But we have been discussing children's learning of numeration systems in which the number words do not give consistent cues (at least in the realm of numbers under 20) about the fact that we count different-sized units in a base-ten system.

We have seen earlier in this chapter that there are other systems, such as the Japanese one, which give much stronger cues to the counting of units of different size and to their additive composition. It is possible that the experience of counting with a regular system helps children to understand the properties of a base-ten system and makes it easier for them to do so than it is for children who have to deal with more capricious systems.

There are several reasons for thinking that the regularity of the system might make a big difference. One is a study by Miller and Stigler (1987) who compared 4-, 5- and 6-year-old children in Taiwan and the United States. The Chinese number system, which the Taiwanese children were learning, is as regular and transparent as the Japanese one.

Miller and Stigler simply asked both groups of children to count: the children counted objects, either arranged randomly or in neat rows, and they counted 'abstractly', which meant that they just counted as far as they could though they were counting nothing in particular.

The Taiwanese children were spectacularly better at both kinds of counting. The vast difference between the two groups was striking enough, but the pattern of differences was even more interesting.

The mistakes that the children made when counting objects were mostly of two kinds, the familiar one-to-one correspondence errors and errors with the sequence of numbers, such as producing numbers in the wrong order or missing a number out. There was no difference at all between the two groups as far as one-to-one errors were concerned, and it is interesting to note that these errors were much more frequent when the children counted the random arrays than the arrays in rows. But there was a significant difference between the groups with respect to the children's ability to produce the conventional count words as they pointed to the objects; the Taiwanese children could count much better.

The differences between the Taiwanese and the US children in the abstract counting task also took a striking pattern. Miller and Stigler let each child go on counting until he or she had made two mistakes: thus they had a measure of how far children can count without falling into serious error. Recall that the irregular English number words are entirely words for numbers between 10 and 20 and for the decades. The Miller and Stigler study showed that the sharpest difference between the two groups was in the number of children who began to make serious mistakes between 10 and 20. Hardly any of the Taiwanese children went wrong at this stage whereas a large number of the American children did.

This last result is rather strong evidence that a large part of the difference between the two groups is the direct effect of the difference in the number words. The US children make more mistakes because they have to deal with a much less helpful set of words: less helpful because it is more of a burden on their memory. They have to remember words like 'twelve' and 'thirteen'. Unlike Chinese children, they cannot generate these words from the constituent numbers 10 and 2 or 10 and 3.

The study plainly raises a question about the US and the Taiwanese children's understanding of the base-ten structure. The American children made more mistakes but we do not know whether that means that the Taiwanese children had a better grasp of the nature of the base-ten system. We need to know not just how well they count, but also how good they are in tasks in which they have to deal with different denominations and apply their understanding of the additive composition of number.

To answer this question we ourselves (Lines and Bryant, forthcoming) set up a study of 6-year-old Taiwanese and English children's understanding of additive composition and counting. In this study we repeated Miller and Stigler's counting tasks, and we also gave the two groups of children our shop task, to see how well they coped with different denominations and how well they could combine these denominations.

The purpose of the shop task, as we have seen, is to analyse children's understanding of additive composition. In this study we included combinations of 1p and 5p as well as combinations of 1p and 10p, all of which are numerical values of coins available both in Taiwan and in England. The items involving combinations of 1p and 5p create a useful control task, because they allow us to see whether the two groups of children differ in their ability to combine different denominations whatever these are or whether they differ only in their success in combining ones and tens.

We reasoned that the Chinese system is so transparent that perhaps Chinese children would behave in the shop task *as if* they understood additive composition when handling 1p and 10p combinations but they could be merely matching the verbal labels to the coins. If this were so, they would perform better on the 1p and 10p items but would not perform any better than the English children on the items that required combinations of 1p and 5p. We had previously found out that English children perform better in the combinations of 20p and 1p coins (which contain more cues to additive composition) than in the 10p and 1p combinations.

A different possibility is that children do not simply match number words to coin values in the shop task. Rather they need to *understand the idea of additive composition* and therefore particular linguistic cues do not radically influence the children's performance. A transparent counting system like the oral Chinese and Japanese numeration systems would facilitate children's learning in a more global fashion, helping them understand the idea of additive composition, and not simply leading to the matching of number words to values. If this is the case, then the Taiwanese children should perform significantly better than the English children both in the items involving combinations of 10p and 1p and in those involving combinations of 5p and 1p.

Three interesting results came out of this study. First, we confirmed the striking difference between speakers of Chinese and English originally reported by Miller and Stigler. The English children were at as much of a disadvantage to their Taiwanese peers as the American children had been in the Miller/Stigler study. This supports the idea that Chinese-speaking children are considerably helped by their number system in learning to count.

The second result concerns the single denominations problems in the shop task. In this task the two groups were at roughly the same level when they had to pay just in denominations of 1p, but the English children were at a disadvantage when they had to pay just in 10p. The Taiwanese children could count in tens much better than the English children, and this no doubt was because the Chinese decade words are much more helpful than the English ones.

Third, the Chinese-speaking children outperformed the English children in both combined denomination problems but this difference was greater when they had to combine 1p with 10p than 1p with 5p. So, here we have both a specific and a general effect. The Chinese children have an advantage over the English children when it comes to combining denominations in general but this effect is particularly strong when decades are involved. It seems that the regularity of the Chinese words for the decade structure helps the Chinese children with additive composition of units of different size in general and with additive composition involving decades in particular.

Another comparison of different number systems was carried out by Nunes et al. (forthcoming), this time involving English and French children. The English and French oral numeration systems involve similar difficulties up to the number 69. From then on, the French system becomes more complex because there are no longer simple combinations of the name of a decade plus ones. The word for 70 is equivalent to 'sixty-ten', followed by sixty-eleven, sixty-twelve etc. up to sixty-nineteen (that is, 79). The word for 80 is equivalent to 'four-twenty' followed by labels up to 'four-twenty-nineteen' (that is, 99). Our question was whether these special irregularities of the French counting system would make the task of understanding the properties of numeration even harder for French children or whether they caused no extra difficulties because the further irregularities only appear with much larger numbers. We reasoned that it is possible that children develop an understanding of additive composition in the realm of smaller numbers (say up to 30–50) and use this understanding when dealing with the larger numbers even if there are further irregularities in the system. If this is the case, French and English children should not differ in their understanding of additive composition. Furthermore, French children should show no further difficulties in composing sums of money in the seventies to nineties than in composing sums in the forties to sixties.

We interviewed 30 French children, 10 at each of three age levels, 5, 6, and 7 years, and compared the performance of 5- and 6-year-olds with that of English children. This is not a straightforward comparison because 5-year-old children in England were in their first year of primary school whereas the French 5-year-olds were in preschool. If English children had an advantage at the age of 5, this difference could result either from their being in school or from their using a more regular system. In order to minimize the effects of schooling, we worked only with English 5-year-olds in their first term in school and with 6-year-old French children also in their first term of school. For some further analyses involving French children only, a group of 7-year-olds was also interviewed.

All children answered, among other tasks, the additive composition task with two types of item, those that used only 1p coins and those that mixed 10p and 1p coins. In addition, the French 6- and 7-year-olds also answered items where the children were asked to pay amounts of money in the eighties either using mixtures of 20p and 1p coins or using mixtures of 10p and 1p coins. These latter items were introduced in order to ascertain whether French children would show greater ease in composing the larger sums of money by using four 20p coins (a composition that parallels their 'quatre-vingt' label for 80) or by using eight 10p coins (a composition that is distanced from the verbal label but is coherent with the understanding of additive composition of numbers built from smaller values). This allowed us to evaluate the possibility that children make direct matches between the verbal labels and the coins in the shop task.

The results of these comparisons are briefly presented below. First, a comparison of the different types of item for the French children demonstrated once again the significance of the distinction between counting and understanding the numeration system. Items that involved only 1f (for *franc*, the French currency) coins were significantly easier than those that involved combinations of coins of different denominations although the value of the sums of money was controlled as in the previous studies. Second, the comparison between French and English children in their first term of school did not produce significant differences. The greater irregularity of the French counting labels does not make the task of understanding additive composition any more difficult for French than for English children. However, it must be recalled that the French children beginning school were older than their English counterparts. Third, it was not more difficult for the French children to compose sums where the values were in the seventies, eighties, and nineties than to compose sums where the values were in the forties, fifties and sixties. This result supports the idea that children can develop their understanding of additive composition in the realm of smaller numbers and apply this understanding to larger numbers even if new irregularities in the numeration system are observed. Finally, French children did not find it any easier to compose sums of money in the eighties by using four 20f coins rather than eight 10f coins. This result once again suggests that children are not simply matching verbal labels to coins in the shop task because the French word 'quatre-vingt' would cue them to using four 20f coins to pay 80 francs but not to using eight 10f coins. In other words, if children understand additive composition, the particular values (5, 10 or 20) that go into the composition do not affect their performance in this task significantly.

To sum up, the studies described here indicate that the regularity of the counting system influences children's learning significantly. The highly regular systems, like Chinese, where the counting of units of different values is clear even in numbers between 10 and 20, afford children better possibilities for understanding additive composition. This facilitation does seem to result partly from the use of particular linguistic cues and partly from a general understanding of additive composition. If a system has further irregularities involving larger numbers, these irregularities do not seem to influence children's learning significantly because they can work out the idea of additive composition within the realm of relatively smaller numbers. Although the difficulty of the task of understanding additive composition varies across cultures with the regularity of the system, children in these different cultures still have to master the same principles in order to understand their number system.

A recent study by Miura et al. (1994), including a comparison of first-grade children from six different countries (People's Republic of China, France, Japan, Korea, Sweden, and the United States), brings further confirmation to these ideas. In the study by Miura et al., the children were asked to give the experimenter several quantities of small bricks, that could be either single bricks or presented in strips of ten bricks glued together. This task, much more similar to a school task than our shop task, revealed that speakers of languages where the base ten of the numeration system is transparent – namely, Chinese, Japanese and Korean – had a strong preference for building the large amounts requested by the experimenter (for example, 42 bricks) using the strips of ten bricks plus single bricks – an efficient strategy for the task. In contrast, the speakers of the languages where the structure of the system is not as clear – namely, French, Swedish and English – had a preference for building the same amounts using single bricks counted one by one. The authors go on to suggest that this may give the Chinese, Japanese and Korean children an overall advantage in learning mathematics in primary school. Although this is a plausible hypothesis, we believe that much more evidence is still needed before we can be certain that the often documented better performance of Japanese and Chinese children in mathematics can be explained mostly on the basis of their use of a more regularly built numeration system.

2   Understanding Written Numbers

We started out our investigation by asking whether it was necessary to know how to write numbers in order to understand the structure of the numeration system. We found out that children and adults who did not know how to write numbers could still understand the invariants of a numeration system with a base. Their understanding of additive composition seemed to be based on the understanding of addition. A natural sequence to our studies was to turn the question around: is the understanding of additive composition necessary for learning how to write and read numbers?

Some reflection about the way in which we write numbers is necessary before we describe the empirical studies. First, it is clear that writing numbers in the way we do involves the concept of units. In the Hindu-Arabic system we use, each digit represents units of a particular value. When we write, for example, '124', 1 indicates the number of hundreds, 2 indicates the number of tens, and 4 indicates the number of ones. Second, each unit is represented by its place in the number from right to left. The digit on the right indicates how many units, the one to left of it indicates how many tens, the one to the left of the tens indicates how many hundreds etc. This convention is known as *place value*, an expression that shows that the relative value is indicated by the place of the digit. Third, if there is an empty unit in the number – for example, the number 1,805 has no counting of tens – a zero is used as a place holder. Thus some aspects of the written numeration system require the understanding of the same principles as the oral system but other aspects – namely, place value and the use of zero as a place holder – are specific to the written system.

This analysis leads us to expect that children who do not understand additive composition will not be able to write and read numbers, but not all children who understand additive composition will necessarily know how to write and read numbers. We can also reasonably expect that, if properly taught, children who understand additive composition will readily learn to write and read numbers.

There is plenty of evidence to show that young children do at first have considerable difficulty in writing large numbers, but until recently there had been little to show what is the source of their problem. Kamii (1980) and Sinclair (1988), for example, demonstrated that 6/7-year-old children have difficulties in interpreting the idea of place value. When shown a two-digit number – say, 16 – and asked to indicate what each digit signified, many children indicated the meaning of each digit as referring to units only, showing one object to correspond to the digit 1 in 16 and six objects to correspond to the digit 6. The children in Kamii's study did so even though they had originally been asked to pick out 16 objects and write out how many objects they had on the table.

However, neither Kamii nor Sinclair investigated children's understanding of additive composition and its relationship to writing numbers or interpreting written numbers. This was the question asked by Terezinha Nunes and her colleague Analucia Schliemann (T. N. Carraher, 1982; T. N. Carraher and Schliemann, 1983). The studies were carried out in Brazil and their aim was to test the hypothesis that children have to understand the additive composition of number before they begin to be able to write and interpret multidigit numbers. To test this hypothesis, they gave the children the shop task to look at their ability to cope with the additive composition of number and also asked them to write and read a set of multidigit numbers.

The children's performance was analysed in terms of whether the children could combine denominations in the shop task, and whether they were proficient or not in writing and interpreting numbers. In principle the children could fall into four possible categories: (1) those who could do neither task at all, (2) those who could manage the additive composition of number task but could neither write nor read the multidigit numbers, (3) those who could do both tasks well, and (4) conversely, those who could read and write the numbers but who failed in the additive composition shop task. However, if it is true that children need to understand additive composition in order to learn to write and read multidigit numbers, it can be predicted that the children will fall into only three of these four possible categories. The hypothesis produces the prediction that the fourth group is an impossibility. There may well be children who can sort out the additive composition problems but cannot yet manage to read and write multidigit numbers, but there should be no children who do well at reading and writing numbers but fail the additive composition task.

The results turned out this way. One hundred children in first and second grade were interviewed and all children fell into one or other of the first three groups: none fell into the fourth.

The children in the first group could neither understand the additive composition of sums of money in the shop task nor write numbers correctly. In the second group were the children who performed well in the additive composition task but still made errors in writing numbers. Their errors, however, were systematic. Most of the time these children represented the hundreds and thousands literally rather than accomplishing a compact representation through place value. For example, when writing the number 'one hundred and twenty' the children tended to produce '10020'. Similarly, when writing 'one thousand one hundred and sixty-one' a common production was '100010061'. Some of the children were able to eliminate some of the zeros in these productions but still did not accomplish a compact representation by place value. Examples of the partial reduction of zeros were 120 written as '1020' and 1161 written as '10161'.

Finally, a third group of children displayed a mastery of both additive composition of sums of money and the conventional writing of numbers.

Nunes et al. (forthcoming) also examined children's productions of written number in England. We asked the English children to write a single-digit number (8), three two-digit numbers (14, 25, 47), two three-digit numbers (108, 129), and one four-digit number (2569). We also asked them to write round numbers (10, 60, 100, 200, 1000). They were also asked to read numbers chosen in an analogous way. We had several hypotheses for this study and will deal with each one in turn. First, we expected that the size of the number would not be the best predictor of its difficulty for the children either in the reading or writing task. Round numbers, such as 10, 100, 200 and 1000 might be more frequently seen by children in everyday life and also involve fewer difficulties because the notion of additive composition is not necessary. Thus more children may write 100 correctly than 47, or 200 than 129, even though 100 and 200 have larger values than 47 and 129, respectively. Figure 3.2 shows the percentage of children reading and writing each of the numbers correctly. The graphs show that, as expected, more children write and read 100 correctly than numbers like 14, 25, 36 and 47. Similarly, more children read and write 200 and 1000 correctly than 129 or 123.

Second, we expected that children would be active learners of the written numeration system and try to generate written representations although they had not been taught how to write two-digit numbers and had not mastered the system. This hypothesis is based on our view that learning mathematics involves the acquisition of generative systems rather than the learning of isolated facts. If this turned out to be the case, we should be able to find a considerable number of children who used their own system to produce written numbers in a relatively consistent, even if not correct, fashion. Thus the children's productions were classified on the basis of the principles that they seemed to be using when they wrote numbers.

Almost all the children were able to write 8 (93 per cent) and 10 (85 per cent) correctly. Only a few children (about 15 per cent) refused to try to write most of the other numbers. Refusals from the other children were selective. About half of the children said that they could not write 2569 but only about 30 per cent said they could

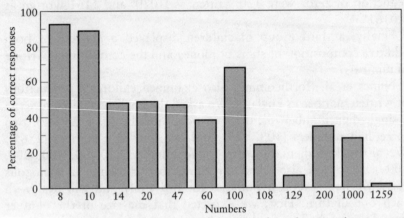

Percentage of 5/6-year-olds writing each number correctly

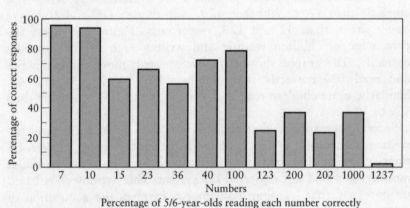

Percentage of 5/6-year-olds reading each number correctly

Figure 3.2 Examples of one-to-one correspondence between numbers and words in children's written numbers

not write 129, the number with the next largest percentage of refusals. This by no means implies that the children knew how to write the other numbers that we dictated. They seemed to feel, though, that they could try.

Some children (4 per cent) appeared to use a one-to-one correspondence between a number word and a digit. This means, for example, that 25 required two digits, 60 was written with one digit, and both

100 and 1000 were written with two digits, one digit signifying 'one' and the second digit signifying 'hundred' or 'thousand'. Alice, who wrote a slightly different list of numbers (she decided to write 40, for example, instead of 60), produced numbers within this system. Gloria used this system only partially, when she chose the pound sign to represent 'thousand' (see figure 3.3).

Many of the children seemed to use two systems, one for the two-digit numbers and one for writing 108, 129, (sometimes) 200, and 2569. The two-digit numbers (25 and 47) plus the round numbers (100, 1000, and sometimes 200) were often *written correctly*. It is not clear to us how the children managed to succeed with two-digit numbers – and, in particular, how they managed to succeed in writing 25 and 47. Although one could argue that simple memory explained their success with the round numbers 100, 200 and 1000, it is unlikely that all two-digit numbers could be memorized without a system that helped the children in their production. Their second system consisted of concatenating a string of numbers corresponding to the number labels, just as we had observed with Brazilian children. Thus 108 was written as 1008 and 2569 was written as 200050069. Sometimes the number of zeros was either increased or decreased. Some examples of this type of production are presented in figure 3.3. For the numbers 108 and 129 about 40 per cent of the children produced this type of writing, which was more frequent than either refusals or correct responses. Thus we can say that this way of writing numbers corresponds to the use of consistent (even if implicit) rules used by children.

Figure 3.4 displays the percentage of productions of writing numbers by concatenation, and the percentages of refusals for some of the numbers used in the study. The productions for numbers which could not be written by the concatenation process are excluded from this figure.

A third type of response included productions that involved other mistakes – such as writing a wrong digit (for example, 129 may have appeared as 159) or inverting the right to left position of the digits (e.g. 47 written as 74). These errors account for a relatively small percentage of productions and don't exceed 21 per cent in any case.

In short, a small portion of children's errors in writing numbers was the result of using the wrong digit or the wrong relative position of digits. The great majority of errors was accounted for by the use of a concatenation rule, which resulted in writing each component of a number word after the other in a sequence. This rule for writing

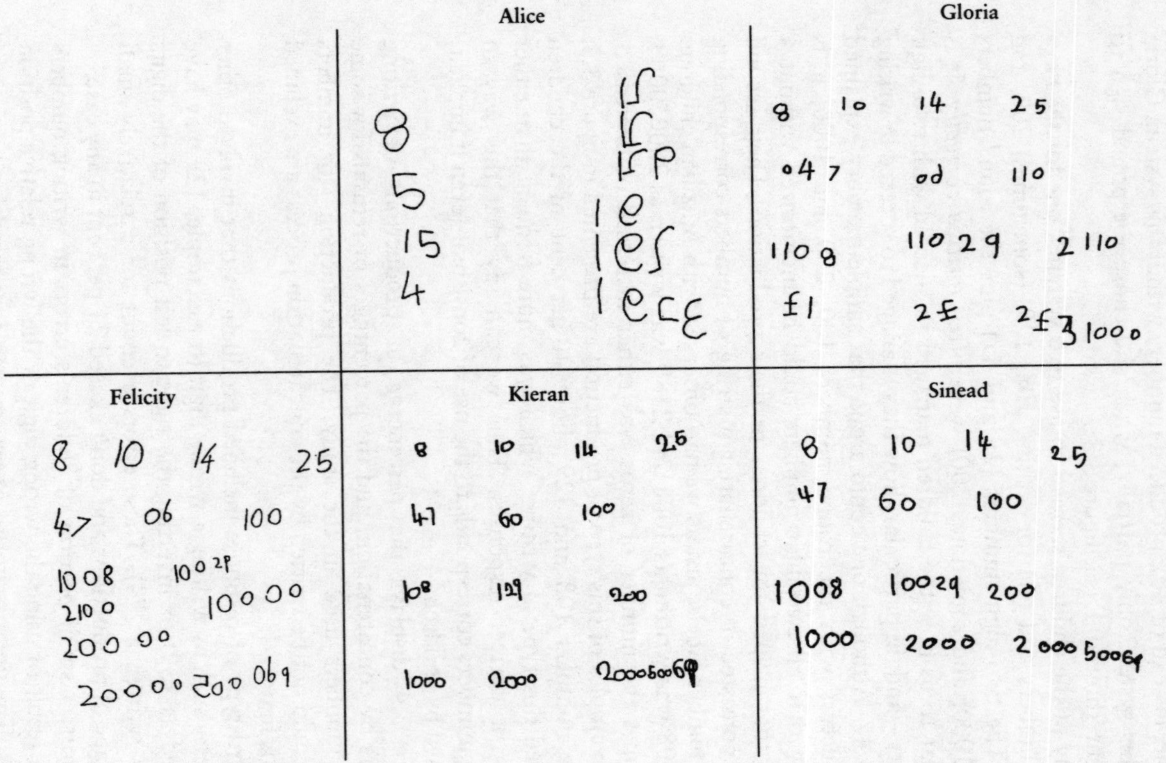

Gloria

8 10 14 25
o4o oo 110
o11o 29 110 210
8 1F 2F 2F 3 1000

Sinead

8 10 14 25
47 60 100
1008 100 29 200 2 000 5009
1000 2000 2 000 000

Alice

(handwritten numerals)

Kieran

(handwritten numerals)

8 10 14 25
47 60 100
8 10q 101 000
1000 2000 2 000 000

Felicity

8 10 14 25
47 60 100
1008 100 2P 800
210 00 2100
200 000 2000 00

Figure 3.3 Different types of error in writing numbers

SOURCE: Nunes et al. (forthcoming)

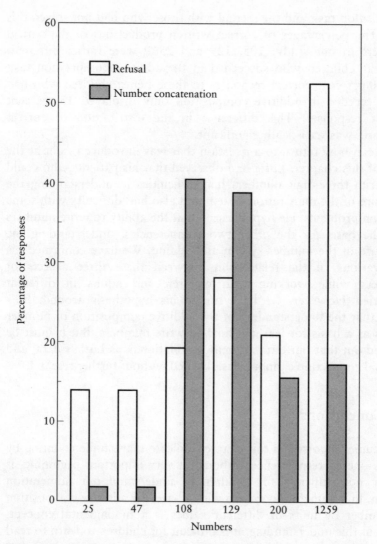

Figure 3.4 Writing numbers: percentages of concatenations and refusals

numbers has also been observed among Italian 6- to 8-year-old children (Power and Dal Martello, 1990) and French and Belgian children (Seron and Fayol, 1994) and confirmed once again among Brazilian children (Silva, 1993).

As a final analysis, we separated the children in our study into two groups, one with children who had been successful in the additive composition task and the second with those who had not solved this task. The percentages of correct written productions of the critical numbers in our study, 108, 129 and 2569 were rather different. Whereas children who succeeded in the additive composition task had 60 per cent correct responses to these items, children who had not succeeded in additive composition only displayed 13 per cent correct responses. This difference in the distribution of correct responses was statistically significant.

We can now return to a question that was introduced right at the start of this chapter. Luria had observed that his patients who could not write three-digit numbers had difficulties in understanding the structure of the numeration system and also had difficulty with some addition problems. He hypothesized that the ability to write numbers was the basis for the other two competencies, understanding the structure of the number system and adding. We have confirmed his observations of the relationship between these three aspects of numbers while working with children and adults in different countries. However, we have turned his hypothesis around. It is likely that the understanding of the additive composition of number works as a basis for learning how to write numbers. But it must be pointed out that our data are only correlational, as Luria's data, and a causal connection cannot be established without further research.

3   Conclusions

The studies reported in this chapter indicate that simple counting by one-to-one correspondence, although a very important beginning, is clearly not sufficient for children to understand our numeration system. In a numeration system with a base, the additive composition of number by units of different values is a fundamental concept. Without this understanding, it is difficult for children to learn to read and write numbers. Additive composition, in turn, seems to rest more on children's understanding of addition than on one-to-one correspondence. Counting, as we saw repeatedly, is not enough for children to understand the numeration system.

There seems to be an ordered way in which children's understanding develops with respect to number understanding. The use of the count-on strategy in addition precedes the understanding of the properties of the numeration system, which serves as a basis for children to learn to read and write numbers. But this sequence does not seem to be a series of prerequisites that the children have to develop on their own. Young children (5-year-olds) can be confronted with addition problems where one addend is not visible. The need to cope with such problems may lead them to discover more efficient addition strategies, which will then constitute a basis for understanding the numeration system. When children use play-money in problem-solving, they become quite comfortable with the idea of exchanging one 10p piece for ten 1p or other such exchanges. They use the ideas of units and additive composition as 'theorems in action' (to use Vergnaud's expression; see Vergnaud, 1985) – that is, unspoken but firmly established knowledge of invariants. These insights will be important in their understanding of the written Hindu-Arabic numeration system. Learning how to read and write numbers will in turn open up new opportunities for children.

In short, these findings indicate that young children can solve simple problems, even if they may initially need to use some sort of visual representation as a support, and that it is important to involve them in problem-solving in order to build a basis for their concept of number to develop beyond counting by one-to-one correspondence. In chapter 4 we will turn to other experiences where young children need to think about the concept of units – their experience with measurement systems.

4

Measurement Systems

Discussions of counting lead on quite naturally to the question of measurement, for there are strong links between the two activities. When young children compare two sets by counting – a task which, as we have seen, is at first quite hard for them to do – they are using number as a measure. Counting here is the formal equivalent of using a ruler. Just as one takes a ruler and puts it first against one quantity, then against the other in order to find out how the two quantities compare, so in the case of two sets of discrete objects one first counts one set and then the other to make the same kind of comparison. In both cases there is an intervening measure: in one that measure is the ruler and in the other the number system itself.

The act of measuring, with a ruler or with a number system, may seem simple enough, but it does involve two different and separable components. The first of these two components is a logical inference which is called the transitive inference. To use a ruler in order to compare two quantities, you have to know that these two quantities can be compared through a common measure, and to grasp this you have to be able to make inferences.

These inferences take a particular form. If A equals B and B equals C, then A must equal C; if A is greater than B and B greater than C, then A must be greater than C. In both cases we infer the relations between A and C, which we never see directly compared with each other, by combining two premises (e.g. A > B, B > C) and in both cases this inference takes the form of comparing A and C through their relations to B. Thus B acts as an intervening measure and it is easy to see that no one can have the slightest idea how a ruler works unless he or she can also make and understand such inferences.

Measurement is a logical act and one has to grasp the logic in order to measure.

The second essential requirement is an understanding of units. When we measure we are concerned with actual quantities as well as with simple relations like 'larger' and 'smaller'. The ruler is divided into inches or centimetres, the thermometer registers degrees, the scales give us ounces or kilograms. The most important and the most basic rule about units of measurement is that, in order to allow for transitive inferences, they have to be a constant quantity. One inch is always the same as another, and it is no use measuring two lengths in hand widths unless the same hand or at any rate the same-sized hand is applied to both quantities.

Units add a very great deal to the power of measurement. They allow us to go beyond the simple transitive inference. They make it possible to ascribe a particular value (6 inches, 50 grams) to a quantity, and with the help of units of measurement we can tell not just that A is larger than C but also that A is twice the length of C or that A is 15 centimetres longer than C.

We can now apply the distinction between universal logical rules and man-made cultural inventions to these two aspects of measurement. It is easy to see that transitive inferences must be the universal basis of measurement: no attempt to measure will succeed unless it conforms to the rules of the transitive inference. Units are another, rather more complex, matter. The actual size of the unit is man-made and arbitrary, and it varies between cultures. We measure distance in miles, others do it in kilometres and our predecessors did it in cubits. Indeed the creation of standardized measures and the immense care and attention devoted to them over the centuries is a great human achievement and has played an important part in the development of agriculture, industry and commerce. Units are often (but not necessarily always) put into systems so that larger amounts will be measured with larger units and smaller ones with smaller units; a conversion rule can then be applied to allow the user of the measurement system to go from smaller to larger units or vice versa. Different units in the same scale always bear a constant relation to each other: there are always 12 inches in a foot, 16 ounces in a pound. It follows too that the relations between different units of measurement of the same dimension must be constant too. There are always (approximately) 2.5 centimetres to 1 inch and 1.6 kilometres to 1 mile. As we shall see later, this constant ratio between different scales of measurement gives us an excellent way of looking at children's understanding of measurement.

However, these ways of organizing units are not universal. Not all systems of measurement use units of the same size. Among the Oksapmin, for example, a body-part measurement system is used to determine the length of bags which the people often carry around. A bag is measured by placing the outstretched hand into it and looking at how far it reaches up: it can be a fist bag, if it reaches up to the fist, an elbow bag, if it reaches up to the elbow, a shoulder bag, if to the shoulder and so on. Further, not all measurements are organized into precise systems but only the most formal ones seem to be. In our own practices in the kitchen, for example, we measure with tea-spoons, tablespoons, cups etc. and do not necessarily know how to convert tablespoons into cups or vice versa.

In spite of the variations in cultural practices, the logic used in connection with the systems is universal. Saxe and Moylan (1982), who described the use of the body-part measures among the Oksap-min, gave an experimental task to unschooled adults by asking them to make comparisons between bags that had been measured against the body of different people, a child and an adult. The two measure-ments had the same value: they were, for example, 'shoulder bags'. The majority of the unschooled adults interviewed (64 per cent) realized that, in spite of the same value having been given to the two bags, the sizes were different. These adults understood both transitive inferences and the logic of units – that is, the need for equal units if transitive inferences are to be made – although their own system of measurement did not rely on units that are constant across people.

Thus in the same way that there are universal aspects in the logic of number (such as conservation) and logical aspects in the particular number system constructed in cultures (additive composition using the base of the system), there are also universal aspects in the logic of measurement (transitive inference) and logical aspects in the systems constructed by cultures (the systems of units). In the following sections we will look at how children come to understand these different sides of measurement systems.

1   Logic and Measurement

It seems right to turn first to children's understanding of the tran-sitive inference as the basis for measurement. But we need not spend a great deal of time on it, for the evidence suggests quite unambiguously that children have little difficulty with this aspect of measurement. Some time ago Peter Bryant and Hanka Kopytynska (1976) gave 5- and 6-year-old children as simple a measuring task as they could think of. They gave them two blocks of wood, each with a hole at the top. The children could not see to the bottom of the holes because these were too narrow, and they were asked whether the holes were the same depth or, if not, which was the deeper. Because simple visual comparisons were out of the question, they had to find some other way of answering. The only other material in front of them was a stick which fitted well into the holes. The stick had marks along it; when it was inserted into one of the holes, these marks made it easy to see and remember how far in the stick had gone.

They wanted to know whether the children would solve the problem of comparing the depths of the holes by using the stick as an intervening measure.

They found that for the most part they did. Most of the children used the stick without any prompt to do so; when they used the stick, their judgements were mostly right. This is a result which has been confirmed many times and has even been shown to be true of younger children in some circumstances (Miller, 1989). The basic idea of an intervening measure is not a difficult one for young schoolchildren, and the transitive inference which underlies the use of these measures seems to come easily to them.

2 Units of Measurement

The evidence on children's dealings with units produces a very different picture. Here we find a mixture of success and failure which suggests that children quickly grasp some aspects of units of measurement but are slow to understand others.

In the rest of this chapter, we will use some research that we have done to analyse children's understanding of the concept of unit in measuring length. We chose to work with length for several reasons. One significant reason is that schoolchildren in England are exposed to two different systems for measuring length, the imperial and the metric. English children, therefore, are familiar both with inches and with centimetres (that is, they hear these terms quite often), and many of the rulers that they use have marks for centimetres along one edge and for inches along the other. This gave us the opportunity to talk to children about alternative conventional measures for the same dimension.

A second reason for picking length was that young children do show interest in comparisons along this dimension. They compare themselves in height, they compare objects (pencils, pieces of chocolate bars etc.), and discuss these comparisons, thereby developing a vocabulary (longer, shorter, larger, smaller) that could be used in our tasks.

Finally, comparisons of length are much easier to carry out directly through perception than comparisons of other dimensions, such as area, volume or weight. If two areas have different shapes, it becomes rather difficult to compare them directly through visual inspection. The possibility of direct perceptual comparison was important for some of the experiments that we carried out on measurement.

Our description of this work is divided into four sections. In the first we will examine how children make logical inferences in situations where they are required to use the concept of unit. In the second we will investigate children's memory of rulers and discuss how their productions inform us about their understanding of measurement. In the third we will examine children's performance in a measurement task in an unusual situation: measuring with a broken ruler. We will conclude the chapter with a brief section on educational implications.

2.1   *Making inferences about relative size*

A pioneer study about children's understanding of the concept of unit was carried out by the Russian developmental psychologist Davydov (1982). His interest was in investigating whether children can keep in mind a unit when they are asked to count. In one task, for example, the children were asked to determine how many large glasses of water were contained in a series of three large and four small glasses. The children were told that each small glass was the same as half of a large glass. Although most of the children could count and even carry out additions of single- and two-digit numbers, many could not say how many large glasses were contained in the whole set of glasses. They simply counted the number of glasses and ignored the fact that two small glasses were needed to make up a large one. These children, Davydov argued, did not understand the multiple relationships between the number, the unit, and the quantity expressed in number-of-units.

We investigated the concept of unit among primary school children in England (Bryant and Nunes, 1994) in a task that differed from that used by Davydov (1982). It seemed to us that there were two possible, alternative sources of the difficulty of Davydov's task. One was the concept of unit itself and the other was the requirement to convert one unit (small glasses) into another (large glasses). The second requirement of course depends on the first and it seemed more likely to us that it was the difficulty of the second requirement that held the children back. Children may overcome the first difficulty without yet mastering how to convert one unit value into the other.

Suppose, for example, that young children were given two ribbons to compare, both of which measure 'eight units' though one ribbon is measured in inches whereas the other is in centimetres (a problem not unlike the Oksapmin's when two bags are 'shoulder bags' but one was measured by a child and the other by an adult). If children understand the idea of a unit, they should quickly grasp that the ribbons are of different sizes. The ribbon measured with larger units is itself the larger one. It is possible that children may understand this relative comparison some time before they can quantify the exact relationship between the two types of units. This was our hypothesis, and we held it for theoretical and for empirical reasons.

In a theoretical analysis of children's performance in some learning experiments, Bryant (1974) had argued that young children can make logical deductions using what he terms *relative codes* before they make similar deductions using *absolute codes*. They are, for example, able to realize that if A is greater than B and B is greater than C, then A is greater than C, before they understand that if they add the difference between A and B to the difference between B and C they will find the difference between A and C. Further empirical results, observed in our shop task, also suggested that children may be able to reason using relative codes and yet be unable to transform one unit into the other for the purposes of quantification. Children who were clearly able to say, for example, that four 1p and four 10p coins cannot buy the same amount of sweets still failed the additive composition task, where the values of the two types of coins had to be coordinated.

So we designed a series of studies in which we asked children to make transitive inferences about the relative sizes of two ribbons when they were given different sorts of measurement information. We interviewed 43 children in the age range 5 to 7 years, all attending the same primary school in Oxford. The children were familiar with both centimetres and inches and this gave us the opportunity to use different-sized units which the children could easily talk about. We presented them with several inference trials in a sort of 'detective game'. We had two sets of ribbons, each set kept in a separate envelope. One of the envelopes contained the child's ribbons, the second one contained the experimenter's. The ribbons were of different colours in each set but across sets they formed pairs of the same colour. The experimenter told the child that he/she had measured the ribbons and was going to give the child a clue so that the child could try to figure out which ribbon was longer or whether they were of the same length.

The trials were divided into two blocks. In the first block, all the ribbons had been measured in centimetres. Thus we started out by showing the children a ruler and indicating what centimetre units were on the ruler. We then asked the children to show on the ruler how long something would be if we said it was '4 centimetres long'. This posed no problem to the children. Then we gave the children information about the ribbons in two different ways. In one type of trial, the information was absolute. For example: 'I measured my yellow ribbon and it was 8 centimetres long. I then measured your yellow ribbon and it was 9 centimetres long. Do you know whether they are they the same length or whether one is longer than the other?' In the other type of trial, the information was a mixture of absolute and relative, but was sufficient for the child to reach a conclusion. For example: 'My green ribbon is longer than 7 centimetres. Yours is 6 centimetres. Are they the same length or is one longer than the other?' This type of trial was considered important as a control for the level of difficulty in the next block of trials, where children might have to rely on a mixture of absolute and relative information in order to succeed. A practice trial of each type of item was given at the outset, and feedback was provided (in all trials) by taking the ribbons out of the envelopes, comparing them, and then discussing the results of this comparison.

In the second block of trials, the child's ribbons had been measured in inches and the experimenter's in centimetres. To ensure that the children realized that these two units are of different sizes, we placed two fragments of a ruler on the table, one indicating centimetres and cut at 5 cm and the second indicating inches and cut at 2 inches. We first explored with the children the differences in the size of the units by showing them how long one inch is, how long one centimetre is, and then calling their attention to the fact that 5 centimetres is just about the same as 2 inches. A practice trial in making inferences followed, in which both ribbons measured three units. We wish to point out here that although we told the child the measurement of each of the ribbons, the children might have to work with a mixture of relative and absolute information in order to reach the correct conclusion. They might reason somewhat like this: 'one ribbon is 3 centimetres but the other ribbon is more than 3 centimetres because inches are bigger than centimetres', still without knowing how to convert inches into centimetres. They would, in this case, be using a mixture of absolute and relative information. This is why we included in the previous block of trials some in which the child was provided with a mixture of relative and absolute information. After the child's response, the ribbons were taken out of the envelopes, compared, and feedback was provided by measuring the ribbons against each other.

The comparison between the different types of trial provided several kinds of information. First, we looked at the use of absolute information versus relative information when the measures had both been taken in centimetres. There was no difference in the children's performance as a function of the type of information they had received, absolute versus a mixture of absolute and relative in this case. Second, we compared trials where both ribbons had been measured in centimetres with those in which one ribbon was measured in centimetres and the other one in inches. The mean number of correct responses for each type of item by age level is presented in figure 4.1. The children's performance improved significantly with age level and the difference between the two types of item was statistically significant. The mean numbers of correct responses for the trials where only centimetres had been used was almost equal to the total number of items – in other words, there was what is called a *ceiling effect*. In contrast, in the trials where different units were used, the mean number of correct responses for 5-year-olds was just over half of the items and even 7-year-olds still made mistakes. However, the performance of the 5-year-olds was significantly above chance level, because there were three possible answers – A and B are of the same length, A is longer or B is longer. The fact that 5-year-olds were not simply answering randomly indicates that at least some of the children realized that the size of the units mattered in this task.

We then analysed the difference in performance when the trials with different units were divided into those where the number of units was the same although their size was different and those in

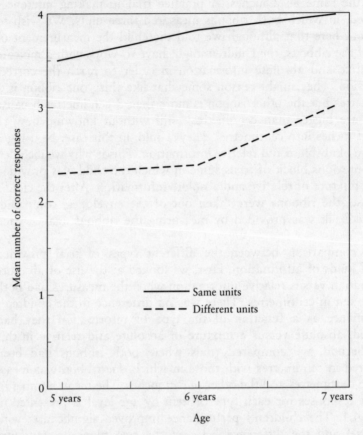

Figure 4.1 Children's responses to items where either different or the same units were used

which both the number and size of units were different. In the first type of item, the children simply had to reason that, if the number of units is the same but their size is different, the larger unit will correspond to a larger object. In the second type of item a conversion of units was required for the comparison to be accurate – a task which is more comparable to that used by Davydov in his studies. Although the children had in front of them rulers which could be used to make these conversions, the task was still difficult. Figure 4.2 indicates the mean number of correct responses for these two types of item. The difference in the children's performance across the two types of item was statistically significant. Although the 7-year-old

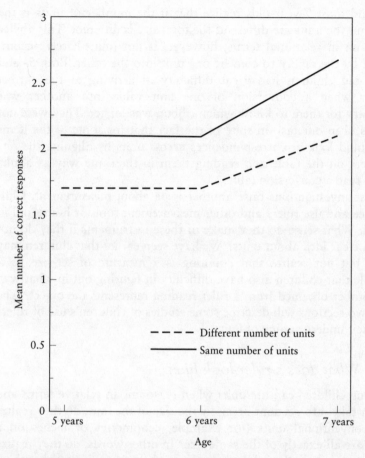

Figure 4.2   Children's responses to items with centimetres and inches and same/different number of units

children did slightly better than the 6- and 5-year-olds, this difference was not statistically significant. The performance of the 5-year-old children was above chance level in the items where the number of units is the same but was not significantly above chance level when a conversion of units was required for the answer to be correct. Not even the 7-year-olds reached as a group the maximum number of correct responses when a conversion of units was required.

In summary, children can use the concept of unit when they make inferences about the relative size of objects. These inferences seem to be based on judgements about relations – that is, some 5- and 6-year-olds and most 7-year-olds realize that if the number of units is the same but the units are different, the total size is different. This ability to reason in relational terms, however, is not immediately accompanied by the ability to convert one unit into the other. Both 5- and 6-year-old children had great difficulty in arriving at the correct answer when a conversion of one unit value into another was necessary for them to know which ribbon was longer. They were not successful in our task in spite of the fact that for some of the items they could look at correspondences across units by aligning the bits of rulers on the table and reading them in the same way as adults would read a conversion table.

These investigations raise another issue about measurement. Children see and use rulers and other measurement tools at home and in school. What sense do they make of these instruments if they do not have a clear idea about units? We have seen earlier that children may count but not realize that counting is a measure of set-size. Is it possible that children also have difficulty in figuring out in what way the number obtained from a ruler reading represents the object? The next two sections will describe some studies of children's use of rulers and their understanding of units.

2.2   *What does a ruler look like?*

If young children can use units when reasoning in relative terms and do not take into account precisely the size of the unit, do they realize that conventional units (for example, centimetres or inches on a ruler) are all exactly of the same size? In other words, do they realize that a number on the ruler – say, the number 5 – indicates that there are five units from the starting-point at zero to the point where 5 is written?

Piaget et al. (1960) suggested that it is possible that young children do not make much sense of the reading they obtain from a ruler. Reading a ruler and saying '5 centimetres' may involve little comprehension of measurement. Children can conceivably be taught to follow a procedure for reading measurements on a ruler and still have little understanding of the logic of measurement.

Nunes et al. (1995) suggested that, if children do not realize the significance of units and the importance of their equality for measurement, it is likely that they would not treat these as important characteristics of rulers and would not know how to coordinate numbers and units on a ruler. If the children were either asked to judge whether some rulers had been drawn properly or to put numbers on a ruler, their behaviour should reflect their lack of awareness of the significance of these features in the construction of rulers. For example, they might not recognize that a ruler with unequal units is not properly constructed, as long as the numbers are placed in the correct counting order. If asked to place the numbers on a ruler with equal units, they might not respect equal intervals themselves.

Nunes et al. worked in this study with 92 first-year pupils (age range 5 to 6 years) from three different classes in a state supported school in Oxford. According to their teachers, the children had rulers available in the classroom but did not often use them for measuring. Measurement activities for their age level were carried out primarily with non-conventional units (handspan and footsize, for example).

All the children answered two tasks presented in a fixed order. In the first task, the children were given a picture of a ruler drawn without the numbers. The picture was of a ruler in centimetres with half-centimetres marked on it because this was the type of ruler available in their classroom. This was given as a group task to 70 children and individually to a sample of 22 children. The researcher started out by asking the children what was drawn on their paper, to which they always answered 'a ruler'. The researcher then asked what was missing and they always recognized that numbers were missing. The children were then asked to put in the numbers the way they would have been on the ruler.

The children's productions in this memory task were analysed in a yes/no fashion by checking three characteristics of their productions: (1) did they use equal spaces when putting in the numbers? (2) did they allow for subdivision of units by leaving blank spaces consistently between the numbers? and (3) did they put a zero at the start or leave a blank space to correspond to the zero? It was expected that children who had mastered the idea of units on a ruler would satisfy two criteria in this task: (1) use equal spaces when putting in the numbers; and (2) allow for a zero at the start. There were no clear predictions for how the children would deal with the possibility of subdivisions of the unit. Figure 4.3 presents some children's productions in this task.

It was observed that some children seemed to write just the sequence of numbers on the ruler without establishing a one-to-one correspondence between numbers and units. Their production did

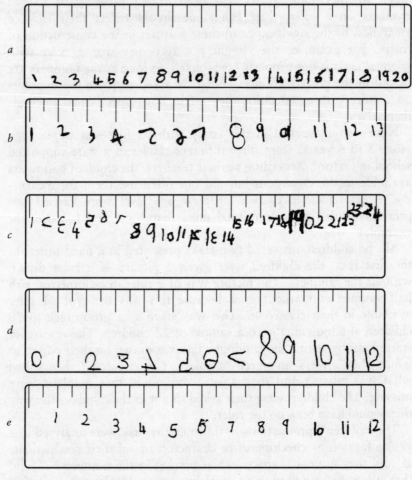

Figure 4.3   Numbers written on a ruler by 5- and 6-year-old children
SOURCE: Nunes et al. (1995)

not reveal any systematic attempt to ensure that each number referred to a unit of the same size as all the others. This lack of regularity in the spaces between the numbers did not appear to result simply from motor coordination difficulties because some rather neat productions reveal no consistent relationship between the numbers and the units, whereas some children who did not completely master the writing of single digits established a clear correspondence between the units and their numbers (compare, for example, *a* and *b* in figure 4.3). Of the

92 children, 60 per cent systematically established a one-to-one correspondence between the units and the numbers and 40 per cent did not.

Half of the children who succeeded in keeping the size of the units constant assigned a number to each subdivision on the ruler, without distinguishing between what corresponded in the drawing to the centimetre and half-centimetre markings, whereas the other half skipped one of the marks and used the idea of subdivision (see figure 4.3). Although this result cannot be interpreted with respect to their understanding of units, it does point out that children's productions are not likely to be simple reproductions of what they see. The rulers available in their classroom had half-centimetre marks on them without any number in correspondence with the 'small lines', as the children often referred to them during the interviews.

One surprising outcome of this study was the very small proportion of children who made an allowance for zero as the starting-point. The great majority of the children (89 per cent) placed the number 1 in correspondence with the first mark on the ruler. This finding raises some doubts about their understanding of units of length on a ruler. First, it is possible that children simply thought of how they count and put the numbers on the ruler in that way. Because we never start from zero when counting, they did not think of using a zero here. But one must then ask: what were they counting? Lines on the ruler or 'centimetre gaps' (as one child explained)? If they were counting lines, they would be justified in starting from 1 but in this case they were not using the same conception of measurement as we do. We think of centimetres as the units and cannot count 'one' before we have used a unit.

We interviewed a sample of children in this task to find out why they put the numbers on the ruler in the way that they did. Unfortunately, only one of them made allowance for the zero. He did so by writing the numbers not in correspondence with the lines but within the spaces between the lines. When asked why he had placed the numbers in that fashion, he explained that he was indicating the 'centimetre gaps'. All the other children did not seem to see any sense in our asking why they had put the numbers on the ruler in the way they did. They either justified the location of the numbers in correspondence with the lines by saying 'this is where the numbers go' or justified their production by checking that the sequence was correct.

Thus the children's productions of rulers support with a different sort of evidence the idea that 5- and 6-year-olds may not fully understand the concept of unit in spite of their exposure to rulers in school.

In the second task, the children were shown some rulers and asked to judge whether they had been drawn properly. The characteristics of the rulers were varied so that we could evaluate what the children took into account. The results are briefly described below.

Two rulers did not have equal units. These were evaluated as not being drawn correctly by the majority of the children: 67 per cent in one example and 56 per cent in the second example. These figures are quite similar to the results we obtained in the first task, where 60 per cent of the children took care to place the numbers on the ruler at equal intervals.

Four other rulers were also used, all of which had equal intervals between the numbers. Two of them were marked, according to the imperial system and the other two were marked in centimetres. The children seemed to have a clear preference for the metric-system rulers, which resembled those available in their classroom: 73 per cent of the answers indicated that the metric system ruler had been drawn correctly whereas only 47 per cent of the answers regarding the imperial rulers indicated them as correctly drawn. It is possible that the children were using a global judgement on the basis of familiarity rather than a more analytical approach. The justifications offered by the children who were interviewed individually appear to confirm this supposition. Some of the children indicated that the imperial ruler was not correct 'because it didn't have enough numbers' or 'it had many lines with no number on them'.

Finally, of these two types of rulers, metric and imperial, one had a zero and the other one had the numeration starting from one. This did not affect significantly children's judgement of whether the rulers had been drawn properly. The percentages of children judging rulers with a zero to be properly done were 71 for the metric and 48 for the imperial ruler whereas the percentages for the rulers without a zero were 76 for the metric and 52 for the imperial. It is possible that many children did not have an approach to the task that was analytical enough to distinguish between rulers with and without a zero. This possibility is supported in the justifications obtained in the interviews, where the zero was used as a criterion by only two (of the 22) children. Of these two, one rejected the rulers with a zero explicitly because they had a zero on them whereas the other rejected the rulers without the zero because they should have had a zero. The other 20 children did not seem to mind very much whether there was or wasn't a zero.

Taken together, the analysis of children's productions when putting the numbers on a ruler and their performance in the judgement task suggest two conclusions. First, it seems that a substantial portion of 5- and 6-year-old children recognize that the spaces between lines/numbers on the ruler must be of the same size. However, they may not appreciate that these regular spaces actually represent the units of measurement. In Davydov's terms, we could say that they have not completely established the multiple correspondences between the units, the numbers, and the measured quantity.

However, we were still left with a doubt. The children in this study did not use rulers in their measurement activities in the classroom. Perhaps they would perform better if they were required to think and discuss the use of rulers rather than simply use what knowledge they already had developed in or out of the classroom. In the next section a study in which children use and discuss how to use rulers will be briefly (and only partially) reported (for a complete description, see Nunes, Light, and Mason, 1993).

2.3 *Measuring with a broken ruler*

Nunes, Light and Mason (1993) carried out another study of children's understanding of measurement in which the children had to read rulers under unusual circumstances but were allowed much more time to consider the difficulty of their task. In this study the children worked in pairs but not face-to-face. Each child in the pair was placed in a different room and had access to the other child only through a telephone. Each child had a piece of paper with a line on it. The task was to figure out which of the two lines was longer or whether they were of the same length. The children were randomly assigned to one of two conditions: either both of the children had a 'good' ruler (control condition) or one of the children had a good ruler and the second had a ruler broken at the 4 cm mark (broken ruler condition). If the children did not understand what reading a ruler means, those assigned to the broken ruler condition would perform very badly. The reading from the broken ruler would have been always off by 4 cm and all their comparisons would come out wrong. A significant difference between the performance of the children in the control condition and the broken ruler condition would therefore be observed. On the other hand, if children can, upon reflection, come to realize what the spaces between the lines/numbers on the ruler mean, they should be able to devise procedures to deal with the systematic error provoked by the use of a broken ruler. For example, they could both start measuring from 4 cm. Alternatively, they could count the centimetres rather than simply read off the measurement or subtract 4 from the value obtained in the broken ruler.

Fifteen pairs of children (working in same-sex same-age-level pairs) in the age range 6 to 8 years from two state-supported schools in Oxford were interviewed under each of these two conditions. They were first given a practice trial, in which they would have the opportunity of getting their strategy together for the remaining trials. They also received feedback in the first three of the six trials. The feedback consisted of giving the children an opportunity to come together and compare directly the length of the lines. When they had made an error, they were encouraged to discuss what had happened and why they had got it wrong.

The children in the broken ruler condition performed slightly worse than those in the control condition but this difference was not significant (see figure 4.4). When the children were split in two groups, younger and older, we still found no significant difference between the conditions and no significant interaction between age and condition. In other words, solving the task in the broken ruler condition was more difficult for both younger and older children but not significantly so.

However, the younger children did not perform significantly above chance level in the broken ruler condition whereas in the control condition their performance was above chance level. This result suggests that young children – in this study, 6-year-olds – could not successfully modify their ruler reading procedure to compensate for the error of measurement introduced by the broken ruler. Their understanding of the units of measurement was not sufficient to overcome this difficulty. The successful pairs most of the time ignored the numbers on the ruler and counted the units marked on it, that is, the centimetres. Only two pairs departed from this practice of counting centimetre gaps: one of the pairs had the idea of using the 'good' ruler in the same way as the broken ruler and start measuring from 4 cm; the second pair subtracted 4 from the measurement obtained with the broken ruler.

The young children made errors even in the control condition, where their mean number of correct responses was five out of six

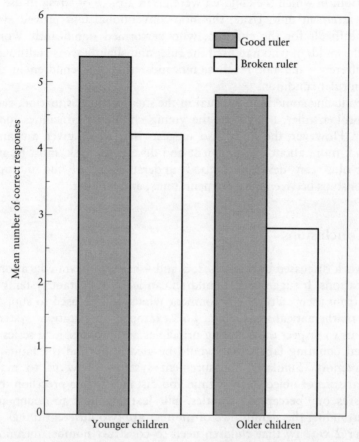

Figure 4.4 Children's correct responses to working out line length with a ruler

trials. Their errors derived from the children in the pair using different starting-points on the ruler for their measurement procedure – for example, one child in the pair might have aligned the zero on the ruler with the end of the line whereas the other one aligned the end of the line with the number 1 on the ruler. These mistakes confirm once again young children's difficulties in understanding measurement.

The results of this study clearly indicate that young children do not easily master the concept of unit. Even when using a conventional measuring instrument such as a ruler, where the units are predefined and clearly marked, they have difficulty in knowing how to use the predetermined units. This study also included a third measurement condition, in which the children were given a piece of string to use as a measurement unit. Using this non-conventional unit proved even more difficult for the children, who performed significantly worse than the children who had used the ruler and slightly worse (although the difference did not reach significance) than the children in the broken ruler condition.

Introducing something unusual in the measurement situation, such as a broken ruler, brings out the young children's difficulties more clearly. However, the study also suggests that, when given a chance to think more about measurement and discuss the task, most 6- and 7-year-olds can develop a good understanding of the multiple relationships between measurement, units, and number.

3   Conclusions

The work discussed in chapters 2, 3 and 4 has significant educational implications. It suggests that children can learn important systems of signs from their cultural environment which will be used to support their mathematical reasoning. For example, numeration systems allow us to respect the counting principles and produce long series of ordered counting labels that would be clearly beyond the limits of our memory. Similarly, measurement systems allow us to make comparisons of objects across time and distance with a precision that surpasses our perceptual abilities. But learning how to count and understanding the significance of number are two different things. In chapter 2 we saw that children need to construct number meanings in order to use counting correctly in connection with the purposes of their activities. If they are counting two sets to find out how many objects there are altogether they have to count differently from the way they would use counting in order to compare the two sets. Young children do not seem to grasp these different uses of counting. We also saw in chapter 3 that being able to produce number labels in one-to-one correspondence with objects and understanding the numeration system are two different accomplishments. It seems that children's understanding of the numeration system is related to their growing understanding of addition rather than to the mastery of one-to-one correspondence principles. Finally, in chapter 4 a new concept that seems significant for the development of young children's mathematical understanding was introduced, the concept of unit.

This concept is clearly basic to children's grasping of measurement systems and arguably of the numeration system also.

These results require that we reflect once again about the three components of concepts which we discussed in chapter 1: invariants, systems of signs, and situations. It is clear that the relationships between these components is rather complex. Situations give meaning to the concepts. In order to understand what counting is for and to adjust counting procedures as a function of the task at hand, for example, children need to use counting in different situations. Their mastery of the system of signs may still be restricted and they may make errors but still they need to use counting and think about when and how to use it.

As they start to be able to generate number words from the regularity of the verbal labels, they can be faced with new counting situations, such as counting money, where additive composition is involved. With this activity comes the need to understand a new invariant property of number, additive composition. The research reviewed here indicates that working with simple addition problems may be a good way of bringing children to construct meaning for additive composition. As children's strategies in solving addition problems change and become more efficient, so does their understanding of additive composition also grow.

Finally, it also seems that measurement activities are important in expanding children's understanding of number. If counting is a special case of measurement where the units are given from the outset, it seems sensible to expand children's number experiences by having them work with measurement systems. This clearly is not a simple task and children do not master units of measurement just from recognizing them on a ruler, for example, and knowing what they are called. They need to be involved in activities where their apparent simplicity is destroyed. We suggest (but so far we have no evidence for it) that children are likely to profit from the need to measure in unusual circumstances, such as using a broken ruler or using rulers that are too short for their purposes, so that they have a measurement problem to solve and need to do more than read the value from the ruler. But educational research is still needed to put this idea to test.

5

Mathematics under Different Names

In chapters 2, 3 and 4 we have been discussing activities of different sorts – counting money, playing detective games with ribbons, comparing line lengths by talking on the telephone – which we claim have something to do with children's mathematical understanding. But are these really mathematical activities?

In this chapter, we will discuss what is 'really mathematical'. We wish to reflect on the nature of mathematical activity. Our aim is to consider different views of what mathematics actually is and how these views influence the teaching of mathematics to children.

This is a fundamental issue and one that has to be faced not only by people involved in the philosophy of education and the psychology of learning but also by mathematics teachers. It is consequently frequently discussed. The points that we ourselves want to contribute to this debate are controversial and we do not claim to have found the answer.

Our aim is to make the point that children's learning of mathematics is not independent of the complex social framework in which they do this learning. In principle it is possible to analyse children's growing understanding of mathematical concepts as a purely cognitive matter, and this route has often been taken by psychologists and philosophers. In practice this kind of analysis is at best limited and at worst quite wrong. We wish to argue that children's progress in school is not simply a matter of cognition. *Our view is that social factors are extremely powerful and must not be forgotten.*

We wish to consider different views of mathematics and what it means to know and to teach mathematics. In this attempt we will draw on incidents and research that have demonstrated the role of

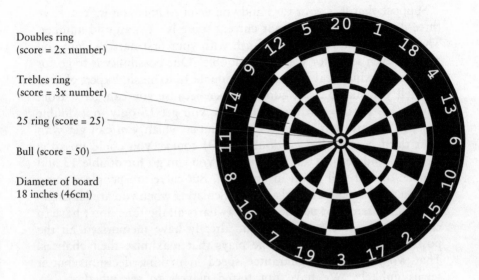

Doubles ring
(score = 2x number)

Trebles ring
(score = 3x number)

25 ring (score = 25)

Bull (score = 50)

Diameter of board
18 inches (46cm)

Figure 5.1   Darts board showing the doubles and trebles rings
SOURCE: *Darts Rules: Technique Advice* (London: Unicorn Press)

social influences on children's and adults' success in solving mathematics problems.

1   Are You Good at Maths?

Recently we talked to members of a darts team, each of whom told us that he was bad at mathematics. How true can this really be?

Playing darts requires rapid and accurate calculation, if not throughout the game, at least in its final stages. A game of darts is played in a sense backwards. Instead of starting from zero and accumulating points, a player starts a darts game with 501 points and needs to get down to exactly zero. When the game starts, players aim to get as many points as possible so that they can get close to zero faster than the others. On each turn they will throw three darts and subtract the score for the turn; this gives them their current score. But according to our informants, when they get down to about 200, they start planning their moves in a more precise fashion. A game must be finished on a double – that is, the last dart must hit those special areas on the board where the value is double the number that is written on the outer ring (see figure 5.1). In what ways does this require computation from the player?

Suppose that it is your turn and you want to finish on it. You have three darts to throw and your current score is 71 – an odd number. That means that you cannot finish with your first dart because you need an even score for your final 'double'. One possibility is to go for a treble 13, which leaves you with a double 16 to finish. Expert players will tell you that 32 is a good number because you can get it from double 16. If you split the 16 (that is, you get 16 only, not double 16) you are still left with an even number which you can get with your third dart by hitting double 8. Of course, you could miss the treble 13 and get just 13. That means you can go for double 13 and double 16 and still finish in one turn. But there are people waiting for you and you can't spend all day calculating when you are playing.

It might seem that people who play darts all the time don't have to calculate any of this; they might already have memorized all the possible ways to finish and the plays that maximize their chances. That would certainly guarantee speed in making decisions but it seems unlikely. We have not tested players to see whether they memorize finishes or not, but we had a look at a list, produced by a darts league, of some ways to finish. Figure 5.2 displays a copy of a portion of this list, which is not exhaustive and does not take into account the sequences of games left if a double or a treble is split. It seems a most discouraging beginning for people who say they are not good with numbers.

We argued in chapter 1 that people often overcome memory problems by understanding a system that can generate correct solutions. It is quite possible that darts players develop a good understanding of how to decompose numbers and that they know what a 'double x' or a 'treble x' is all the way to doubles and trebles of 20 in the same way that most of us know multiples of 10. With this knowledge and their understanding of how to decompose numbers, they may also operate on other calculations that have nothing to do with the darts board. One member of the darts team told us that he uses 'darts numbers' to solve all other types of calculation. His own example was that if he has to solve something that involves 7×17, he thinks of this in terms of treble 17 (51) plus treble 17 plus 17. His own analysis of this process is that he does it this way because 'he doesn't know how to multiply'.

If we try to describe his knowledge in terms of theorems in action or the principles of multiplication that he must understand in order to devise this method (which almost certainly he did not learn in school), we come to a quite different conclusion. Multiplication is

Suggested best ways to finish

3 Dart Finishes

Score	1st dart	2nd dart	3rd dart
170	3x20	3x20	Bull
167	3x19	3x20	Bull
164	3x20	3x20	Bull
161	3x17	3x20	Bull
160	3x20	3x20	2x20
158	3x20	3x20	2x19
157	3x19	3x20	2x20
156	3x20	3x20	2x18
155	3x20	3x19	2x19
154	3x18	3x20	2x20
153	3x20	3x19	2x18
152	3x20	3x20	2x16
151	3x17	3x20	2x20
150	3x20	3x18	2x18
149	3x19	3x20	2x16
148	3x16	3x20	2x20
147	3x20	3x17	2x18
146	3x20	3x18	2x16
145	3x20	3x15	2x20
144	3x20	3x20	2x12
143	3x20	3x17	2x16
142	3x20	3x14	2x20
141	3x20	3x15	2x18
140	3x20	3x16	2x16
139	3x19	3x14	2x20
138	3x20	3x18	2x12
137	3x19	3x16	2x16
136	3x20	3x20	2x8
135	3x20	3x15	2x15
134	3x20	3x14	2x16
133	3x20	3x19	2x8
132	3x20	3x16	2x12
131	3x20	3x13	2x16
130	3x20	3x18	2x8
129	3x19	3x16	2x12
128	3x20	3x20	2x4
127	3x20	3x17	2x8
126	3x20	2x15	2x18
125	3x20	25	2x20
124	3x20	3x16	2x8
123	3x19	3x14	2x12
122	3x20	2x15	2x16
121	3x17	3x10	2x20
120	3x20	20	2x20
119	3x19	3x10	2x16
118	3x20	18	2x20
117	3x19	20	2x20
116	3x20	20	2x19
115	3x19	18	2x20
114	3x20	18	2x18
113	3x19	16	2x20
112	3x20	20	2x1
111	3x17	20	2x20
110	3x20	18	2x16
109	3x19	20	2x16
108	3x20	16	2x16
107	3x19	18	2x16
106	3x20	14	2x16
105	3x15	20	2x20
104	3x18	18	2x16
103	3x17	20	2x16
102	3x20	10	2x16
101	3x17	18	2x16
100	3x20	2x20	
99	3x19	10	2x16

Below 99 the game may be finished with only 2 darts.

Suggested best ways to finish

2 Dart Finishes

Score	1st dart	2nd dart
110	3x20	Bull
107	3x19	Bull
104	3x18	Bull
101	3x17	Bull
100	3x20	2x20
98	3x20	2x19
97	3x19	2x20
96	3x20	2x18
95	3x19	2x19
94	3x18	2x20
93	3x19	2x18
92	3x20	2x16
91	3x17	2x20
90	3x18	2x18
89	3x19	2x16
88	3x16	2x20
87	3x18	2x16
86	3x18	2x16
85	3x15	2x20
84	3x20	2x12
83	3x17	2x16
82	3x14	2x20
81	3x15	2x18
80	3x16	2x16
79	3x17	2x14
78	3x18	2x12
77	3x19	2x10
76	3x20	2x8
75	3x15	2x15
74	3x14	2x16
73	3x19	2x8
72	3x16	2x12
71	3x13	2x16
70	3x10	2x20
69	3x19	2x6
68	3x20	2x4
67	3x17	2x8
66	2x15	2x18
65	25	2x20
64	3x16	2x8
63	3x17	2x6
62	2x15	2x16
61	25	2x18
60	20	2x20
59	19	2x20
58	18	2x20
57	17	2x20
56	16	2x20
55	15	2x20
54	18	2x18
53	13	2x20
52	2x	2x16
51	19	2x16
50	18	2x16
49	17	2x16
48	16	2x16
47	15	2x16
46	14	2x16
45	13	2x16
44	12	2x16
43	11	2x16
42	10	2x16
41	9	2x16

Figure 5.2 Suggested best ways to finish a game of darts
SOURCE: *Darts Rules: Technique Advice* (London: Unicorn Press).

defined by a property called *distributivity* (among other properties). What distributivity means is that if we multiply one number by 7, each unit of that number must be multiplied by 7 and then all the products added together. When we multiply following the procedure we learned in school – that is, in the way our expert darts player claimed not to know – we implicitly use the property of distributivity. According to the procedure we learned at school, we write 17 with 7 underneath, and then sequentially multiply 7×7 and 7×10, adding the intermediary products to obtain the final answer.

Our choice takes advantage of the knowledge of the multiplication facts we learned in school. It is likely that we know the 7-times table and this is what we use. Our darts player has a different choice that uses other multiplication facts that he knows well: the 3-times table up to 20. The 7 times table he analyses into $n \times 3 + n \times 3 + n\, (\times 1)$. The principle is the same; the partitioning of the number is different. The theorems in action underlying the procedure the expert player claims not to know are the same theorems in action that he uses with his spontaneously developed procedure.

But then why should he think he does not know how to multiply if he can actually *invent* a new way of solving multiplication questions which suits him better than the school way? Why should people think of themselves as bad at a mathematical task when they can do it in their own way? In the next sections we will consider some ideas that relate to this issue.

2   Mathematics as a Socially Defined Activity

Mathematics, like literature, music, sports and science, is a cultural product and a culturally defined activity. The boundaries of what is mathematics and what is not mathematics are also culturally defined. Growing up in a Western society, we have learned much about this social definition. Below are some beliefs that have become part of how people in our society view mathematics.

- Mathematics is a special kind of activity and any other activity is, by definition, not mathematics.
- Mathematics is learned in school – consequently, people who have not gone to school don't know any mathematics.
- Mathematics is something one gets qualifications in – if you don't have any qualifications, you can't possibly know much mathematics.
- Mathematics is abstract and is not about the everyday world – therefore you don't learn about mathematics in everyday life.
- Mathematics is difficult; few people can get qualifications in mathematics – that means that few people know mathematics.

- Mathematics is used by mathematicians, some scientists, and some higher-level technically qualified people (mostly men!) – these are the people who know mathematics.

It is true that mathematics is a special kind of socially defined activity – just as selling and buying, playing darts, and building houses. This is why we think of these latter activities as 'not mathematics'. But do all the other ideas listed above follow from the fact that mathematics is a special kind of activity? Is it correct that mathematics can only be learned in school and that there is nothing about mathematics that is learned in other socially defined activities? We don't think so.

Mathematics has a double status – it is a particular kind of activity but it is also a form of knowledge. This means that mathematical knowledge can be learned and used outside school and outside what we define as 'mathematics'. We started out in chapter 1 by saying that mathematics is not simply a discipline but also a way of thinking. This is why mathematics, just as literacy, is something that should be made available to all. Yet the social definition of mathematics ends up making us blind to mathematical knowledge that is embedded in other activities. We learn some forms of mathematical knowledge in school and become blind to the importance of others which are not taught there.

Fortunately, in the last two decades or so, anthropologists, psychologists and mathematics educators have striven to become more aware of other forms of mathematical knowledge. Our attempt is not to review the work in this domain exhaustively but to present a selection of work that is particularly relevant to the later chapters in this book.

2.1 *When the new mathematics was brought to an old culture*

Sometime in the 1960s Gay and Cole (1967) became involved in a project about mathematics teaching and learning among the Kpelle in Liberia. The Kpelle play a game in which two rows of eight stones each are set up. One person is sent away and the others choose a stone. When the person comes back, he/she is allowed to ask four questions in order to find out which stone was chosen. The researchers observed the Kpelle playing this game and decided they could also play it. They were sent away and, when they came back, they rearranged the stones according to a series of moves that would bring the chosen stone to the head of one of the lines after three shifts. While they made their plays, they noticed that the group of villagers was laughing at them. The villagers seemed sure that they could not possibly get the answer. Gay and Cole report: 'They were utterly amazed when we pointed at the correct stone. As it turned out, they were amazed because we made the moves in a way different from their traditional procedure. They had memorized a set of procedures for moving the stones. The principle was the same as the one we used, but the application was slightly different' (Gay and Cole, 1967, p. 28).

Gay and Cole used this lesson about not being fooled by particular procedures but rather concentrating on underlying principles in their own subsequent work. In their studies of mathematics among the Kpelle, they did not investigate the Kpelle villagers' knowledge of Western mathematics. They studied how the Kpelle organize and classify objects into sets, how they count and reason in terms of relations of equality and inequality, how they describe space, and how they operate with numbers in ways that correspond to our operations of addition, subtraction, multiplication and division. It was Kpelle tradition that had to be taken as a starting-point if the task was to understand how the Kpelle reason about number and measurement, and in order to understand the Kpelle reasoning about number and measurement, it was necessary to understand their world view.

Let us take one of their analyses of mathematical reasoning among the Kpelle. It concerns measurement. According to Gay and Cole, the Kpelle use a measure if it is needed, and otherwise they estimate. They measure the length of cloth and rope, for example, in arm-spans. They also measure sticks and short objects in hand-spans. Long distances are not measured in these units but may be described in terms of the time that it takes to travel them. Presumably because these different measures are used in the course of different activities, the Kpelle do not seem to connect these different units of measurement of length into an overall system as we do with centimetres, metres and kilometres. What this means is that when the Kpelle traditional adults use their smaller unit of hand-spans to estimate shorter lengths, such as that of a stick (something in the 4 to 32 inches range), they perform markedly differently than when they use this same unit to estimate longer distances (between 72 and 162 inches). When Gay and Cole looked at the accuracy with which

Kpelle adults estimated short distances in hand-spans they found that the average error was below a half hand-span. But when the task was to estimate longer distances in hand-spans the Kpelle informants tended to overestimate the values by somewhere between 40 and 90 per cent. This rather poor showing contrasted sharply with their performance in estimating the same distances in arm-spans, the conventional unit for longer distances: in this case their errors of estimation were smaller than 30 per cent.

In contrast, US adult subjects performing the same tasks showed a much smaller difference in their performance when estimating shorter and longer distances. Gay and Cole report that, although these US adults were not as familiar with the use of hand-spans as a measure, they were more familiar with the notion of converting from one measurement to another, and seemed to use this resource to solve the task: they seemed to translate hand-spans into some value in feet and inches, which they then used to estimate the distances.

These results indicate that, although Kpelle adults were able to work with the concept of unit (discussed in chapter 4) when they estimated length, their lack of familiarity with conversions across units for different orders of magnitude of distances was a disadvantage when they had to work with small units for estimating larger distances.

Gay and Cole also investigated the Kpelle system for measuring volume. Rice is a staple food for them and is measured in a number of ways which are interconnected. The smallest measure for buying and selling is the *kopi*, a term derived from the word 'cup' and a measure roughly equivalent to two cups. It is used in two values, one for selling and one for buying; it is the difference between these two measures that gives the profit margin of the trader. This measure of volume corresponds roughly to one pound in terms of weight and is sometimes also referred to in this way. Two larger units used for measuring rice are a *boke*, which corresponds to 24 cups of rice, and a *tin*, that corresponds to 44 cups. The largest measure is a *boro* (a bag), which contains nearly 100 cups of rice.

Gay and Cole found the system to be consistent by checking the volumes against the prices of rice for the different amounts. Traditional Kpelle adults and American adults were compared when estimating amounts of rice, as they had been with respect to length. The results of this comparison are rather distinct from those in the length study. The Kpelle adults were very accurate in their use of the *kopi* as a measure whereas the US adults performed quite poorly, especially when a relatively large amount of rice was involved.

It is possible (although Gay and Cole do not offer specific evidence for this) that the existence of a cultural practice of conversion of measures of volume is at least in part responsible for the Kpelle adults' ability to estimate volume with accuracy. In turn, the lack of such cross-references in the system for measuring length would explain the local efficiency of each unit, for shorter and longer lengths, without much conversion of one into the other as a strategy in solving such tasks.

Gay and Cole clearly indicate the need to be cautious when drawing general conclusions about people's ability in one sort of mathematical knowledge, such as measurement, in a general way. We may observe rather different types of performance for the same subjects, as they did in the case of the Kpelle, and these differences are not easily discounted as different degrees of difficulty in the task. Whereas for the Kpelle subjects the length tasks were harder than the volume tasks, just the opposite was observed for the US subjects. Culturally developed systems of signs can be used to support performance when they are available, but the same subjects will appear to be lacking in ability where there are no such systems in their culture. Mathematical knowledge may thus become connected to the activities through which that knowledge is acquired.

The next question we want to address is how common is this connection between mathematical knowledge and specific situations. Perhaps playing darts and dealing with rice are isolated examples which should not be used to make general points about mathematical knowledge. In section 3 we discuss other examples of the interconnection between the learning context and the mathematics learned in different situations.

3   Street Mathematics and School Mathematics

Terezinha Nunes and her colleagues in Brazil (Nunes, Schliemann and Carraher, 1993) carried out an extensive programme of research on the relationship between the learning context and the form of mathematics learned. Their starting point was a phenomenon which was a puzzle for any psychologist concerned with children's learning of mathematics in school. This puzzle concerns the failure rates of Brazilian working class children in mathematics. Working class children do rather poorly in mathematics in school and if they fail they must resit the grade level. The rate of failure in maths can be over 30 per cent in grade 2 (T. N. Carraher and Schliemann, 1983). However, working class children are often engaged in what is called the 'informal' or the 'invisible economy'. Their activities in this sector of the economy take the form of selling small items in street corners (sweets, soft drinks, fruits etc.) or in street markets, either on their own or as help for the family.

This was the puzzle. How could these same children who fail elementary school mathematics succeed as vendors? Do they not carry out the transactions themselves? Or is it that the children who are vendors are those who succeed in school?

In order to discover whether the children really didn't do the maths in the streets or whether it was those who did do maths in the streets that succeeded in school, five young street vendors were interviewed, four boys and one girl in the age range 9–15 years, with levels of schooling varying from years 1 to 8. The children were spotted by the interviewers while they carried out their vending activity and the interviewers initially posed as customers. Several different purchases would be proposed in this interaction and questions were also asked about the amount of change. At the end of the interaction, after some purchases were carried out, the children were told that the interviewers were interested in how they solved mathematical problems and asked whether they would be willing to solve some problems later. None of them refused and the interviewers went back at most one week later and gave the children school-type problems – word problems and computation exercises – which involved the same arithmetic that the children had worked with when each of them solved problems in the street market. In this way, it was possible to answer the two questions raised above: (1) did the young street vendors really succeed in using elementary mathematics in the streets?; and (2) were they the same ones who failed in mathematics in school?

The results of this study were striking. The answer to both questions was clearly 'yes'. The children were very successful in street mathematics and solved 98 per cent of the 63 problems correctly. In contrast, they only solved 74 per cent of the word problems and 37 per cent of the computation exercises correctly. Thus the same children succeeded in the streets and failed at school: the rates of success were significantly different.

Further analysis showed that the children used rather different approaches to problem-solving on the two occasions when they were interviewed. In the streets they seemed basically to use oral methods: they spoke as they calculated and did not write anything down. Most of the problems set out in the school-like fashion were attempted by the children through written algorithms. Below are two examples of the same calculation each answered by the same child across the two situations, one of an addition and one of a multiplication (adapted from Carraher et. al., 1985).

Example 1

Street market problem.
INTERVIEWER: I'll take two coconuts [at CR$40.00 each. Pays with a Cr$500.00 bill]. What do I get back?
CHILD: [Before reaching for the customer's change] 80, 90, 100, 420.

When the same child was asked to solve the computation exercise 420 + 80 later on, the problem was presented orally and the child wrote down 42 on one line, 8 underneath and wrote 130 as the result. She was not asked to explain her procedure but she had explained a similar problem earlier on and we assume that she had used here the same procedure, where she seemed to mix the multiplication and addition rules (a not unusual confusion among elementary school children, which has also been documented by Miller and Paredes, 1990). She added across the numbers but took 8 into the computation twice. She seems to have computed 8 + 2 = 10, carry the one, 1 + 4 + 8 = 13. In this way, 130 is obtained. The interviewer then asked her to explain how she got that answer and she corrected it in the process of explaining.

Example 2

Street market problem
INTERVIEWER: I'm going to take four coconuts [at Cr$35.00 each]. How much is that?
CHILD: Three will be 105, plus 30, that's 135 . . . one coconut is 35 . . . that is . . . 140.

In the second interview, the same child solved 35 × 4 by writing the numbers down, one on the first line and the second one underneath, and explained the process out loud: '4 times 5, 20, carry the 2; 2 plus 3 is 5, times 4 is 20.' He obtained 200 as the result.
When we contrast the children's solutions in the streets and in the

schools, we have to pay attention to two aspects, the system of signs that they use and the principles that underlie the moves in the calculation. We find, just as we did when we analysed the darts players' calculations, that the moves in the calculation are different in the street methods and in the methods which the children clearly failed to learn at school, but we also find that the principles used are the same in both cases.

In the addition example, the child's verbalisation indicates what logical moves she must have been using. She must have thought of 420 being added on to 80 in parts. She first added 10, then another 10, and then 100 four times. She used the procedure of decomposition. The principle or theorem in action implicitly used was the associativity of addition, which allows us to decompose a number into parts and add the parts sequentially. She needs exactly the same principle in order to understand the school algorithm for addition, where she has to add first the units, then the tens, and then the hundreds.

In the multiplication example, like the darts player, the street vendor used the property of distributivity. Multiplying by 4 was seen as the same as multiplying by 3 and then adding once again the number to be multiplied. The school-taught procedure, a *bug* (that is, a fault in the procedure) gets into the child's computation. Instead of multiplying 4 by 3 and then adding the 2 that he had carried from the previous step, he adds first and multiplies later.

A series of subsequent studies led Nunes, Schliemann and Carraher (1993) to suggest, among others, one significant reason for the children's success in the streets and failure in school: the system of signs that the children use when they calculate. In the streets they use oral arithmetic. Representation of the numbers in oral arithmetic allows them to calculate and to think of the values that they are working with at the same time. When tens and hundreds are added, for example, *they are spoken of as tens and hundreds*. In contrast, in written arithmetic we set the meaning of numbers aside during calculation. We operate with digits and speak about them as if they were all units, following the same rules as we move from units to tens and hundreds. This approach seems to detach the children from the meaning of what they are trying to calculate and thereby makes it easier for bugs to appear in their solutions.

Later we will consider again the role of systems of signs in the development of mathematical concepts. Suffice it to say at this point that it is important to consider such systems used by children when they solve mathematical problems. The moves that can be carried out with one system of signs may not be easily carried out with another even if the logical principles implicitly used when operating with each system are the same.

So far in this chapter we have considered the possibility that mathematics is a culturally defined activity and that mathematical knowledge can be found in many activities which are usually defined in the culture as something other than mathematics. Our conversations with the darts players have shown that people who view themselves as *not knowing* something in mathematics – for example, multiplication – may confidently use this knowledge in an activity that is not defined as mathematics. Gay and Cole have taught us that we need to look beyond the surface of mathematical problem-solving: we need to look for principles, to be able to identify what sort of mathematical knowledge people display when they are doing things which are not socially defined as maths. The work with the Brazilian street vendors illustrates that these points are not mere curiosities about mathematics: they have an impact on children's future chances because they can actually affect how well they do in school. The street vendors who fail in school mathematics lose chances in life as a consequence of this failure and their school teachers may actually think that their failure was a consequence of their cognitive incapacity. But their knowledge of street mathematics teaches us otherwise. In the last section of this chapter we will have a look at how society seems to deal with this conflict between knowing that people may be good at maths in some contexts and bad at the same maths in others.

4 Practical and Theoretical Maths and the Ownership of Knowledge

Psychologists such as Ceci and Liker (1986), Goodnow (1986) and Scribner (1986) and anthropologists such as Lave (1988; 1990) have claimed that the distinction between practical and academic intelligence which is commonly made in Western societies is also socially and culturally constructed. In their analysis of adults' thinking and solving problems in diverse situations, they find no cognitive criteria that can tease theoretical and practical intelligence apart. They oppose the old idea that academic intelligence is abstract and therefore applicable everywhere whereas practical intelligence is connected to particular contexts and thus restricted to the practical activity where it was learned. Transfer of school-learned techniques to solve everyday problems is as limited as the use of everyday techniques in school (see Lave, 1988; Nunes, Schliemann and Carraher, 1993). Why then is school-learned knowledge so often more valued? Why do people feel, as recorded in the Cockcroft report (Cockcroft, 1982), that they do not know the right way of solving mathematical problems if they do not use the procedures learned in school but others learned outside school?

Goodnow (1990) has suggested that in the process of socialization of thought that takes place both in and out of school, we do not simply learn to solve problems: 'we learn also what problems are considered worth solving, and what counts as an elegant rather than simply an acceptable solution. We do not simply acquire knowledge. We learn also that some particular pieces of knowledge are expected of us, that some can be happily ignored, and that some are inappropriate for all but a few to own' (1990, p. 259). Some forms of knowledge are socially marked as owned by certain people and we acquire these forms of knowledge if we identify with the owner group and want to become one of them. Some problems are socially construed as 'significant' and 'worthwhile' and others as 'trivial', some arguments are 'elegant' and others 'clever' or even 'too clever by half'. 'Some skills and some areas of knowledge belong to some people more than to others' (1990, p. 264), as can be recognized from expressions such as 'women's issues', 'Western science', 'Eastern philosophy' and 'Chinese medicine'. Goodnow goes on to suggest that this aspect of the socialization of reasoning is not transmitted explicitly but is mostly learned 'through messages that are implicit in the routine arrangements of living and are conveyed with particular force and richness through discourse – through comments on a child's actions, expressions of concern or satisfaction, and, on occasion, the explicit statement of a rule' (Goodnow, 1990, p. 281; see also Shweder, 1982).

We probably become blind or dismissive with forms of mathematical knowledge learned outside school through this same sort of socialization process. In school we are only taught arithmetical procedures which are based on the written symbols. The implicit lesson is that this form of solution is the one worth learning about. Furthermore, what is not written in a test or exam cannot deserve recognition. The routine of tests which consist of written displays of knowledge prevents other forms of reasoning from being recognized, and for students who identify with academic values written displays become the only ones worth thinking about. It is also possible to reject academic values as too far from reality (see Willis, 1977) and seek a different kind of identity, that values practical work and skills in everyday life.

De Abreu et al. (forthcoming) investigated the understanding of ownership of different sorts of mathematical knowledge among teachers and pupils in a rural community in northeastern Brazil. In her first study (De Abreu and Carraher, 1989), she described the forms of mathematical knowledge that are used in the planting and harvesting of sugar cane, a very important economic activity in the community she studied. A variety of mathematical concepts that go well beyond computation strategies play a part in the work of the labourers in sugar cane plantations.

They are, for example, paid by areas worked during the cleaning and tilling of soil. Because these areas are usually not arranged in neatly organized rectangles, or even in triangles, trapezoids or parallelograms, they have developed procedures for calculating area using the measurements of the sides which are radically different from those taught in school.

To take one other example, during harvest the sugar cane is tied into bundles and transported to the site of sugar production. Workers are paid by weight harvested but weighing each bundle would be time-consuming. Averages are then calculated after the intentional sampling of a small, a medium, and a larger bundle harvested.

The sugar cane workers have acquired a rich knowledge of mathematical concepts through activities such as these: but they do not usually represent this knowledge in writing because most of them are unschooled and also because they have to do the calculations on the spot. Through further interviews and investigations into the oral tradition, De Abreu (1994) was able to find out more about their conceptions of the different forms of mathematical knowledge. The knowledge used outside school, in the sugar cane plantation activities or in everyday life, was branded by the users themselves as 'practical' and different from the sort of mathematical knowledge learned in school. Thus she observed among the sugar cane workers the same sort of phenomenon as described earlier with the darts players: an efficient form of mathematics being carried out orally and the concurrent denial of mathematical knowledge.

In another study, this time with schoolchildren, De Abreu (1994) investigated the possibility of there being a hierarchy of knowledge with school mathematics at the top of the hierarchy. She wanted to know whether those who had mastered school mathematics also mastered street mathematics while only some of those who mastered street mathematics reached a good understanding of school mathematics. She selected pupils for her study in such a way that approximately half of them were considered by their teachers to be good in mathematics; the other half were considered weak. She then evaluated their knowledge of mathematical concepts both in school types of problems and in imaginary, everyday problems.

If a hierarchy of knowledge were an adequate description of the relationship between school and street mathematics, some combinations of performance, but not others, would be possible. For example, it would be possible for children to be good at both forms of knowledge, bad at both forms of knowledge, or good at street mathematics but bad at school mathematics. However, it should be impossible to find children who are good at school mathematics but bad at street mathematics.

In fact, De Abreu found all four combinations of knowledge displayed in her pupils. This is a result that allows us to disregard the possibility that these two forms of knowledge are hierarchically organized.

De Abreu also investigated the value that the teachers and children ascribed to the two forms of knowledge, and the influence that their views had on teaching and learning in school. She reported that, like the adults in the community, the children also looked on street and school mathematics as having a different intrinsic value. When the children were asked to solve problems and encouraged to use different strategies to approach the problems, they often said that the strategies that they used for solving problems outside the school were 'not really right', even though they were aware of the fact that they obtained correct answers through these procedures.

The teachers who knew about the sort of mathematical knowledge that their pupils used outside school shared the children's views on the relative value of the two forms of mathematical knowledge. One teacher even mentioned that her own father, an unschooled man who had worked in the sugar cane fields, was more efficient than she was in solving problems involving mathematics in everyday life. However, she saw his knowledge as 'practical', whereas the sort of knowledge that she aimed at teaching in school was, in her view, the only adequate form of mathematics. Another teacher, who fully recognized the existence of a different form of mathematical knowledge outside school, was asked whether she encouraged the children to use this knowledge in school. She answered that this would not be in the children's best interest: they were in school to learn school mathematics, the form of knowledge that would allow them to be something other than a sugar cane worker.

In short, the distinction between academic and applied intelligence seems to be part of the social process of construction of ownership of knowledge. It is, we think, impossible to order school arithmetic and street arithmetic into a hierarchy in which one has a higher place than the other. However, because one form of practice is taught in school and the other is not, the school-taught procedures are valued and viewed as 'the right way' whereas those procedures not taught in school are consequently devalued.

5   Conclusions

We started this chapter with the question 'are you good at maths?'. It seems at first sight like a simple question, with a 'yes' or 'no' answer. But in fact it raises some complex issues. Most people are used to thinking that mathematical knowledge is a consequence of being good or not good at maths at school. However, learning in school is not simply a cognitive matter. It is part of becoming a particular kind of person and, as Goodnow (1990) points out, there are resistances both in offering and in taking knowledge that is owned by specific groups. Mathematics knowledge is a social category of knowledge, and it is one which we might have to revise if we wish to achieve the ideal of mathematics for all.

The possibility that we need to revise our notion of what mathematics knowledge is and of how it is to be acquired is already recognized by some mathematics educators. These are the ones who, in Lave's words, 'are likely to describe conventional school maths learning as the all too mechanical transmission of a collection of facts to be learned by rote, a process devoid of creative contributions by the learner' (Lave, 1990, p. 309). They seek the creation in the school classroom of a community of thinkers who are asked to do what mathematicians do (for discussions of this question, see Schoenfeld, 1987; 1988). This is a significant effort towards the reform of the definition of *school mathematics* but there is still a need to reconsider the social definition of mathematics as 'the activity of mathematicians'. The ownership of mathematical knowledge could be redistributed by concentrating on the principles used in reasoning rather than on particular mathematical moves, as Gay and Cole were able to do when studying mathematics among the Kpelle. If giving up the distinction between practical and academic mathematical knowledge allows us to recognize children's reasoning abilities better and to help them develop these abilities in school, this loss of ownership will be certainly worth pursuing.

6

Giving Meaning to Addition and Subtraction

Children are usually taught addition and subtraction quite a time before the other arithmetical operations, but there is none the less a lot for them to learn and understand about these two basic parts of mathematics. Of course they will have to conquer certain procedures, such as carrying and borrowing in multidigit addition and subtraction, and they will certainly learn a host of 'facts', such as $3 + 2 = 5$, which will help them whenever they have to add or take away either in their heads or on paper. But there is much more to learn than that; addition and subtraction are quite complicated concepts, and until children grasp the conceptual basis of these operations they will be unable to use any procedures that they are taught or any facts that they pick up at school.

In the past the teaching and learning of procedures, particularly with multidigit numbers, was the main concern of investigations of addition and subtraction. A great deal of research was carried out on the best way to help children understand, for example, subtraction with borrowing (see, for example, Resnick 1982; 1983; Van Lehn, 1983). This theme has received much less attention recently, and now the major focus of research on adding and subtracting is on problem-solving and on the basic conceptual understanding of these two operations. This will be the main concern of this chapter.

In the first section we will consider the concepts of addition and subtraction in relationship to the three fundamental aspects of mathematical concepts – situations, representations and invariants – which we discussed in chapter 1. The sections that follow will report some research findings that illustrate how children come to master the concepts of addition and subtraction. In the final section we will turn to educational implications.

1   Situations, Representations and Invariants in the Concepts of Addition and Subtraction

We have already touched on some aspects of the concept of addition in preceding chapters. In these we discussed the fact that children as young as 5 or 6 years of age can solve some addition problems through a simple extension of counting and with the help of their imagination in pretend-play. For example, if they are asked to pretend that some blocks on the table are sweets, they can solve problems like 'Mary had five sweets. Her grandmother gave her four sweets. How many sweets does she have now?' Most 5-year-old children solve this problem by counting out five blocks, then four more, and then counting them all together. We have also discussed the idea that this concrete-looking problem-solving behaviour already encompasses some abstraction. In order to find the answer in this way, the children must assume that whatever results are obtained with the blocks would be obtained also with the sweets.

Young children, it seems, solve subtraction problems in the same way as they solve addition problems. Riley et al. (1983) gave comparable addition and subtraction problems to young American children and allowed them to solve these problems using blocks as a support. The subtraction problem: 'Joe had eight marbles. Then he gave five marbles to Tom. How many does he have now?' was solved with the same rate of success as the parallel addition problem above. Six-year-old children made very few mistakes in either kind of problem when the numbers were small and they were allowed to use blocks as a support: 87 per cent of their answers to the addition problem and 100 per cent of their answers to the subtraction problem were correct.

However, these children's high rate of success does not necessarily mean that they had mastered the concepts of addition and subtraction. The questions that they were asked concerned one type of situation only. In every case they were asked to transform one quantity by adding to it or subtracting from it. In research on problem-solving, this kind of task is usually referred to as a *change situation*. But there are other addition and subtraction situations which have different levels of difficulty for young children. These are the part–whole and the comparison situations.

In *part–whole situations* the numbers refer to sets of objects; there is no change to any quantity. An example of a part–whole task would be: 'Five of the fish that Martin has in his aquarium are yellow and three are red. How many fish does he have in his aquarium altogether?'

In the third type of situation children are asked to quantify *comparisons*. For example, 'Joe has eight marbles and Tom has five. Who has more marbles? (an easy question) How many more marbles does Joe have than Tom? (a difficult question)'

The difficulty of a problem is determined not only by the situation but also by the *invariants* of addition and subtraction or the *operations of thought* (Vergnaud, 1982) that have to be understood by the children in order to solve a particular problem. Change problems like one of those presented above are quite easy, but there are other change problems which are rather difficult for young children. An example is the following problem-type: 'Joe had five marbles. Then Tom gave him some more marbles. Now Joe has eight marbles. How many marbles did Tom give him?' The difficulty of a problem of this type is that it is an additive problem but one of the addends is missing.

There are different ways to solve missing-addend problems. One is to use blocks or fingers. A child could count out five fingers (or blocks), keep track of where this set of five ended but go on counting up to eight, and then count once again only those elements which were added on to the five to get up to eight. This solution is an explicit representation of the actions in the problem and can be efficiently used by children who could not tell you what arithmetic operation is needed to solve this problem – as Marton and Neuman (1990) have observed with Swedish children and we have also observed with Brazilian children (T. N. Carraher and Bryant, 1987).

Another way to solve the missing-addend problem is by subtraction, a problem solving strategy that depends on the child's understanding of subtraction as the inverse of addition. In the example that we have been using, this would mean working out that the answer can be reached by subtracting the initial state, 5, from the end state, 8. Of course, to do this, the child needs to understand an invariant of addition/subtraction – their inverse relationship – and also to carry out an operation of thought (that is, apply this inverse transformation) before calculating the result of the arithmetic operation. This kind of solution can be implemented with the support of fingers or of blocks, just as the previous one can, but this is not a direct representation of the problem situation. Before the computation, the mental operation of inverting the transformation must be carried out in order to connect the additive situation with a subtractive solution.

The analysis of the invariants presented above allows us to predict that additive-change problems where the change is unknown should be more difficult than change problems where direct modelling of the situation leads to the correct solution even if the sum the children need to do is exactly the same. This prediction is supported by the results of Riley et al.'s (1983) study with kindergartners and first-grade children in the United States. As we have seen, subtraction problems and missing-addend problems can be solved by exactly the same operation of subtraction, but one type of problem is a great deal easier than the other. The kindergarten children were right 61 per cent of the time and the first-graders 56 per cent of the time when solving problems where the additive-change was unknown and their task was to work out what the change had been; yet their success in subtraction problems where direct modelling was possible was 100 per cent. The need to carry out an operation of thought based on the inverse property of addition and subtraction before computing the result of the arithmetic operation significantly increased the difficulty of the problem.

A third problem type involving change situations through addition is possible. An example of this type is: 'Joe had some marbles. Then Tom gave him five more marbles. Now Joe has eight marbles. How many marbles did Joe have in the beginning?' Let us consider the invariants which children need to understand in order to solve this problem and compare it with the preceding problem. Inversion is required for both problems, because in both an additive situation is described with one of the addends missing. However, this latter situation, called *additive-change with start unknown*, requires that children recognize one more invariant of addition: commutativity (that is, $a + b = b + a$). If the child tries to represent the problem situation directly with fingers or blocks, he or she needs to add 5 on to 'some' blocks to obtain 8. One way to do this would be by trial and error. The child may try starting up with 2, add 5, and count the total to check if there are now 8. Some children actually try to solve the problem in this manner, but they rarely succeed. A second way is to model the problem, but also implicitly to use the property of commutativity of addition. That means that the child presupposes that 'adding some on to 5' is the same as 'adding 5 on to some'. Because it is easier to add 'some on to 5' until 8 is obtained, the child can proceed in this way and still find the answer to the problem by modelling the situation. Finally, a third route is to use two operations of thought, commutativity and inversion, and arrive at the solution through subtraction.

This analysis of the invariants involved in the solution of additive-change with start unknown problems suggests that change-problems with start unknown should be the most difficult type of change problem. More invariants must be understood for this problem to be solved than for the other two types, and therefore it should be more difficult even when the arithmetic operation is kept constant. Riley et al.'s results support this prediction: in their study change problems in which the start was unknown were solved correctly by only 9 per cent of the kindergartners and 28 per cent of the first-grade children.

There are also interesting differences in the level of difficulty between various change-unknown problems. When the situation is additive (Joe had three marbles and then Tom gave him some more marbles. Now he has eight. How many did Tom give him?), the solution can be obtained in two ways: (1) through modelling without inversion (how much do we need to add on to 5 to get to 8); or (2) through inversion plus the arithmetic operation of subtraction. If children rely only on superficial cues from the problem (*Tom gave him some more marbles*), they will add and make a mistake. In contrast, when the situation is subtractive and the change is unknown (Joe had eight marbles. Then *he gave away some marbles to Tom*. Now Joe has three marbles. How many marbles did he give to Tom?), children will succeed if they follow the superficial cues in the problems, but of course they are succeeding for the wrong reasons. This allows us to predict that this type of subtraction problem will not differ significantly from the simple subtraction problems and will be easier than additive-situation change-unknown problems, where following superficial linguistic cues leads to failure. This is in fact what happens when we look at children's success in solving change-unknown problems: additive situations result in a lower percentage of correct responses than subtractive situations (see figure 6.1).

Inversion is required, however, with the problems in which the start is unknown both in the additive and the subtractive situation. In both cases, following superficial linguistic cues in the problem results in error. Thus we expect start-unknown problems to be more difficult for children regardless of whether the situation is additive or subtractive.

Figure 6.1 summarizes the results of children's success in solving distinct types of problems where addition and subtraction are the arithmetic operation required.

The results clearly support the theoretical approach discussed above: figure 6.1 shows that the analysis of situations and the invariants used in solving a problem jointly influence the difficulty of a problem.

But these are not the only determinants of success in addition and subtraction tasks for young children. It is also important to know what resources the children are using to implement the computation procedures – that is, what tools for thought· or systems of signs are available to them.

Carpenter and Moser (1982), for example, showed that young US children who had not yet received instruction on how to solve addition and subtraction problems performed much better when they could use blocks to implement the solution than when no blocks were available. They looked only at children's performance in part–whole problems in this comparison and they held problem-type constant. The rate of success of these young preschoolers who had had no instruction in arithmetic when solving small-number problems with blocks was 78.5 per cent correct answers. When they had no objects to help them to implement the computation, the figure fell to 68 per cent correct. The differences were more marked when the numbers were larger – that is, when the numbers were above 10 and the use of fingers became awkward. The rate of success for problems solved with the support of blocks was 60.5 per cent correct responses in contrast with 36.5 per cent correct responses without the support of blocks.

The use of fingers and of other objects to support calculations is important before instruction and remains so during the children's first years of school. Carpenter and Moser (1982) found that the difference disappeared after instruction for numbers under ten but persisted for large-number problems. The first-grade children (6-year-olds) in their study were right 84 per cent of the time in large-number problems when objects were available and 66 per cent of the time when they were not.

Terezinha Nunes and Analucia Schliemann (T. N. Carraher and Schliemann, 1985) also analysed the role of the systems of signs used to support computation when Brazilian children in the first two

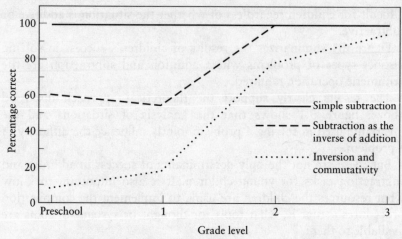

Percentage of correct responses for problems requiring subtraction but different numbers of invariants

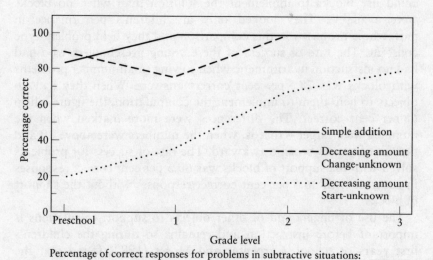

Percentage of correct responses for problems in subtractive situations: change-unknown differs from start-unknown

Figure 6.1 Children's rate of success in different kinds of addition and subtraction tasks

SOURCE: Riley et al. (1983)

grades of school were asked to solve addition and subtraction computation exercises with numbers above ten. The children were significantly less likely to succeed if they used the written computation routines that they had been taught in school, involving carrying and borrowing, than if they used other systems of signs and other methods to calculate. Among the methods that were successful, two were most common: (1) the children represented the numbers through fingers or marks on paper (no concrete objects were provided) and counted them as they would have done with concrete objects; (2) the children computed by decomposition, using number facts that they already knew as intermediary steps to find the solution (for example, $5 + 8$ was solved as 'five plus five is ten, plus three, thirteen'). Thus the use of written numbers and algorithms based on written numbers seemed a less effective support for children's implementation of their solution than either manipulatives (fingers, marks on paper) or oral numbers.

In these latter studies, the problem situations were held constant and only the means of implementing the computation were changed. In the Carpenter and Moser (1982) study the systems of signs available to the children were manipulated by the experimenters, who either offered or did not offer the blocks to be used in calculation. In the study by Carraher and Schliemann (T. Nunes Carraher and Schliemann, 1985), the children were solving computation exercises and they either tried to use the methods that they had been taught at school or they produced other representations for the numbers themselves. When the situation is held constant, computation procedures are still influenced by the representational tools or the systems of signs the children use in solving problems.

In brief, this overall analysis of addition and subtraction concepts suggests that, in order to analyse children's concepts, we need to take into account simultaneously the situations described in problems, the operations of thought or invariants needed to solve particular problems, and the systems of signs that the children are using when they are asked to solve problems. Thus children's understanding of addition and subtraction develops as they master more problem situations through the utilization of a larger variety of procedures that rely on different invariants as theorems in action and draw on a variety of systems of signs.

After this brief overview, we will consider each aspect of the concepts of addition and subtraction in turn. This separation for analytical purposes must not be interpreted as a suggestion that the different aspects of addition and subtraction are isolated one from the other. They should be considered together when we are trying to understand the development of children's knowledge of addition and subtraction.

2   What Might Numbers Refer to in Addition and Subtraction Situations? A Detailed Analysis of Number Meanings

When numbers refer to objects in a situation, they make much more sense to young children than when they do not refer to anything at all. Hughes (1986) documented young children's difficulty in understanding simple addition and subtraction sums when numbers are presented to them without referring to situations that could make the numbers meaningful.

He asked nursery school children (3–5 years of age) to solve addition and subtraction questions in different experimental conditions. In one condition, the children first counted how many blocks were inside a box and then saw how many blocks Hughes put into the box or took out of it – for example, there were two bricks in the box and then one more was put into it. The children were asked how many bricks were in the box at the end. In a second condition, parallel problems were posed but this time about an imaginary box. Thus the children were asked to imagine that there were two bricks in a box and then one brick was placed inside, and then asked how many bricks would be inside the box altogether. In a third type of situation, the imaginary shop, the children were presented with problems such as: 'If there was one child in a shop and then two children went into the shop, how many children would be in the shop then?' Finally, the children were also presented with computation exercises, where they were simply asked what is 2 and 1 more (or 2 plus 1 or 2 and then 1 more).

In none of the task-conditions could the children use blocks to solve the problems (but they could, of course, use their fingers if they wished). The only difference between the various conditions was whether the children were given a situation that they could think about in order to give meaning to the question.

Hughes used very small numbers, such as those in the examples above, and also some slightly larger ones which were nevertheless still small numbers (where the starting-point involved 5 or more) in all of these conditions. He observed that the children had the highest rate of success when the box was present, intermediary rates of success but still rather high when they had to imagine the box or the shop, but very low rates of success when no situation was described to give the computation some meaning, which was the case in the

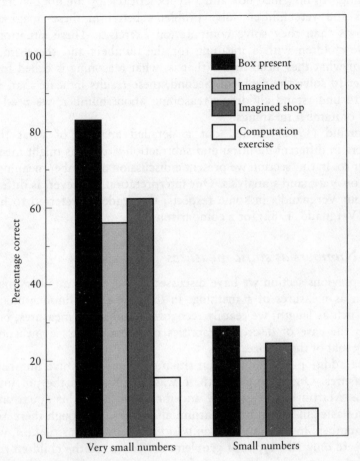

Figure 6.2 Children's responses for problems in different conditions with very small and small numbers

SOURCE: data from Hughes (1986)

computation exercises. This pattern was observed both for very small and for small number problems. Hughes's results are summarized in figure 6.2.

The results of Hughes's study are very important for our understanding of children's conceptual development in addition and subtraction. First, as he clearly suggests, these results indicate that we need more sophisticated theories about children's understanding of number than the often-used dichotomy between concrete and abstract reasoning. An imagined box and a hypothetical shop are not concrete objects and yet children solve problems better in these imagined situations than they solve computation exercises. These situations provide children with a meaning for the numbers and therefore a sense of what they need to do (that is, what reasoning is called for) in order to solve the problem. Second, these results indicate that, in order to understand children's reasoning about number, we need a theory of number meanings.

Vergnaud (1982) carried out a detailed analysis of what the numbers in different addition and subtraction situations might mean or refer to. In this section we present a discussion of number meanings based on Vergnaud's analysis. Our interpretation, however, is different from Vergnaud's in some respects; the reader is referred to his work (Vergnaud, 1982) for a comparison.

2.1   *Numbers as static measures*

In the previous section we have discussed the idea that numbers may be seen as measures of something. In the case of continuous quantities, such as length, we readily recognize numbers as measures, but also in the case of discrete quantities numbers express a measure, namely that of the set size.

Some addition and subtraction situations simply involve numbers as measures. One example of these was mentioned in the previous section: 'Martin has five yellow and three red fish in his aquarium. Martin has eight fish in his aquarium altogether.' Although there are three numbers in the simplest *composition of measures situation*, we can create only two types of problem: either we tell the children the size of the parts and ask them to find out the whole or we tell them the size of the whole and one of the parts and ask them to find the other part.

2.2   *Numbers that measure transformations*

Change problems (which we discussed at length in the previous section) involve two types of number-meanings: static measures and transformations. In the situation 'Joe had three marbles. Then Tom gave him five more marbles. Now Joe has eight marbles,' three and eight refer to static measures and five refers to a transformation.

Problems involving three static measures and those involving two static measures connected by a transformation might seem very similar to an adult. For example, one could say that the latter problem can also be thought of as involving simply a composition of sets of marbles, those that Joe had and those that Tom gave to him. Conversely, an adult could also argue that problems with static measures can be solved by an imagined transformation, whereby the child thinks of one set being added to the other (add the red fish to the yellow ones that are already in the aquarium to find the total) or a set being taken away (take the red fish out of the aquarium and count the yellow ones to know how many yellow fishes you have). So, is there any reason to distinguish between numbers as static measures and numbers as transformations?

Two kinds of evidence suggest that it is important to consider measures and transformations as distinct at least from the viewpoint of children's developing understanding of mathematical concepts. The first kind concerns children's understanding of the invariants of addition in the context of these different number meanings. The second kind relates to children's rate of success in solving problems with a subtraction transformation, in contrast to static part–whole measures problems when they know the whole and one of the parts.

The understanding of invariants with different number meanings Rachel Wright (1994; see also George, 1992) carried out a study in London in which she investigated whether different types of number meanings influence young children's (5 to 8 years of age) understanding of the commutativity of addition. She hypothesized that children might understand commutativity earlier in situations that involve three static measures within a part–whole relationship than in situations involving two static measures connected by a transformation. She reasoned that in part–whole situations the elements being added, the two parts, are of the same type whereas in a transformation problem the elements being added are of a different nature – one is a measure and the other a transformation. In composition of measures situations where the children know the two parts and want to find out the whole, in order to understand commutativity, the children just need to realize that it does not matter where you start counting a total set; whether you start from one part or the other, the number will always be the same. This is a simple counting principle that appears to be mastered by most 5-year-olds (see Gelman and Meck, 1983, for example). In the problems where two static measures are connected by a transformation, children may need to use a notion of compensation: if you start out with less than another person but then you get more, you can end up with the same amount. Although young children seem to understand that less added to less results in less, and that more added to more results in more, they have some difficulty in realizing that less added to more leads to the same amount in the end if the differences compensate exactly for one another.

Wright (1994) used an ingenious method to see whether the children understood the commutativity of addition. She asked the children to 'be the teacher' and mark the solutions that three children had written for a series of problems in a test. She presented each problem orally to the children and showed them the computations that each of the three children had carried out. The computations were only indicated (for example, $5 + 3$); the final answer was not written down. Playing teacher, the children had to tick the computations that would be correct for solving the problem and cross the wrong ones. If they were not sure whether the answer would be correct, they could place a question mark by the solution.

The crucial problems for Wright's hypothesis involved either the addition of static measures or change situations with the result unknown. Some control-problems involving subtraction were used to make the series more varied. The target answers for analysis (supposedly provided by three different children) to the addition problems either indicated an addition with the addends written in the order in which they appeared in the situation or they indicated an addition where the addends had been written in the reverse order (the second part plus the first one, for composition of static measures, and the transformation plus the initial state, for change problems). Some incorrect answers were also included – for example, indicating addition where subtraction was required or vice versa.

Wright (1994) also varied number size and used small numbers (with addends of one digit only and adding up to at most 15) and large numbers (with two-digit addends adding up to at least 50). She made three predictions concerning the development of children's understanding of commutativity. First, she expected to observe a developmental trend in the acquisition of commutativity, with younger children (Year 1, 5/6-year-olds) demonstrating less understanding of commutativity than the older (Year 2 and 3) children. This hypothesis could be tested by looking at the 'assessment errors' made by the children when they were playing the role of teacher. If the children had not yet mastered the idea of commutativity, they would accept as 'correct' significantly more solutions in which the addends were indicated in the same order as they appear in the situation – the a + b solutions – than when the addends were indicated in the reverse order – the b + a solutions. In other words, they would make assessment errors and mark as wrong the correct b + a solution. This prediction was supported by her findings. The children made significantly more assessment errors when the answers were of the b + a type than when they were of the a + b type and also younger children made significantly more assessment errors than older children.

Her second prediction was that if children understand commutativity better in the context of addition of static measures, then they would show a tendency to mark as 'correct' b + a solutions in the addition of static measures more often than in the change problems. This prediction was also clearly supported by her findings: a significantly larger number of assessment errors was observed in the change problems than in the addition of static measures.

Her third prediction was that these trends would be independent of number size. This is a negative prediction since it is that a particular factor – number size – will have no effect. Negative results are not usually convincing evidence, but number size often does affect children's performance in problem-solving significantly, and so a failure to find such an effect would be surprising. In the event the prediction was confirmed: number size had no effect.

Thus we conclude that it is necessary to distinguish between number as a static measure and number as a measure of transformation when we study children's conceptual development because the property of commutativity of addition is more readily recognized when numbers are measures of sets than when they are measures of transformations.

Further evidence for the need to make this distinction comes from studies of children's success in problem-solving which are briefly reviewed below.

Problem-solving with different number meanings We have seen that young children understand commutativity better in the context of adding static measures than in the context of change problems where transformations are involved. It could be argued that it is simply easier to solve static-measures problems in general because all that is involved in these problems is an understanding of part–whole relations whereas in change problems there is a composition of static measures (the initial and the final state) linked by a transformation. However, a closer look at children's problem-solving procedures and their rate of success in solving problems tells us that the situation is more complex than that.

As Wright (1994) cogently argued, the simplicity of commutativity in the context of adding static measures may be related to the fact that children recognize quite early the irrelevance of order in counting. It is likely that children understand that all they are doing when they add the parts is counting the elements together because this is actually how young children solve addition problems. The addition of parts is in this sense a direct extension of counting. However, there is no immediate connection between counting and finding the value of a part when the other part and the whole are known; an intermediary transformation is required, taking away the known subset from the whole. In contrast, in change-subtraction problems there is a direct connection between the situation described in the problem and the arithmetic operation to be performed when solving the problem. Thus subtraction carried in a change-subtraction problem can be solved by direct modelling of the situation whereas subtraction to find the value of the second part when the whole and one part are known appears to be more akin to taking subtraction as the inverse of addition. If this analysis is correct, the latter type of problem must be significantly more difficult than change-subtraction problems with result unknown.

This expectation is supported by the analysis of children's success rates in the different types of problems of relevance here. Table 6.1 presents a summary of the relevant results observed by Riley et al. (1983). The rate of success when children are asked to find the part in part–whole problems is quite similar to their success in using subtraction as the inverse of addition in change problems. Thus transforming a situation with three static measures into one where a transformation connects two static measures involves difficulties for children and therefore these two types of problem must be kept separate in an analysis of number meanings.

In summary, the analysis of number meanings and the empirical evidence from children's understanding of addition and subtraction presented so far indicates that we must distinguish between numbers that refer to static measures and those that refer to transformations. Children find it easier to understand commutativity of addition in problems where both numbers refer to static measures. On the other hand, they find it easier to understand the idea of subtraction in the

Table 6.1 Children's rate of success in different kinds of addition and subtraction tasks

Problem type	Percentage of correct responses			
	Kindergarten	Grate 1	Grade 2	Grade 3
Simple addition				
Change problem with result unknown	87	100	100	100
Adding two static measures	100	100	100	100
Simple subtraction				
Change problem with result unknown	100	100	100	100
Inverse subtraction				
Find a part when whole and other part are known	22	39	70	100

SOURCE: Adapted from Riley et al. (1983)

context of problems where a transformation is involved. In the next section another meaning for numbers will be considered: numbers as measures of static relations.

2.3 *Numbers that measure static relations*

There is still one type of addition/subtraction situation that we have not discussed – comparison situations where the measure of a static relationship is involved. A comparison involves two static measures and a static relation. An example of a comparison problem is: 'Joe has eight marbles. Tom has three marbles (the two static measures). How many more marbles does Joe have than Tom?' (the static relation). Research on comparison problems indicates that they are rather difficult for young schoolchildren and also tells us a great deal about the reasons for this difficulty. We will review below the major issues in the analysis of these problems and some significant empirical findings.

Static relations versus transformations Establishing relationships between comparison situations and arithmetic operations is not a simple matter. In change problems, where things are added or taken away, children can easily figure out what actions they need to carry out to solve a problem with the support of blocks or their fingers. The actions carried out on the symbolic objects are analogous to those that would be carried out with the objects themselves. When problems involve static comparisons, however, the connection between the situation and an operation on symbolic objects that would lead to problem solution is not immediately clear because nothing is added or taken away from either of the sets.

It is possible to phrase problems that involve comparing sets in a different way so that static relations are no longer involved. For example, the problem above could be phrased differently: 'Joe has eight marbles. Tom has three marbles. How many marbles must we give to Tom so that he will have the same number of marbles as Joe?' If the problem is presented in this way, it is no longer the same problem. Instead of thinking about a static relation, the child is asked to figure out a transformation that connects two static measures. This latter type of problem is referred to in the literature as an *equalizing problem*, being distinguished from the static comparisons exactly because it involves a transformation.

A contrast between equalizing problems and change problems illustrates the importance of considering all aspects of a problem together when we want to make predictions about problem difficulty. An equalizing problem is in some ways similar to a change-unknown problem; the question is to find out how much to add to *a* to make it equal to *b*. But it intuitively seems that it is easier for children to realize what it is that they need to do in an equalize problem than in a change-unknown problem if we think of the questions actually asked – that is, the verbal representation of the situation that we present to the children. In the equalizing problem the question is directly about how much to add to one set to make it equal to the other set, whereas in the change-unknown problem the question is much less direct. (In this latter type of problem the question is 'How much did Tom give to Joe?' when the problem is 'Joe had three marbles, Tom gave him some, now he has eight marbles.') These considerations lead to the prediction that equalising problems will be more similar to the easiest type of change problems than to the change-unknown problems. This is in fact what Carpenter et al. (1981) found: in their study, 91 per cent of the first-graders solved equalizing problems correctly when they had blocks available whereas only 72 per cent of the additive-situation change-unknown problems were correctly solved.

It has been consistently found that equalizing problems are easy for 6/7-year-old children whereas comparison problems are difficult. Cividanes-Lago (1993) and Hudson (1983) independently observed very high rates of success in diverse experiments about equalizing problems using several forms of presentation. Hudson presented 6/7-year-old children in the United States (first-graders) with illustrations where two sets of items were displayed – for example, birds and worms, children and balloons etc. (see figure 6.3 for an example). Half of the problems were presented as comparison problems (e.g. how many more birds than worms?) and the other half were presented through a question that suggested to the children the idea of using a one-to-one correspondence reasoning (e.g. if all the birds race and try to get a worm, how many birds won't get worms?). Hudson observed 100 per cent correct responses to the 'won't get' questions and only 64 per cent correct responses to the comparison questions.

Hudson suggested that the difference in the children's rate of correct responses was a consequence of their difficulty in understanding 'more' and 'less'. When the problems were presented without the comparatives, in the 'won't get' form, the children were successful. However, an alternative explanation needs to be considered: that the strategies that 6/7-year-olds have for solving 'won't get' and equalizing problems are not easily connected with their understanding of arithmetic operations and with the idea of numbers as static measures.

Hudson's linguistic hypothesis (as pointed out by Cividanes-Lago, 1993) cannot account for the fact that 6/7-year-olds are successful in answering the question 'who has more/less?' but fail in the quantification of the difference. 'More' and 'less' are understood as comparative terms but in order to quantify the difference between the sets it is necessary to connect an action on objects with the situation where the question refers to a static relation. When the question is changed from a comparison to an equalizing question, children succeed. The question 'How many more do we have to give to Tom so that he has as many as Joe?' helps the children think of a procedure to obtain an answer.

Similarly, in the 'won't get' question, there is a clear indication of what the children need to do with the objects to answer the question: they need to make two matching sets and count out the remaining

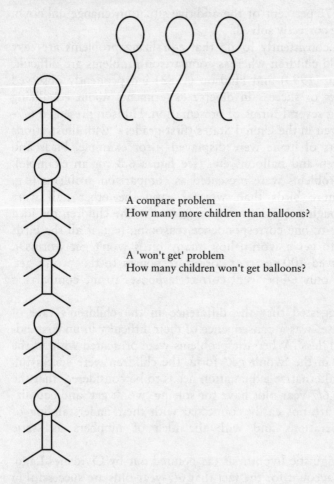

A compare problem
How many more children than balloons?

A 'won't get' problem
How many children won't get balloons?

Figure 6.3   The material used in Hudson's children and balloons task
SOURCE: Hudson (1983)

objects in the larger set. In fact this is exactly how the successful children solve them. Hudson (1983) analysed children's strategies in solving the 'won't get' problems and noted that approximately 40 per cent of the successful children exhibited observable strategies. Of these, the great majority (77 out of 97 children) either established correspondences across the sets of objects and then counted the objects left without a pair in the other set or counted out the smaller set, counted an equivalent number in the second set (that is, created a corresponding set within the larger set), and then counted out the remaining objects. These correspondence strategies are in some sense cued by the 'won't get' question but are unlikely to be easily connected with children's notions of addition and subtraction because their initial conceptions of addition and subtraction are based on increasing or decreasing a quantity.

The analysis of children's strategies in the equalizing and 'won't get' problems prompted us to investigate in greater detail how children eventually come to succeed in solving comparison problems. This work is described in the next section.

How do young children solve comparison problems? Previous studies (e.g., Riley et al. 1983; Hudson, 1983) had indicated that young children don't make random errors when they answer comparison problems. When they are asked the question 'How many more marbles does Tom have than Joe?', the typical wrong answer is to say the total number of marbles that Tom has – that is, the number for the larger set. Similarly, when asked 'How many less marbles does Joe have than Tom?' the typical wrong answer is to say the total number in the set with fewer marbles. This type of error suggested to us that the children know what 'more' and 'less' mean in terms of comparisons but they cannot get this knowledge connected with a strategy to quantify the difference. If that were the case, teaching children how to solve comparison problems could take the route of leading them to establish a connection between the strategies they have at their disposal for solving equalizing and 'won't get' problems and their concepts of addition and subtraction. In spite of the difficulty of comparative problems for young children, this form of teaching should be relatively simple and successful. On the other hand, if the hypothesis set out by Hudson (1983) were correct – that is, that children have difficulty in understanding comparative terms – teaching should take a rather different form because what children would need to learn is what comparative terms mean.

An answer to the question why children make errors in comparative problems is therefore of considerable educational significance. It is also important for our better understanding of the development of addition and subtraction concepts. In our view, children develop an initial concept of addition and subtraction that is related to putting sets together and taking them apart and this concept is not easily connected to the meaning of number as a measure of a static relationship. Independently of their understanding of addition and subtraction, young children also develop an understanding of equality related to one-to-one correspondence, which allows them to answer 'won't get' problems. However, as long as these concepts are not connected, they will find comparison problems difficult. When they come to see the relationship between the two schemas that they already have, they should be able to relate comparison problems to the operations of addition and subtraction. Concept development in this case would result from establishing connections between concepts already understood in one situation and their use in another set of situations.

In order to test whether it is possible to facilitate the establishment of a connection between one-to-one correspondence strategies in a static situation and addition/subtraction as actions that involve change, we carried out a training study where we attempted to provoke this connection (Nunes and Bryant, 1991). The study included a pre-test, in which we investigated the children's ability to solve different types of comparison problems; a training phase, in which we attempted to lead the children to make the connection between their one-to-one correspondence strategy and the idea of addition/subtraction in the context of one type of comparison problem; and a post-test, in which we analysed children's success in solving the type of problem they had been taught about and their use of their newly acquired understanding to solve other types of comparison problems not included in the training phase. We will describe below first the different types of comparison problem and then the results of this study.

Different types of comparison problems   When we discussed change situations, it became clear that different types of problems with different levels of difficulty can be created in such situations. We saw, for example, that change-unknown problems and start-unknown problems require different operations of thought before the arithmetic operation can be determined. The same applies to comparison situations, where different types of problems can be generated.

A comparison situation involves two sets and a static relation. A comparison problem may therefore have the static relation or either of the sets as the unknown. In contrast to the part–whole situation, where it makes no difference which of the subsets is unknown, in a comparison situation problems are quite different depending on which of the subsets is unknown. In a comparison situation, one of the sets works as the referent for the comparison. When the referent is unknown, the problem is more difficult. A contrast between the problems is instructive:

- **Comparison situations referent unknown:** Joe has eight marbles. He has five more marbles than Tom. How many marbles does Tom have?
- **Comparison situation, referent known:** Tom has three marbles. Joe has five marbles more than Tom. How many marbles does Joe have?

In order to consider the operations of thought involved in solving these comparison problems, we can make an analogy to the change problems discussed earlier. In a comparison problem where the referent is unknown, the child needs to 'add 5 to some' and make sure the result is 8. Thus this is analogous to a start-unknown problem. In the comparison problem with the referent known, the child needs to 'add 5 to 3'. This analogy leads us to expect that, when the referent is unknown, comparison problems are significantly more difficult for children. This hypothesis is supported in a general fashion by the results reported by Riley et al. (1983), summarized in figure 6.4 (but note that for kindergarten children, where there is a floor effect, there is no significant difference between the two problem types).

Establishing a connection between one-to-one correspondence strategies and addition/subtraction   In our training study (Nunes and Bryant, 1991) we wanted to lead children to establish a connection between their understanding of one-to-one correspondence and addition/subtraction as a means of quantifying the static relation in a comparison problem. Thus we needed first to make sure that the participants in the study understood that building sets in one-to-one correspondence leads to the formation of equal sets.

In order to ensure that the children understood one-to-one correspondence, all children were given a screening task, in which they were initially asked to share 16 pretend-sweets between themselves and the experimenter equally. The experimenter then asked them to count out their own set and find out how many sweets they had. Finally the experimenter covered his/her own set and asked the children how many sweets the experimenter had. Only 8 per cent of the children did not immediately make the inference about the

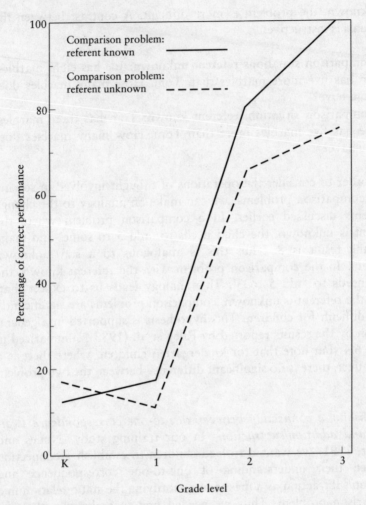

Figure 6.4 Children's responses in different types of comparison problems: percentages by problem type and grade level
SOURCE: data from Riley et al. (1983)

number of sweets that the experimenter had. These children were not included in the study.

The study involved 180 Brazilian children in the age range 5 to 7 years, attending preschool (5/6 years) or Year 1 (7 years) in an independent school in Recife, Brazil. All the children were pre- and post-tested in a set of comparison problems. In the pre- and post-test the children were asked to solve four comparison problems, two of which had the static relation as the unknown (how many more does A have than B?) and two where the referent set was unknown (A has five more than B. How many does B have?).

Between the pre- and post-test, all children answered a series of six comparison problems that were presented to them in three different conditions to which they had been randomly assigned. The children in the *control condition* simply had to answer the same six comparison problems presented to the other groups. Like the children in the other groups, they had some blocks to use as pretend-sweets in trying to figure out the answer. They were told to build the two sets of sweets (e.g. 'You have eight and I have five sweets'), asked the comparison question ('How many more sweets do you have than I have'), and were given feedback by the experimenter, who told them the correct answer after each trial if they had made a mistake.

Two experimental conditions were created. For both we devised a situation in which the sets were initially equal and then one of the sets was changed, either by addition or by subtraction, with the child being asked about the static relationship immediately after this change. The experimental conditions started out with the experimenter asking the child to give the same number of pretend-sweets to the child and to the experimenter – for example, five. When the two equal sets were constructed, the experimenter said: 'But you were a very good girl/boy today. I think that I will give you three more sweets [the experimenter then added three sweets to the child's array]. How many sweets do you have more than I have?' Alternatively in some trials we told the child that he/she had been very naughty and some sweets would have to be taken away. Through this procedure, we expected the children to establish a connection between their knowledge of one-to-one correspondence and the idea of addition/subtraction.

The two experimental conditions varied in one respect. In one condition the equal sets were built through a *spatial one-to-one correspondence* procedure. In this condition we asked the child to set aside, say, five sweets for him/herself and then indicated that the same number should be set aside for the experimenter through spatial correspondence ('now give me just as many sweets as you have and put them in a row like this' – gesturing to indicate the spatial correspondence). In the second experimental condition, the equal sets were built through a *temporal one-to-one correspondence* procedure. In this condition, the experimenter and the child each had a box in which to keep their sweets. The child was asked to put a sweet in his/

her box at the same time as the experimenter did the same until they had five each. As in the control condition, the children were given feedback and told the correct answer if they made a mistake during the teaching phase.

Thus all three groups of children answered the same number of comparison questions between the pre- and post-tests and received feedback by being told the correct answer whenever they were wrong. All the comparison problems in this phase involved a question about the static relation ('how many more/less do you have than I have?'). Their experience differed only in terms of whether they just had feedback or whether they had participated in a teaching phase that aimed at developing a connection between one-to-one correspondence strategies and addition/subtraction.

The results of this study are summarized in figure 6.5, where the mean numbers of correct responses in the pre- and post-test for the children in the three groups are presented for each age level.

The results indicated that all three groups did significantly better in the post-test than in the pre-test. Thus simply asking the children to answer the series of problems and giving them feedback about the correct response had a positive effect on their performance. However, the group that profited most was the experimental group working in the *spatial correspondence condition*: both preschoolers and Year 1 children assigned to this group performed significantly better than the children assigned to the other two groups of the same age level. The preschool children who participated in the spatial correspondence teaching condition did as well as the Year 1 children in the other two groups. Year 1 children in the spatial correspondence condition accomplished 78 per cent correct responses, a level of success that indicates that they were able to solve both problems in which they had been instructed (static relation missing) and those in which they had not been instructed (referent set missing). In contrast, children in all other groups basically progressed only on the problems that had been included in the teaching phase.

These results are encouraging both from the theoretical and from the educational viewpoint. Theoretically they strongly support the idea that young children come to solve comparison problems by coordinating two strategies that they already had at their disposal. They understand addition/subtraction in some situations but not in others where addition/subtraction could be used. By making a connection between two things they already knew, the children come to understand something new.

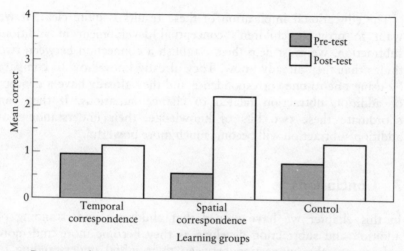

Percentage of correct responses by learning group in the pre- and post-test for 5/6-year-old children

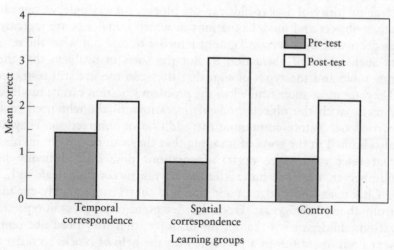

Percentage of correct responses by learning group in the pre- and post-test for 6/7-year-old children

Figure 6.5 Children's responses in pre- and post-tests for comparison problems

The educational implication of these results is quite clear. If we want to promote children's conceptual development in addition/subtraction, we must help them establish a connection between two things that they already know. They already know how to compare by using one-to-one correspondence and they already have a concept of addition/subtraction related to change situations. If they can coordinate these two bits of knowledge, their understanding of addition/subtraction will become much more powerful.

3   Conclusions

In this chapter we have argued that children's understanding of addition and subtraction develops as they become more and more able to see the connection between their initial understanding of addition and subtraction and new situations, and as they become able to use different systems of signs (or tools for thought) when reasoning about addition and subtraction. The developments that we have discussed are briefly summarized below.

Preschool children do not seem to find it difficult to relate their understanding of number as a measure of set size to their conception of addition/subtraction as an increase/decrease in quantities. The large majority of 5-year-olds can use blocks, for example, as signs for other objects and model situations in which initial sets are increased or decreased by a certain amount in order to find out what the result of such addition/subtraction is. But the sorts of problem that they can solve and the types of sign that they can use are still restricted. They are most successful when the problem situation can be modelled directly with the objects and no operations of thought need to be carried out before computing the addition or subtraction. They are also limited in the sorts of meaning that they can deal with: numbers that refer to set size or transformations pose little difficulty but numbers that refer to static relations are not successfully dealt with.

Children's knowledge of addition and subtraction quickly expands from about 5 to 7 years. From the viewpoint of progress in representation, children soon realize, for example, that they need not represent both quantities in a problem with the help of blocks in order to add them. They can use a number word to represent the first addend and count on from there, representing only the second addend with blocks or fingers. As we saw in chapter 3, this insight about addition is related to their understanding of numbers in a new way because it is connected to their understanding of the property of additive composition of numbers.

Children's knowledge of addition also expands in terms of the properties of addition. To understand addition and subtraction as the inverse of each other is a significant achievement and it allows children to solve missing-addend problems where the amount of change has to be figured out from the starting-point and the result. A second property of addition that children also come to understand between 5 and 7 years is commutativity. Although their understanding of it is restricted initially to the part–whole context, it later becomes applied to change situations. This progress seems to be instrumental in their mastery of different types of problems in change situations, such as those problems in which the starting set is unknown and has to be calculated.

Finally, children develop several strategies for working with numbers, but these strategies seem initially to be connected to different situations. They use one-to-one correspondence in order to construct equivalent sets. The correspondence can be either direct, through the pairing of objects, or mediated by counting, where each set is constructed by counting up to the same number. Children use addition and subtraction in situations that involve numbers as measures of set size and numbers as measures of transformations. But they use neither of these operations when they have to deal with numbers as measures of the static relationship between two sets: young children are not successful in solving comparison problems where a static relation between sets is involved. However, they can be easily led to coordinate the strategies that they already have, and thus learn to solve comparison problems. This seems to be the last step in the development in their understanding of addition and subtraction situations with natural numbers – but these concepts will go on developing, as they need later on to deal with directed (that is, positive and negative) numbers.

7

The Progress to
Multiplication and Division

A common view of multiplication and division is that these are simply
different arithmetic operations which children should be taught after
they have learned addition and subtraction. According to this view,
there need be no major change in children's reasoning in order for
them to learn how and when to carry out multiplication and division.
This view was challenged by Piaget and his colleagues (see, for
example, Piaget, Grize, Szeminska and Bangh, 1977), who suggested
that understanding multiplication and division represents a significant
qualitative change in children's thinking.

There certainly are significant discontinuities between addition and
subtraction on the one hand and multiplication and division on the
other, as Piaget and his colleagues stressed, but there are some
significant continuities too. The main theme of this chapter will be
that the continuities and discontinuities are as important as each
other, and both need to be thoroughly charted if we are to understand
the many steps that every child has to take towards a full understanding of multiplication.

We will discuss the number meanings involved in multiplicative
reasoning, the situations in which they appear, and the development
of children's understanding of these situations and number meanings.
There is, it should be noted, a certain amount of controversy here.
There is certainly much less agreement about how to classify types of
multiplication and division problems than there is about addition
and subtraction, and our own classification might not be universally
accepted. Our aim will be to describe children's progressive understanding of the operations of thought, the systems of signs, and the

situations which are connected to the concepts of multiplication and division.

We must start with some reflection on the new number meanings and the new kinds of situation that children encounter when they begin to learn about multiplication. The first section of this chapter will set out the different number meanings that are involved in multiplicative reasoning and these will form a framework for the sections that follow. In the second and third sections we will examine the development of children's understanding of situations which involve multiplication and division. We shall distinguish three types of situation, but we will discuss only the first two types now, and will leave the third to chapter 8. We decided to make this separation partly for a practical reason, which is to keep the chapter reasonably short, but also for a conceptual reason: the third situation leads immediately to the concept of fractions, which is a distinctive topic and deserves its own chapter.

We must begin with a word of caution. Multiplicative reasoning is a complicated topic because it takes different forms and it deals with many different situations, and that means that the empirical research on this topic is complicated too. So, in order to make sense of the empirical work, we must first spend some time setting up a conceptual framework for the analysis of children's reasoning and only then go on to review the research. Thus this chapter will differ in style from the preceding ones. Up to now it was possible to build the concepts and the vocabulary needed slowly through the chapter: with multiplication and division we stray so far from common sense and everyday vocabulary that we have to agree on a set of terms and conceptual distinctions at the outset. We hope that the same curiosity about children's understanding of mathematical concepts that made us persist in searching for a synthesis of different types of multiplicative reasoning situations will also keep the reader going through this challenging introductory section.

Our goal is to understand why it is that the same children can seem extremely clever with some forms of multiplicative reasoning and yet fail dismally when trying to solve other problems that seem at first to be at the same level of difficulty as, if not actually easier than, the problems that they manage with great success.

1   Multiplication, Division, and New Number Meanings

It is common practice in schools to teach addition before multiplication. There are several possible reasons for this. One is the general belief, which, as we shall see, is correct, that multiplication is more difficult than addition. Another is the idea that addition leads on to multiplication because some aspects of addition form the basis of multiplication. To some extent this is also right, since one way of solving multiplication sums is through repeated addition. You can work out the answer to 3×270 by adding 270 three times. Similar relations exist between subtraction and division sums: you can work out the answer to $270 \div 90$ by seeing how many times you must subtract 90 from 270 to reach zero. But it would be wrong to treat multiplication as just another, rather complicated, form of addition, or division as just another form of subtraction.

The reason for this is that there is much more to understanding multiplication and division than computing sums. The child must learn about and understand an entirely new set of number meanings and a new set of invariants, all of which are related to multiplication and division but not to addition and subtraction. In this section we will concentrate on the types of situation that produce these new meanings and invariants, and we will contrast these with situations which involve additive reasoning.

Let us first summarize briefly the number meanings and situations involved in additive reasoning. Additive reasoning is about situations in which objects (or sets of objects) are put together or separated. All the number meanings in additive situations are directly related to set size and to the actions of joining or separating objects and sets. Number as a measure of sets involves putting objects into a set where the starting-point is zero; number as a measure of transformations relates to the set that is joined to/separated from another set; number as a measure of a static relation (in comparison problems) relates to the set that would have to be joined to/separated from another in order to make two sets equal in number.

Situations which give rise to multiplicative reasoning are different because they do not involve the actions of joining and separating. We will distinguish three main kinds of multiplicative situation: (1) one-to-many correspondence situations; (2) situations which involve relationships between variables; and (3) situations which involve sharing, division, and splitting.

1.1 *The one-to-many correspondence situations*

The simplest sort of multiplicative situation is probably one in which there is one-to-many correspondence between two sets. Some every-day examples of one-to-many correspondence are: one car has four wheels (1-to-4), one child has two feet (l-to-2), one table can sit 6 people (1-to-6) etc. There are some continuities between these multiplicative situations and additive situations. The most salient is that some of the number meanings here are also connected to sets: 'one car', 'four wheels', 'one table', 'six parents' etc. also refer to set size. However, there are four differences of great significance.

First, the multiplicative situations involve a constant relation of one-to-many correspondence between two sets. This constant one-to-many correspondence is the invariant in the situation, a type of invariant which is not present in additive reasoning. The one-to-many correspondence is the basis for a new mathematical concept, the concept of *ratio*. In order to keep, for example, the correspondence '1 car to 4 wheels' constant, each time we add one car to the set of cars we must add 4 wheels to the set of wheels – that is, we add different numbers of objects to each set. This contrasts with the additive situation where, in order to keep the difference between two sets constant, we add the same number of objects to each set.

This reasoning leads us to the second difference: the actions carried out to maintain a ratio invariant are not joining/separating but *replicating* (to use Kieren's (1994) expression) and its inverse. Replicating is not like joining, where any amount can be added to one set. Replicating involves adding to each set the corresponding unit for the set so that the invariant one-to-many correspondence is maintained. For example, in the relation 'one car has four wheels', the unit to be considered in the set of cars is one, whereas the unit in the set of wheels is a composite unit of four wheels. The inverse of replicating is removing corresponding units from each set. If we remove one car we must remove four wheels, in order to maintain the $1:4$ ratio between cars and wheels.

The third difference is that a ratio remains constant when replication is carried out even if the number of cars and the number of wheels change. In a set where there are 3 cars and 12 wheels, the ratio is still $1:4$. This is the case because a ratio does not represent the number of objects in either set but is an expression of the relation between the two sets.

Finally, a new number meaning can be identified in the number of times that a replication is carried out. For example, if we start with the simple situation where we have 1 car and 4 wheels and replicate this starting situation six times, '6' refers to the number of replications – called the *scalar factor*. A scalar factor is neither about cars nor about wheels; it does not refer to the number of objects in the sets but to the number of replications relating two set sizes of the same type. 'Six' expresses the relation between 1 and 6 cars and between 4 and 24 wheels. For the ratio to remain constant, the same scalar factor must be applied to each set.

It is worth pointing out that ratios do not need to involve a unit: for example, a recipe may involve a 2 : 3 ratio between the number of eggs and of cups of flour. When you increase the number of cups, you also need to increase the number of eggs so that the ratio remains constant.

The number meanings in one-to-many correspondence situations are schematically represented in figure 7.1. In short, one-to-many correspondence situations involve the development of two new number meanings: *ratio*, which is expressed by a pair of numbers that remains invariant in a situation even if the set size varies, and the *scalar factor*, that refers to the number of replications applied to both sets maintaining the ratio constant. It should be clear that neither of these meanings relates to set size: the ratio and the scalar factor remain constant even when set sizes vary.

1.2   *Situations that involve relationships between variables – that is, co-variation*

A different type of number meaning in multiplicative reasoning can be found in situations in which two (or more) variables co-vary either as a consequence of convention or of causation. *Convention* here means 'agreed upon co-variation' which can be altered by new agreements. An example of a conventional situation is: one kilo of sugar costs £1.60, ½ kilo costs £0.80. *Causation* refers to the impact of one variable on another; we do not expect to be able to change causal relations by agreement. For example, if you hang a weight of 20 grams at the end of a certain spring, the spring will stretch 15 cm. If you hang a 10 gram weight, it will stretch 7.5 cm.

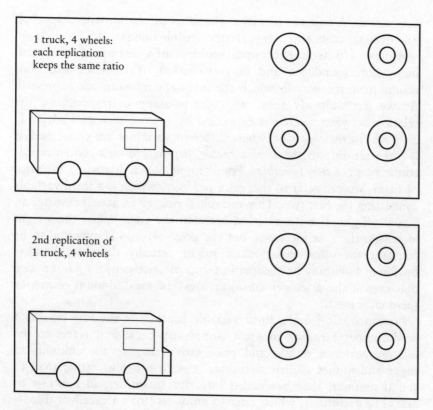

1 truck, 4 wheels:
each replication
keeps the same ratio

2nd replication of
1 truck, 4 wheels

Figure 7.1 One-to-many correspondence

There are some similarities but also some differences between this second type of multiplicative situation and the first. An important one is that it is possible to use the same sort of operation, replicating and its inverse, when solving problems about relationships between two variables and problems which involve one-to-many correspondence between sets. Consequently, the number of replications – that is, the scalar factor – is an important number meaning in both kinds of multiplicative situation. If you buy 20 times as much sugar, you should pay 20 times as much money: the relationship between the two variables is not changed by the number of replications.

However, there are also significant differences. First, the numbers in the second type of situation refer to *values on variables* and not to sets. Sets are made of discontinuous elements and variables are continuous. Thus *fractional values* emerge naturally in the context of variables whereas we are confined to whole numbers when speaking about sets. 'A half car has two wheels' is nonsense, whereas 'a half kilo of sugar costs 80p' is a perfectly sensible thing to say.

A second difference between multiplicative reasoning in one-to-many correspondence and in co-variation of variables situations results from the way in which the invariant relations are expressed. As we have already seen, with one-to-many correspondence the relation between the sets is expressed by a ratio, such as $1 : 4$, $1 : 2$, $2 : 3$ etc. In the situation where different variables are concerned, it is often sensible to speak of *a factor, a function or a third variable connecting the two variables*. For example, when discussing the price of sugar, we can refer to the 'price per kilo', which is a third variable connecting the first two. This variable is neither an actual cost nor an actual weight, but the relation between the two. When the weight increases, the cost increases, but the price-per-kilo is expected to be constant (in some situations it might actually decrease, because buying in bulk may be cheaper in terms of price-per-kilo – but notice that even if the price-per-kilo decreases, the total amount of money spent increases).

Price per kilo (or the third variable connecting the first two) is a new number meaning of great complexity because it refers to the relation between weight and price rather than to the amounts of sugar and money. When quantities refer to relations rather than to actual amount, they are called *intensive quantities*, in contrast to *extensive quantities*, which refer to amounts (for an excellent discussion of extensive and intensive quantities, see Schwartz, 1988). Similarly, when we speak of the effect of hanging a weight at the end of a spring, we can speak of a 'stretching factor', which is not the same as the weight or the increase in length at any point, but is a constant relation between these two variables. This stretch factor does not change (at least up to the point where the spring loses its shape!) with the increase in the amount of weight put on the spring. The stretch factor can be used, for example, to compare springs (which spring has a higher stretch factor?). In the same way, we use price per kilo to decide which is the 'best buy'.

These number meanings in co-variation situations are presented schematically in figure 7.2.

Before we finish this section, we must note that we have restricted the discussion so far to situations in which only two variables are involved at the outset or, as well, a third variable which relates the initial two. But this simple type of situation stands here for a host of others in which more than two variables need to be considered from

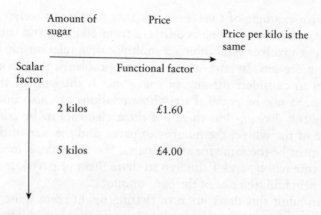

Figure 7.2 Number meanings in co-variation situations

the outset. Vergnaud (1983) provides us with a good example: the total amount of money collected by a farmer from the milk production in his farm depends on several variables – the number of cows that he has, the average production of milk per cow per day, the number of days, and the price of milk. Without taking all of these variables into account, the farmer cannot try to estimate his income. Problems that involve multiple proportions are clearly more complex. But the principles are the same as in the situations that we have just discussed and we need only acknowledge the existence of more complex situations without having to create a separate category of multiplication situations (for further discussion of different types of co-variation situations, see Vergnaud, 1983).

In summary, even if children understand one-to-many correspondence, they probably need to build some different concepts in order to deal with situations where a relationship between two variables is involved. The novelties in dealing with relationships between variables relate to *fractions of units of measurement*, which appear in these situations because variables, unlike sets, are continuous quantities, and to a new type of number meaning that expresses the relation between the two variables, *a factor, a function or an intensive quantity*.

1.3 *Situations that involve sharing and successive splits*

The activity of sharing provides us with a third type of situation that involves multiplicative reasoning. Sharing involves the distribution of a set – for example of sweets – amongst a number of recipients – for example, children. Sharing is different from addition and subtraction because it involves establishing a multiplicative relationship between two or more sets. In part–whole additive problems, there is only one relation to consider: the size of the whole is the sum of the parts, which need not be equal. Part–whole relations are also involved in sharing and division but there are three elements to be considered: the size of the whole, the number of parts, and the size of the parts, which must be the same for all the parts. For example, if there are 20 sweets (the whole) and 4 children to share them (4 parts), there are 5 sweets per child (the size of the part, or *quota*).

To an adult this description of sharing might seem quite reminiscent of one-to-many correspondence situations, but children might not think in the same way as adults do about the two situations. There is a number of reasons why they may treat them as quite different. One is that the action of distribution is the starting-point and the most basic and obvious aspect of sharing, whereas in one-to-many correspondence situations this action is in the past, as with 1 car–4 wheels.

Another difference between the two situations lies in the fact that with sharing children need to come to grips with the relationships between three sets (or variables): the total number of sweets, the number of children, and the number of sweets per child. If you keep the number of children the same and increase the number of sweets, there will be more sweets per child; but, if you keep the number of sweets the same and increase the number of children, there will be fewer sweets per child. There is a direct relation between total number of sweets and sweets-per-child but an inverse relation between number of children and sweets-per-child. Thus there are new relationships to be understood with sharing and successive splits which are not present in the one-to-many correspondence situation, where the ratio is fixed from the outset. Correa and Bryant (1994) have suggested that understanding this inverse relationship is a basic step in going beyond the simple activity of sharing to the understanding of division.

A third reason for drawing a line between one-to-many correspondence situations and division by sharing is that a division may naturally result in fractions whereas one-to-many correspondence situations are more clearly connected to whole numbers, as we showed earlier. If there were 6 chocolate bars and 9 children, each child would end up with 1½ bars of chocolate. Fractions are not only a new sort of number meaning but also a new sort of number – an issue which will be discussed in detail in chapter 8.

Yet another reason for contrasting sharing and division with one-to-many correspondence and co-variation situations arises from the actions and operations carried out in these different situations. One-to-many correspondence and co-variation situations have in common the fact that the basic action that links several pairs of numbers is replication (or its inverse). As the scalar factor (or number of replications) changes, the relationship between the sets or between the variables remains constant: there is a constant ratio in the one-to-many correspondence situations and a constant function (or factor) in the co-variation situations.

Division situations are different: when division is performed successively on a set or object, *these successive divisions provoke a chance in the relationship between the whole and the parts.* This is rather complicated but might be clarified by visualizing the process, as Confrey (1994) suggests, as a tree diagram, like the one presented in figure 7.3. We will use interchangeably the terms 'successive splits' and 'successive divisions' during this discussion; many of the ideas presented here were initially developed by Confrey, who uses the expression 'splits' with a broader meaning than division.

The initial situation at the top contains one chocolate cake, which is split the first time around into two pieces. If each piece is split a second time (two successive divisions), there will be four pieces. Three splits lead to eight pieces; four splits will give sixteen pieces. We can readily see that there are three sorts of number meaning in this situation: the number of splits (or divisions), the number of parts in each division, and the size of the parts. In the tree diagram of figure 7.3, we have four splits, into two parts each time, giving pieces which are one-sixteenth of the whole.

Confrey (1994) pointed out that successive divisions clearly differ from the preceding multiplicative situations in many ways. First, there is a new number meaning which indicates the rate of change. For example, cutting into two (a 2-split) and cutting into three (a 3-split) represent different rates in the growth of number of pieces. One 2-split gives two pieces, two 2-splits give four pieces. This rate of growth contrasts with: one 3-split gives three pieces, two 3-splits give nine pieces. Second, the result of such splits differs from the result of replicating. Replicating gives an arithmetic progression – if the relationship 1 : 2 is replicated, for example, we have the following sequence: one person needs two shoes, two people need four shoes,

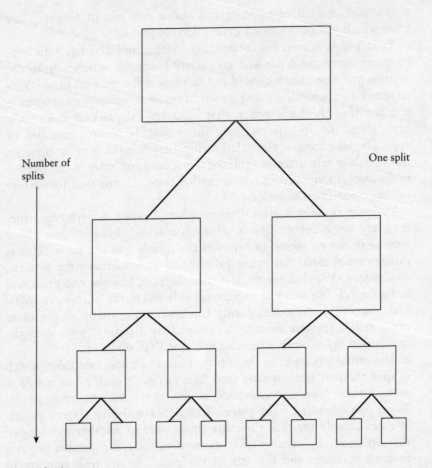

Number of splits

One split

One 2-split: 2 parts
Two 2-splits: 4 parts
Three 2-splits: 8 parts

Figure 7.3   Successive splits and divisions

three people need six shoes, four people need eight shoes. The sequence in the number of shoes is 2, 4, 6, 8 etc. Splitting gives a geometrical progression. The sequence in the number of pieces after each 2-split is 2, 4, 8, 16 etc.

To summarize: sharing is an action that relates to the operation of division and to the possibility of successive splits. We distinguish sharing as an action from division as an operation because under-standing division goes beyond the action of sharing: it involves the realization of the inverse relation between the number of recipients and the size of their quota (as suggested by Correa and Bryant, 1994). These part–whole relations are rather different from the part–whole relations involved in additive situations. When division is applied successively, the situations become more complex. A series of divisions or successive splits shows a progression that differs from the preceding multiplication situations. The number of successive divisions does not have the same meaning as the number of successive replications: with replication there is no change in the relation between the variables whereas with division there is change in the part–whole relation.

1.4 *Overview*

The common-sense view that multiplication is nothing but repeated addition, and division is nothing but repeated subtraction, does not seem to be sustainable after a careful reflection about situations that involve multiplicative reasoning. There are certainly links between additive and multiplicative reasoning, and the actual calculation of multiplication and division sums can be done through repeated addition and subtraction. But several new concepts emerge in multiplicative reasoning, which are not needed in the understanding of additive situations. *Ratio* is a new form of number meaning expressing a one-to-many correspondence situation. A ratio is expressed not by one number but by pairs of numbers. In order to maintain the ratio fixed and add more elements, *replicating* rather than joining is the action to be carried out. The number of replications is known as a *scalar factor*.

In multiplicative situations where the relationship between two variables is concerned, a new number meaning emerges, *a factor, function, or an intensive quantity connecting the two variables.* Multiplicative situations which involve the relation between variables can become more complex as the number of variables in the situations increases (for further discussion of the difference between one-to-many correspondence and co-variation situations, see Greer, 1992; 1994).

Finally, another sort of action, *sharing* involves a new view of part–whole relations, which differs from such relations in additive situations. In sharing, there are three values to be considered: the total, the number of recipients, and the quota (or the size of the share). The quota and the number of recipients are in inverse relation to each other: as one grows, the other decreases. Sharing also involves a new type of number, fractions, which will be considered in chapter 8. To complicate matters even further, it is possible to work with situations where *successive divisions or splits* are involved. Successive splits are related to the emergence of new relations and number meanings, such as *rate of change* and *number of splits* (for further discussion of splits, see Confrey, 1994; Kieren, 1994).

With our classification completed we will now review some of the work that describes children's developing understanding of these new number meanings.

2   Children's Understanding of Multiplicative Situations

Our main theme in this chapter is that there are many different levels of multiplicative reasoning, and that children take their first steps on the multiplicative ladder at quite a young age. One rather dramatic way of illustrating this theme can be found in Piaget's work. Most people who mention Piaget's ideas about multiplication concentrate on his writings on late development. There is a tendency to view multiplication rather narrowly as intrinsically related to the concept of proportionality and Piaget's later work on proportions (Inhelder and Piaget, 1958) indicates that proportionality is only mastered by young adolescents (10/11 years).

However, Piaget (1965) also suggested that children as young as 5/6 years deal with elementary ideas about multiplication, such as one-to-many correspondence, surprisingly well. This apparent contradiction seems to us a good place to begin our analysis of how the ideas of multiplication and division might at first appear in the child's thinking.

The discussion of the origin of children's understanding of multiplicative reasoning will be organized around the three different sorts of multiplicative situation.

2.1   *One-to-many correspondence situations*

Young children's multiplicative reasoning: how does it all start?   Piaget (1965) suggested that children's first ideas of multiplication come from the development of the correspondence scheme and its use in transitive inferences. He reasoned that children who can understand one-to-one correspondence and also transitivity should also be able to grasp one-to-many correspondences. When children at the age of 5–6 years realize that if A = B and C = B. then A = C, they should also be able to understand that if A = 2B and A = C, then C = 2B.

Couched in such formal language this idea might seem a complicated one, but Piaget's method for investigating children's understanding of these relationships was simple enough. He asked children to set up one-to-one correspondence and also one-to-many correspondence between different sets of objects. In one task the children were asked to put one large blue flower in each of ten vases first; then the blue flowers were removed, arranged into a single bunch, and the children put one small pink flower in each vase. Next the pink flowers were also removed and arranged into a single bunch. Thus the children knew that the number of blue flowers (A) was equal to the number of vases (B) and they also knew that the number of pink flowers (C) was equal to the number of vases. However, the blue and pink flowers were of different sizes so that children could not easily compare the number of flowers in the two sets visually. The bunch with large blue flowers looked different from the bunch with small pink flowers. The children would have to understand one-to-one correspondence to be able to conclude that the two sets of flowers were equal in number.

According to Piaget, the children's responses to this situation fell into two categories: either the children recognized that the number of flowers in the blue and pink bunches was the same and justified their deduction on the basis of the correspondence between each set of flowers and the set of vases, or they failed to recognize the necessity of this numerical equivalence even when the interviewer pointed out that each bunch of flowers could be put back in the vases, one flower per vase.

Piaget then gave the same children another task which demanded the reasoning that if A = 2B and C = A, then C = 2B. The children were asked what would happen if the same pink and blue flowers were now put back in the vases and shared equally between them. How many flowers would there be in each vase? If the children were not sure of the relation between flowers (A) and vases (B), they could see for themselves by putting the flowers into the vases: they could see that there are two flowers in each vase (A = 2B).

The flowers were then set aside but the vases stayed in sight and the children were asked to pick from a box of thin plastic tubes the right number (C) of tubes for there to be one tube for each flower. The children knew that there were two flowers in each vase and only one flower was to be placed in each tube (C = A). Piaget wanted to find out whether they would understand the need to take twice as many tubes as vases (C = 2B).

The children reacted in three different ways to Piaget's task. Some of them did not *anticipate* that there would be two flowers in each vase and did not realize either that they needed to take out two tubes for each vase on the table in order to have one tube for each flower, even after they had placed the flowers into the vases and had found for themselves that there were two flowers per vase. These children did not use the vases to estimate how many tubes they needed to take out of the box. These tended to be the children who in the earlier task had not realized that there were as many blue as pink flowers. They did not make the transitive inference in the one-to-one correspondence situation and they were not able to understand the one-to-two correspondence between vases and flowers.

The second type of reaction took the form of children not anticipating the one-to-two correspondence between the total number of flowers and vases but managing at any rate to grasp this correspondence as they carried out the action of putting the flowers into the vases. These children started by placing the flowers into the vases one by one but then changed to putting them in two at a time. In the second part of the task these children started by setting the tubes in one-to-one correspondence with the vases, but then realized the need for two tubes to each vase. However, when a similar problem, which involved one-to-three correspondence, was presented immediately afterwards, they did not anticipate the relationships between the sets.

The third type of reaction according to Piaget is to anticipate the relationships in the one-to-many correspondence. An example of a reaction of this third type is presented below (adapted from Piaget, 1965, p. 218):

GROS [*5 years, 10 months, who had succeeded in making the inference that the number of blue and pink flowers was the same, was then asked how many flowers would be in each vase if they were now all put back into the vase*]:   One blue and one pink.
INTERVIEWER: How many is that?
G: Two.
I: And if I added these [*a new set of flowers placed in one-to-one*

correspondence with the vases] how many would there be in each vase?

G: Three.

I: Why?

G: I'd put one, one, one.

I: And now suppose we wanted to put them in these tubes that will only hold one flower?

G: *took three sets of tubes in correspondence with the set of vases.*

On the basis of this third type of reaction Piaget suggests that children as young as 5 to 6 years can already understand some aspects of multiplicative relations. Of course the children were not asked to calculate totals in these problems; they simply had to apply transitive reasoning to the different one-to-many correspondence situations. Nevertheless Piaget emphatically claimed that these relationships are multiplicative rather than additive because the value of each new set of flowers, in this example, was being considered in relation to the basic set of vases (1 × 2; 1 × 3 etc.). His conclusion seems well founded to us.

Piaget sought the origin of the idea of multiplication in the one-to-many correspondence scheme but the work of his that we have just described is about only the very beginnings of the concept of one-to-many correspondence. There is more to be understood about this form of correspondence, and we turn now to the possibility that children learn more about it as they grow older. In this section we will deal with their ability to order different one-to-many correspondence ratios and also to equate sets which involve different ratios, and in the following sections we will look at children's ability to calculate absolute values through one-to-many correspondence.

In order to reason about one-to-many correspondence the child must be able to understand the relation between different one-to-many ratios and particularly about their ordering. With two blue flowers and three pink flowers for each vase, there will be more pink than blue flowers. When there are two pink flowers for each of eight vases and two blue flowers for every nine vases, there will be more blue flowers than pink flowers. The product in a multiplication situation of the one-to-many correspondence type depends both on the number of elements in the basic set and on the ratio (given the same basic set).

Work on this form of knowledge is scarce, but some evidence is now available. Ekaterina Kornilaki (in preparation) presented some multiplicative problems to young children in reception classes (5/6 years) in London. The children were required to order sets that had different ratios with respect to a reference set. They were asked to compare, for example, the total number of bags inside two equal sets of five toy lorries; they knew that the lorries in one set contained two bags each and that those in the other set contained three bags each. She found that the majority of the children were successful in these tasks, even though they could not see the sets they were ordering.

Kornilaki's studies about ordering lead us to the second issue. If sets ordered on the basis of multiplication are different, would young children know how to make them equal by correspondence procedures? In other words, would they realize that the same ratio must be applied for equality to be obtained? Frydman and Bryant (1988) have provided an initial answer to this question in a study where they asked 4/5-year-olds to distribute pretend-sweets equally to two dolls. These children had no difficulty in building equivalent sets if the sweets were all in units of one and they did do so by one-to-one correspondence (one for A, one for B and so on). However, when they were told that one doll liked all her sweets in two units at a time (double units) while the other liked hers in ones (single units), as illustrated in figure 7.4, but that both should be given the same total number of sweets, these young children made many mistakes.

In order to make the two sets equal, the children needed each time to give two single units to one doll while giving one double unit to the other. But Frydman and Bryant found that most of the 4-year-old children, and even some 5-year-olds, distributed units to the two dolls on a one unit for A, one for B basis irrespective of the sweets' values in terms of units. The result, of course, was that they ended up giving one doll twice as many units as the other. Only 4 per cent of the 4-year-olds and 70 per cent of the 5-year-olds succeeded in this task.

There are two ways of thinking about these failures. One is that they demonstrate a striking weakness in children's understanding of one-to-many relations. The other is that the children may have got on the wrong track because they did not properly understand that the double units were the equivalent of two single sweets.

In a following experiment Frydman and Bryant looked at the second of these two possibilities by making children more aware of the fact that the double units are equal in amount to two of the single units. They gave a group of 4-year-old children three tasks – a pre-test, an experimental task, and a post-test. The pre- and post-tests

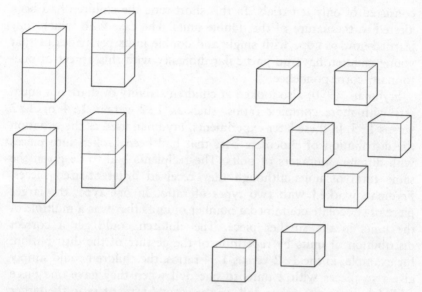

Figure 7.4 Sharing 'singles' and 'doubles' to two recipients: the material used in Frydman and Bryant's task

were exactly the same as the singles/doubles sharing task which we have described already and which proved so difficult for this age group. The intervening experimental task took the same form except that colour cues were introduced. The double-sweets were presented in two colours: each double-sweet contained one blue and one yellow sweet, while the singles came in yellow or blue. The aim of introducing these colours was to emphasize the fact that the doubles consisted of exactly two sweets: if the children's original difficulties with the task were due to their not appreciating that the double units consisted of two sweets, then the blue/yellow arrangement ought to help them.

This new arrangement had a clear effect. The children managed very poorly in the pre-test in which there were no colour cues, but with the colour cues most of them succeeded in giving two units to the doll receiving single units whenever they gave just one unit to the doll receiving doubles. This was a striking change, but the most important result in this study came in the post-test, in which these colour cues were no longer available (all the sweets were the same colour). The children who had been put through the experimental task with the colour cues, now for the most part did extremely well in the post-test as well, even though the experimental task had consisted of only ten trials. In this short time the children had been alerted to the nature of the double units. The ease with which they learned how to cope with single and double units persuades us that young children have no particular difficulty with this aspect of one-to-many correspondence.

Frydman (1990) also looked at children's ability to share out equal sets with more complex ratios, such as $1:2$ versus $1:4$ or $1:2$ versus $1:3$. In these later experiments, Frydman used as the situation the distribution of chocolate bars that had been broken into pieces with different numbers of units. The recipients had to be given the same total of units although they received different-sized pieces. Frydman worked with two types of ratio. In one type, the larger piece of chocolate contained a number of units that was a multiple of the units in the smaller piece. The children could get a correct distribution of units by repetition of the gesture of the distribution: for example, in the $1:2$ versus $1:4$ ratios, the children could simply give two pieces with 2 units to one doll when they gave one piece with 4 units to the other doll. In the second type of ratio the larger piece was not a multiple of the smaller one in terms of the units it contained. Thus no simple repetition of the gesture of distribution was possible: for example, in the situation of the $1:2$ versus $1:3$ ratio, if the children gave two doubles to one doll when they gave a triple to the other doll, the total number of units would differ. In this latter case, as Frydman pointed out, the children had to find a common multiple, giving three doubles to one doll when they gave two triples to the other doll. Following Piaget, Kaufmann and Bourquin (1977), Frydman expected that the second type of problem would be significantly more difficult than the first. The reason for this difference is that the first type can be solved with additive reasoning: two 2-unit pieces added together form one 4-unit piece. If the children realize this, they can adjust their actions of distribution by putting out two 2-unit pieces for each 4-unit piece and thereby obtain the same totals. They do not need to anticipate other relations involving the different units: the 4-unit can be composed of two 2-units by addition.

In contrast, the solution to the ratios where a common multiple must be found is not easily solved by additive reasoning: there is not a simple conversion of one unit into the other. Thus the composition of equal totals must be obtained by anticipation. It does not seem likely that young children can easily work out that if they add up the three doubles given to one doll that makes six and if they add up two triples given to the doll that also makes six. This calculation requires a double counting of pieces and units that may tax young children's counting skills considerably. Alternatively, they could realize that 3×2 and 2×3 is all the same, if they understand the idea of commutativity of multiplication, and anticipate the solution right from the start, but that also seems likely to be hard for young children.

Frydman's results confirmed these expectations: 86 per cent of the responses given by 5-year-olds and 97 per cent of those given by 6-year-olds were correct when the problems could be solved on the basis of additive reasoning. In contrast, only 22 per cent of the 5-year-olds' responses and 47 per cent of the responses given by 6-year-olds were correct. It must not be forgotten that the 5- and 6-year-old children failed to create two equal amounts of chocolate by using double and triple pieces in spite of the fact that they could assemble the doubles and triples into equal-sized pieces of six in total, if they so wished, before the distribution, and were encouraged to do so (but were not allowed to break up the pieces into units). In principle, they could also have got the right answer by keeping a running count of how many pieces each doll had. Thus their lack of success is rather significant. The easier problems demonstrate the continuity between additive and multiplicative reasoning; the more difficult ones highlight the need to distinguish between additive and multiplicative reasoning.

In summary, it seems that children as young as 5 years (but even a good percentage of 4-year-olds, if they receive support) can succeed in solving a variety of problems which involve one-to-many correspondence: they can understand transitive inferences based on one-to-many correspondences (that is, if $A = 2B$ and $C = A$, then $C = 2B$), they can order sets on the basis of their ratio with respect to a reference set, and they can develop procedures to obtain equal sets when the numbers are small and the ratios bear a simple relation to each other. When relations become more complex, even 6-year-old children have difficulty in coordinating relations across ratios.

We wish to stress that all of these studies concern the understanding of *relations* in the context of one-to-many correspondence problems, but we have not looked at children's ability to solve quantitative problems in this context. Peter Bryant (1974), on the basis of a rather different set of experiments, suggested that young children are much better at working with relations than at solving problems that involve considering absolute values. We will now examine the evidence on children's ability to solve multiplicative reasoning problems when they are asked to give the absolute value of one set.

Solving quantitative problems in one-to-one correspondence situations Our analysis of situations, systems of signs, and invariants leads us to the possibility that children might find it easier to deal with relations on the basis of one-to-many correspondence than with problems in which they have to calculate a value. In order to solve a quantitative multiplication problem, children need more than an understanding of relationships: they must also organize their counting activity in a new way. They need to be able to carry out replications and to know how to count the appropriate units in each of the sets.

Leslie Steffe (1994) investigated 8-year-old children's ability to carry out the double-counting required in replicating one-to-many correspondences. He asked them to solve problems in which objects were laid out in one-to-many correspondence but the children could see only some of them. As an example, there were six rows of three blocks but only one row was visible and five were hidden. The children were asked: 'We have six rows, and three blocks in each row; how many blocks would that be?' Steffe observed that the children who solved this sort of problem would, for example, point to each of the blocks and count the six corresponding rows: while tapping on the table at each block, the child would count 6, 12, 18. Steffe suggested that children develop a schema whereby each of the visible blocks can be used to represent the composite unit of six that takes into account the six rows. He also reports that not all 8-year-olds had developed this strategy of double-counting.

Steffe's work involved a series of case studies in which he interviewed the children on different occasions about problems, all of which took the same form as the one that we have just described. But there is also another type of one-to-many correspondence problem which is rather more complex, such as the following one: 'Mary has three different skirts and four different blouses; how many different outfits can she wear by changing around her skirts and blouses?'

Perla Nesher (1988) pointed out that this kind of problem is more complex for at least two reasons. First, the problem involves two basic sets – skirts and blouses – plus a third set of outfits. The outfits are identified by the combination of each element in one basic set (for example, the skirts) with each element of the other set (the blouses).

Second, the one-to-many correspondence is not explicitly indicated in the verbal formulation. It is up to the problem-solver to figure out that, for each skirt there are four possible changes of blouses – that is, four possible outfits. This sort of problem – often referred to as a *Cartesian product problem* – has consistently been found to be more difficult than other one-to-many correspondence problems (see, for example, Brown, 1981).

Because of this greater difficulty, we decided to investigate how children come to master this problem: would they use strategies that justify the classification of Cartesian product problems as one-to-many correspondence problems? Brown, who documented the difference in level of difficulty between these and other one-to-many correspondence problems, could not provide information on the children's problem-solving method because the problems were given in written form and the children simply had to tick the sum that would lead to the correct solution.

We observed 8- and 9-year-old children ($n = 32$) solving four multiplication problems in Oxford (Bryant et al., 1992), two of which were simple one-to-many correspondence and the other two Cartesian product problems. The children were presented with the problems and at the same time they were given appropriate materials that they could use to solve them. For example, in one of the Cartesian product problems, where the children had to figure out how many different outfits you can get by changing around 6 shorts and 4 t-shirts, they were given miniature shorts and t-shirts of different colours to try to work out the solution. With this procedure, we expected that the children would be able to show us what they were thinking about when they solved the problem. We were concerned that the children might simply do with the objects what was indicated in the problem – combine the shorts and trousers, put four yoghurt cups into 6 bags etc. – and count the elements. So, in order to ensure that the children could solve the problem by reasoning mathematically, and not simply by imitating the situation in the problem and counting, they were randomly distributed into two groups. One group was given all the material that they needed (in this example, 6 shorts and 4 t-shirts): all that they had to do was to think how to manipulate the materials and, for example, count the outfits as they moved the shorts and t-shirts into different combinations. In the second group, the children only had a subset of the materials – in this example, 2 shorts and 4 t-shirts. They could use the subset to create a model for thinking – that is, they could figure out with the subset that each pair of shorts could be put into 1-to-4 correspondence with the t-shirts – but they could not count each outfit for all the 6 pairs of shorts.

We expected that: (1) simple one-to-many correspondence problems would be easier for 8- and 9-year-olds irrespective of whether they had all the materials they needed to create the situation or just a sample of materials; (2) children who had all the materials to recreate the situation would be, as a group, more successful in solving the problems than those who only had a sample and needed to complete their reasoning without the support of objects; and (3) that the children would profit significantly more from the support of the whole set of materials when solving more difficult problems.

The results of this study are summarized in figure 7.5. Most 8- and 9-year-olds were able to solve the simple one-to-many correspondence problems when they had the complete set of materials to support them, but the 8-year-olds got less than half of the answers correct when they only had a sample of materials and needed to work out the solution through reasoning. In the Cartesian product problems, none of the 8-year-olds responded correctly without the support of all the materials needed to set up the solution; their rate of improvement with the materials was still negligible. These more complex problems were still rather difficult even for 9-year-olds, who were right about 55 per cent of the time when they had all the materials needed to represent the situation. The differences between the conditions (with all materials/with only a sample of the materials), between age levels (8 versus 9 years), and between types of problems are statistically significant.

The ways in which the children manipulated the materials supported the idea that the Cartesian product problems are, in effect, one-to-many correspondence problems where the children need to identify the correspondences implicit in the description of the situation. Three examples are given below.

The first is of Sarah's solution, which was typical of the successful children. She was included in the group who had the full set of materials needed to represent the situation.

INTERVIEWER: Now this girl had 6 pairs of shorts of different colours, you see? Blue, green, brown, yellow, black and red. She also had t-shirts in different colours, blue, green, black and white. By changing around which t-shirts she put on with the different shorts, she could have different outfits, couldn't she? For example, one day she could

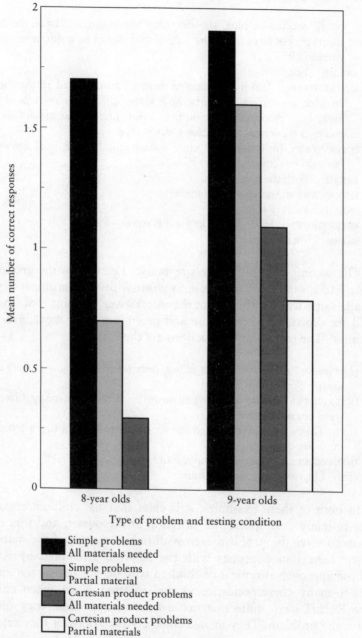

Figure 7.5 Children's success with one-to-many correspondence and Cartesian product problems

SOURCE: Bryant et al. (1992)

be all dressed in blue, the next day she could still have the blue shorts on but have the white t-shirt, that would be a different outfit, wouldn't it?

SARAH: Yes.

INTERVIEWER: And if she changed them all around, had all the shorts on with the different t-shirts, how many different ways would she look, how many different outfits? *Sarah first moves all the shorts and puts them next to the blue t-shirt*:   Six.

INTERVIEWER [mistaking the child's comment for the final answer]:   How do you know . . .?

SARAH: With the blue t-shirt.

INTERVIEWER: And with all of them?

SARAH: Twenty-four.

INTERVIEWER: How do you know it is twenty-four?

SARAH: Six times four.

The second example is Lee's response. Lee was in the group who only had a sample of materials to work with. The problem is posed in the same way as above, but the interviewer explains that 'this boy had six shorts, these two, blue and green, and four more, and these t-shirts'. The remaining instructions are the same.

[*Lee doesn't move the objects about, only takes one of the t-shirts and says*]:   Six.

INTERVIEWER [*unsure of what Lee meant*]:   Is that how many different ways he could look?

LEE: Thirty. He could change the six shorts today. Six times four for the other days.

INTERVIEWER: What is six times four?

LEE: Oh, not thirty, twenty-four.

In both of these examples, it is clear that the children create the one-to-many correspondence situation at the outset, and this allows them to solve the problem even with only a sample of the materials. Their behaviour contrasts with the solution attempted by Rachel, whose approach is typical of children who do not realize the implicit one-to-many correspondence in the situation. Even when children like Rachel were quite systematic in their approach, they did not solve the problem. They missed some combinations or they repeated others.

Rachel made at first 6 pairs by aligning all the shorts and changing two of the t-shirts around: Six.

INTERVIEWER: You've changed some of the t-shirts but you haven't yet had all the shorts on with all the t-shirts, have you?

Rachel aligns the t-shirts and makes four pairs, leaving two shorts without a t-shirt: Four. [Pause]: No. [*She aligns the shorts again, makes four pairs, then moves two t-shirts to make pairs with the other shorts*]: Six. [*She then moves the four t-shirts so as to make new pairs and says*]: Ten.

INTERVIEWER: How do you know she can get ten different looking outfits?

RACHEL: Because she's got ten bits of clothes and everyday she could change.

Rachel's lack of success is rather instructive. If we had obtained her only answer (ten), without observing her attempts to solve the problem, we could have mistakenly interpreted it as simply carrying out the wrong operation. However, her behaviour indicates that she did not set out to add but to find the different outfits through recombinations of the elements. Because she did not organize her attempts in a one-to-many correspondence way, the pairings that she carried out seemed limited by the number of elements present. Her addition (she's got ten bits of clothes) seems to have been carried out after the fact, to justify the answer she had reached.

In short, it seems that the successful children recognize the need to establish a one-to-many correspondence between one pair of shorts, for example, and all the t-shirts, and then they figure out that, for 6 shorts, there should be 6×4 possible outfits.

Conclusions The data on children's ability to solve quantitative problems which involve one-to-many correspondence situations clearly indicate that solving problems with absolute numbers is much harder than reasoning about relations. Although children as young as 4 or 5 years of age can reason about relations which involve one-to-many correspondences, it seems that even the simplest problems are not completely mastered by age 8. Steffe's case studies showed that 8 year old children can carry out mental replications of one-to-many correspondence situations through double-counting of units of different values; his subjects were able to solve problems while seeing only one row of bricks which they used to represent all the six rows in the problem. Similarly, in our work with Luisa Morgado (Bryant et al., 1992) we observed that a substantial portion of 8-year-olds even managed to solve the simple one-to-many correspondence problems without the complete set of materials to reconstruct the problem. However, only by the age of about 9 years do children recognize the implicit one-to-many correspondences in the more complex, Cartesian product problems. Those children who represent the one-to-many correspondence in these complex problems are likely to succeed; those who do not, usually do not solve the problem.

This pattern of results suggests some new ideas about teaching children multiplication. First, the fact that young children have a good understanding of relations involved in multiplication indicates that they can be brought to talk about these relations and explore them in the classroom long before they are able to solve quantitative problems. It seems likely to us that the experience of exploring relations, even without quantification, will increase children's awareness of one-to-many correspondence.

Second, we now know that children can work with manipulative materials under different conditions in the classroom: not just with complete sets of materials, that will allow them to represent the multiplication fully, but also with a sample of materials, so that they are required to expand their mathematical reasoning beyond what they can represent with the materials. A partial representation allows them to form a model for thinking, but requires that the final solution is obtained through reasoning and not just through manipulation.

Finally, when children are able to solve simple one-to-many correspondence problems, it may be worthwhile to give them more complex problems, where the correspondence is not explicitly stated. The progress required of children when they solve Cartesian product problems can be seen as a new level of analysis using the schema of one-to-many correspondence: they need to figure out that this is a way of approaching the problem by analysing the situation itself. This need to discover a relation from the meaning of the situation (instead of being told what the relation is) can lead the children to expand their understanding of one-to-many correspondence.

2.2 Co-variation of variables and the understanding of functions

Piaget's work on multiplicative reasoning can be divided roughly into two sets of research. In one set there is his early work on one-to-many correspondence which we have described already and which shows considerable acumen on the part of quite young children. The other set, which is much better known, consists of a series of studies on the understanding of the co-variation of variables.

Piaget, whose central interest was in the development of logical and scientific reasoning, looked at young people's understanding of co-variation in the context of scientific concepts. For example, he investigated children's understanding of the proportional relations in the projection of shadows, in the understanding of equilibrium in a T-shaped balance scale and in the concept of probability. These are difficult concepts and, in his research on them, he consistently reported that young people's understanding of proportional relations between variables is a relatively late achievement.

At the time that Piaget carried out this pioneering work, he did not expect that the content of a problem would have an effect on how children reason. However, it is certainly possible that children's difficulties with proportions in these problems stems from the complexity of the content of the problem rather than from the mathematical relations. The test is to give proportional problems in more familiar and thus easier contexts.

Several researchers, among them Karplus et al. (1983), Noelting (1980a; 1980b), and Hart (1984) presented students with proportional problems which had more familiar contents. In this new wave of investigations, the problems did not involve complex scientific concepts but nevertheless they tended not to involve relations which children are likely to reflect about in everyday life or view as requiring mathematical reasoning for the solution.

Karplus and his colleagues, for example, devised a task known as the Mr Tall and Mr Short problem. Mr Tall and Mr Short were two stick figures drawn on paper. Mr Tall was described as being 6 buttons in height whereas Mr Short measured 4 buttons. When Mr Short was measured in paper clips, his height was 6 paper clips. The students were asked to calculate Mr Tall's size in paper clips. The children knew about different ways of measuring, and therefore this situation can be viewed as being more familiar to them than those used by Piaget. Nevertheless, even 12- and 14-year-olds performed very poorly in this task, and this suggests that understanding the co-variation of variables is at least as difficult as Piaget himself suggested. However, it is unlikely that children often engage in conversion of measurements. In everyday life we rely on standard measures, and usually have no need to carry out conversions because the same measures are used all around us. Thus the familiarity of measurement, of paper clips, and of buttons does not make the problem into one of the sort that is itself familiar to children.

Noelting's task is known as the 'orange juice problem'. He gave children descriptions of various mixtures of orange juice in terms of amounts of orange concentrate and water, and asked them to judge whether two different total quantities of mixture would taste the same: for example, would 3 cups of concentrate and 2 cups of water taste the same as 4 cups of concentrate and 3 cups of water? Here, too, the content of the problem was certainly quite familiar. Most 6- to 7-year-old children have a certain understanding that the more water, the less of an orangey taste, and were able to demonstrate this understanding in the easiest comparisons. For example, 78 per cent of the 6-year-olds and 86 per cent of the 8-year-olds were able to indicate which of the two mixtures would taste more orangey in items exemplified by the following comparison: 3 cups of concentrate and 1 cup of water versus 2 cups of concentrate and 1 cup of water. However, even the 10- and 12-year-old pupils had problems with the more difficult items. For example, in items exemplified by the comparison of 3 cups of concentrate and 2 cups of water versus 4 cups of concentrate and 3 cups of water, less than 25 per cent of the 10-year-olds and 67 per cent of the 12-year-olds succeeded. These results too suggest a difficulty on the part of young children with the use of proportions in co-variation. But it seems unlikely that this is a situation which young children would ever think of as mathematical: when making orange juice, they are probably happy to add water slowly and taste the juice until the flavour is just right, rather than to think of mathematical proportions. Although the situation is certainly familiar, it is not a familiar mathematical situation.

Hart (1988) worked with enlargement problems: if you want to enlarge a rectangle that measures 6 by 9 centimetres and make the base now equal to 15 centimetres, what should be the height of the rectangle so that it looks the same shape, just larger? This was also an extremely difficult problem for young children. In her series of enlargement problems, the level of success was 28 per cent and 42 per cent, respectively, for the 13- and 15-year-olds in the easiest problems and 8 per cent and 20 per cent in the hardest ones. Again, enlargement and shrinking problems may be familiar to children when they draw. However their thinking about such manoeuvres is probably completely non-mathematical: they might be happy with visual feedback and re-working the dimensions, rubbing out and trying it again, when enlarging or reducing the size of drawings.

In short, this second wave of research involved problems which are relatively familiar to children but with which they would be unlikely to use calculations in their everyday lives. Further work has indicated that when situations are part of everyday practices where numbers are significant and computation is usual, performance seems to be considerably better.

Kaput and Maxwell West (1994), for example, observed that price and speed problems, which in everyday life really are treated as problems that involve computation, are significantly easier than enlargement problems: the rate of success in price and speed problems among US sixth-graders was more than ten times the rate of success of the same children in enlargement problems. These results demonstrate something of great significance: *there are clear differences in performance by the same children across problems that involve different contents*. It is therefore important that we keep these differences in mind as we discuss the development of the understanding of functional relations between variables.

We will now consider several aspects of how children come to understand proportional relations between variables. We will first examine children's understanding of functional relations without quantification. Next, children's methods of solution to quantification problems will be analysed. The final section briefly considers the evidence on children's understanding of the intensive quantities or the functional value that connects two variables.

Understanding functional relations We saw earlier that children understand one-to-many relations and use this understanding to make inferences before they can solve quantitative problems about the same situations. Therefore, it would not be surprising to find that children have some understanding of co-variation before they can solve quantitative problems in the same sort of situation.

There are many situations in everyday life where children readily assume that two variables change together: the older you get, the bigger you get (a relation reported from conversations with young children by Singer (et al., forthcoming); the more sweets you buy, the more you pay; the more you run, the more you get tired. Bryant (1974), Muller (1978), and Van den Brink and Streefland (1978) have independently observed that young children make judgements about proportional relations in some contexts. Van den Brink and Streefland, for example, noted that, in spontaneous conversations about pictures, children use a natural framework of proportional size relations to evaluate the adequacy of pictures: they can, for example, argue that one element in a picture is proportionally too big if compared to another element.

Spinillo and Bryant (1991) provided more systematic evidence to support the idea that children can make judgements based on co-variation when looking at pictures. They asked children whose ages ranged from 5 to 8 years to look at a picture that represented a box with a particular proportion of white and blue bricks inside. The children were then shown two boxes, one which contained the same proportion of white-to-blue bricks and another which contained a different proportion. The picture was much smaller than the boxes, and the bricks were said to have been rearranged in the box after the picture was taken: whereas in the picture the white and blue stripes formed by the bricks were horizontal, they were vertical in the boxes or vice versa. These perceptual differences ensured that the children could not simply carry out a perceptual box-to-picture match.

The 7- and 8-year-old children seemed to realize that the more blue there was in the picture the more blue there should be in the box in proportion to the amount of white. Within certain limits they could use these proportional judgements and choose the correct box. The limits concerned the half-boundary. For example, if more than half of the bricks in the picture were blue, the children assumed that the box that corresponded to the picture had to have more blue than white bricks. They were systematically correct if one of the boxes either had half or less than half blue bricks because they could eliminate that box and choose the correct one. However, the children were much less successful if both boxes had more than half blue bricks. A simple ordering of relations was no longer possible and the children's rate of errors increased significantly.

The evidence provided by Spinillo and Bryant shows clearly that the children could solve this co-variation problem under certain conditions. However, it is not yet clear how the children's success in tasks like this, which do not involve quantification, should be interpreted: do they realize that there is a *proportional* relation between the variables or do they make a general assumption of co-variation? A host of functional relations could exist between two variables that vary together. Proportional (or linear) relations, where the functional value connecting the two variables does not change as the value of the variables changes, are a particular case. For this reason, we cannot necessarily consider the children's general assumption of co-variation as evidence for their understanding of proportional relations. Quantification might play a fundamental role in children's understanding of the precise nature of proportional relations from the start: not any co-variation but only a particular form of co-variation is a proportional relation.

In some cases where children assume that two things change together, they actually do bear a proportional relation. In other cases, they do not: it is not necessarily true that the older you get, the bigger you get throughout all stages in your life. It may be that, when children make these assumptions about co-variation, it is not adequate to describe their thinking as 'understanding proportional relations'. Mathematically, when you speak about a functional relation, you should also know what type of function. We will use as a criterion for the understanding of proportional relations between variables children's realization that there is a third value – a factor, an intensive quantity – relating the two variables and that, for any pair of numbers, this value must be the same. Understanding the functional operator as the invariant in the situation will be our focus of attention in this section.

Because we are concerned here only with linear relationships, the age–height connection offers an instructive contrasting case. It is clearly not true that the relation between age and height is such that knowing your age and multiplying it by a fixed functional value will help us discover how tall you are. Even if, on the average, you can get a good estimate of height as a function of age in childhood, children's growth is not homogenous: it speeds up and slows down, and it stops altogether later on. The relationship between age and height is not even roughly proportional after adolescence. This is not a detail: it is a central issue. In order to understand functional relations, children need to consider *how the variables actually relate.* The idea of function requires more precision than a gross assumption of co-variation. The mathematics carried out is a way of modelling – that is, imitating with symbols in order to make predictions – the relations between the variables. The choice of a proportional model where the relations are not proportional is as much a mistake as it is to add when the situation calls for multiplication.

Solving quantitative problems of proportional relations between variables   It is quite difficult to determine when and in the context of which problems children first start to understand proportional relations between variables. This difficulty relates to the fact that children can use their understanding of one-to-many correspondence situations in order to solve problems which involve the relations between variables without necessarily becoming aware of the func-

Table 7.1 The onion soup problem

Onion soup recipe for 8 persons
  8 onions
  2 pints of water
  4 chicken soup cubes
  2 dessert spoons butter
  ½ pint cream

I am cooking for 4 people.
  (i) How much water do I need?
  (ii) How many chicken soup cubes do I need?

I am cooking for 6 people.
  (iii) How much water do I need?
  (iv) How many chicken soup cubes do I need?
  (v) How much cream do I need?

---

tional relation between the variables. One-to-many correspondence situations obviously offer a good starting point for children because the two classes of situations are related. If you treat problems about proportional relations between variables in the same way as one-to-many correspondence situations and use replicating (or its inverse) to find the solution, you will come up with the correct answer in many situations – but you might get stuck in others.

Many researchers have shown that children are at first successful with problems that involve the relation between two variables by using replication (or its inverse). Hart (1984), for example, asked young people in the age range of 13 to 15 years to solve her onion soup problem (see table 7.1), where a recipe for 8 persons is given and the question is how much of the different ingredients to use when making the recipe for 4 and then 6 persons.

A recipe can be thought of in different ways. It can be thought of as involving fixed ratios among the ingredients – for example, there should be ½ pint of water for each chicken soup cube – but it can also be thought about in functional terms, where the amount of each ingredient is a function of the number of persons. When the question put to the students is how to adapt the recipe for different numbers of persons, they need to think of amount per person.

Hart interviewed the young people about how they solved this question and observed that the great majority of the answers to questions (i) and (ii) were obtained by halving – that is, by the inverse of replicating. The young people between 13 and 15 years were quite successful in answering these questions: over 90 per cent of the answers were correct in each of these three age levels.

Questions (iii) and (iv) were most often also solved by replicating. The subjects had already found the amounts needed for 4 people; the amounts needed for 6 people were obtained by finding half of what one needs for 4 persons and then adding the two intermediary results. Because 6 persons is 4 + 2 persons, the amount of water and chicken soup cubes needed are what you need for 4 plus what you need for 2 people. The method of solution used here is again replicating and its inverse. The rate of success dropped for the 6 person questions in contrast to the 4 person questions but not dramatically: the percentage of correct responses for each of the age groups in these two questions varied between 75 and 88 per cent.

Success rates dropped significantly, however, when the youngsters tried to find out the amount of cream (question v) using the same method: $\frac{1}{2}$ of $\frac{1}{2}$ is $\frac{1}{4}$ – that means, for 4 people, use $\frac{1}{4}$ pint cream; for 6 people, apparently the youngsters wanted to find a fraction that is halfway between $\frac{1}{2}$ and $\frac{1}{4}$ but most were not successful in doing so. Correct responses were now about 20–24 per cent. The replication reasoning is correct but the arithmetic required to solve the problem is not simple, and the pupils end up by not finding the correct answer.

The term for solutions obtained by replication (or its inverse) is *scalar solutions*, because they use the scalar factor as the invariant. Scalar solutions contrast with *functional solutions*, where the functional factor is the invariant used in calculation. Although the two types of solution lead to the same answer, they appear to reflect different ways of thinking about the problem. The scalar solution can stem directly from one-to-many correspondence problems whereas the functional solution relies on establishing a multiplicative connection between the variables. Hart does not report the results of this study in terms of numbers of children, but in a larger survey of over 2,000 children, whose written answers she analysed, she reported that possibly only about 1 per cent used the functional solution.

Some aspects of Hart's study can be clearly interpreted but others not. It is clear that young people realized the appropriateness of solving proportional problems by using the scalar factor: they succeeded with this method as long as they could carry out the arithmetic involved. But it is not clear why they did not use the functional solution. In Hart's onion soup problem, the arithmetic required to find the functional factor for the amount of cream would have been very awkward: the pupils would need to know how to divide ½ by 8 to figure out the amount of cream per person and then multiply the result by 6 – and perhaps calculating with fractions is what they did not know. Perhaps it was the difficulty of the arithmetic that blocked their functional reasoning.

However, some studies have controlled for the difficulty of the arithmetic and found this same preference for scalar over functional solutions. Nunes, Schliemann and Carraher (1993), for example, gave a series of proportions problems to secondary school students from a fishing town in northeastern Brazil, and systematically varied the difficulty of the arithmetic needed for implementing a functional or a scalar solution. Half of the problems would be solved using simpler arithmetic through a scalar approach and the other half through a functional approach (the study is only partially described here; for more detail, see Nunes, Schliemann and Carraher, 1993). The problems were about the relationship between the weight of unprocessed and processed seafood. For example, one problem stated that 'there is a kind of shrimp that yields 3 kilos of shelled and cooked shrimp for each 18 kilos of shrimp that you catch; if a customer wanted 2 kilos of cooked and shelled shrimp, how much would the fisherman have to catch?' In this problem, the arithmetic needed to implement the scalar solution is awkward but the arithmetic for the functional solution is simple. The scalar solution requires applying inverse replications in order to bring the value of processed food from 3 to 2 kilos. In contrast, the functional solution is easy: 18 kilos of unprocessed shrimp yield 3 kilos of processed shrimp – that is, the functional factor is 6. Nunes, Schliemann and Carraher report that the performance of secondary school students dropped drastically in problems where the scalar solution involved more difficult arithmetic than functional solutions (such as the problem above) in comparison to those where the scalar solution was easily implemented. Success rates were 70 per cent when the scalar solution was easy and about 30 per cent when the functional solution was easy to implement but the scalar one was difficult. Thus, when the arithmetic is controlled for, students do better when they can use a scalar instead of a functional solution.

This preference for scalar solutions has been reported by several different authors in the literature in a variety of tasks: Karplus et al.,

(1983), Kaput and Maxwell West (1994), Lybeck (1985), and Vergnaud (1988). Kaput and Maxwell West (1994) also report that, if a problem about relations between variables is presented as a one-to-many correspondence problem, it is more easily solved than if the correspondence has to be discovered by the pupils.

Taken together, these results lead us to two conclusions. First, it is in principle possible (and necessary, as we will see later) to distinguish between situations that involve one-to-many correspondence and those that involve a proportional relation between variables. However, this distinction does not loom large in the reasoning of youngsters of 10/11 years of age. Their strategy for solving both kinds of problem seems to be the same. Our second conclusion is that presenting the problem as a one-to-many correspondence situation helps children to find a solution because it avoids the need for them to identify the functional factor.

However all these studies leave a basic question unanswered. Why do youngsters so consistently fail to adopt functional solutions? There are two possible reasons for this failure. One is that they don't understand the *mathematical ideas* of the logic of functional relationships, and in fact this is what was suggested by Piaget and his colleagues, as we saw earlier. The other is that they don't understand enough about the *content of the problem* – that is, they don't understand the content well enough to realize that there is a constant relation between the two variables. It seems unreasonable to expect the concept of function to develop in contexts about which the children do not know very much. Without being assured that the children know about the relationships in the situation, we do not know how to analyse their mathematics. Therefore we need to consider situations that young people deal with mathematically in everyday life in order to study the development of the concept of functional relations.

In the next section, we will describe a study in which children's understanding of functions was analysed in a context where their everyday mathematical practice was also known. This study allows us to weigh the significance of knowledge about the content of a problem and of mathematics instruction for children's performance in functional problems.

Proportional situations understood in practice The concept of function involves mathematical ideas but also ideas about the situation itself – the facts, so to speak, about the relationship between the variables. But there is little evidence on children's problem-solving strategies in co-variation problems where the relations between variables are familiar and the situation is conceived of as involving calculation. It seems a reasonable assumption that the amount–price relation is a context conceived of as involving calculation and well understood in everyday life. We have noted earlier that pupils do perform better in amount–price problems. But they might have different degrees of involvement in situations where these relations are central to their participation in an everyday activity. For example, children who sell things in the streets as peddlers may have a greater degree of involvement with the mathematics of amount–price relations than those who do not. This might have repercussions for how vendors and non-vendors solve mathematical problems about the amount–price relation.

This possibility was investigated by Geoffrey Saxe (1991) in a study in which he compared Brazilian children who were street vendors with North American non-vendors all of whom were schoolchildren. Saxe gave his subjects two sets of problems (described in detail below) involving proportional profit from selling candy; one set could be solved through one-to-many correspondence reasoning and the second one could not.

The street vendors ($n = 23$) were children from poor families in the northeast of Brazil, who were participating in informal economic activities in order to boost the family's income. They had had little or no schooling: none had attended school beyond second grade. Thus they had only been taught elementary arithmetic, and they had left school before proportional problems would have been part of their curriculum. This sample was not a selective one in terms of intellectual development: dropping out of school or not attending school altogether is not uncommon within this social group in Brazil, where drop-out rates are about 30 per cent after the first year of schooling (Cunha, 1979). The schools attended by poor children have little in terms of material resources and the teachers themselves have rarely been educated beyond secondary school: primary school teachers are prepared in the last three years of a specialized route at secondary school level. Thus whatever the vendors know about the proportional nature of relations between amount and price must be intrinsically connected to their involvement in the everyday activity as candy-sellers.

The schooled, non-street vendors ($n = 17$) were pupils from a highly regarded private laboratory school attached to a university in the United States; they were attending the equivalent of grades 5 or 6. The maths curriculum for the US children was described by Saxe as emphasizing a guided discovery approach to mathematics education, where teachers value mathematics and try to integrate it into various parts of the curriculum. The teaching about proportions offered to these youngsters was not specifically described.

The study allowed at least a rough comparison of the relative impact of two different aspects of children's experience for their understanding of proportionality: the non-vendors, schooled children had learned the relevant arithmetic and mathematical concepts whereas the vendors who were non-schooled children had to consider the relationships between the variables that make sense in practice.

We should like to make the comment that strict comparisons between the two groups in Saxe's study are rather difficult because of differences in the pattern of the children's ages. The actual means of the two groups did not differ much; the mean age of the street vendors was 10.8 years and of the school children 11.1 years. However, the variation in age in the US non-vendor, school children group was rather small (standard deviation = 0.5) whereas it was considerable in the case of the street sellers standard deviation = 1) and this group included subjects from 5 to 15 years. In his detailed analyses of the vendors' performance, Saxe found a significant association between age and success in these problems. Therefore, a poorer performance by the vendors as a group might be expected and we will try to consider age as far as the results reported by Saxe allow us to.

The children were asked to solve a series of problems that related to the activity of candy-selling. The street vendors were familiar with this activity; the US children received extra instructions on how some children in Brazil sell candy in the streets and were put through a trial procedure to get them involved in the types of question that they would have to answer subsequently: for example, they were shown some Brazilian notes, told their value and asked to recognize them later, and also practised counting amounts of money in the Brazilian notes they had seen before.

The candy-selling problems were of two types:

1   Best-profit problems, in which the *one-to-many correspondences were explicitly stated* and the children were asked to judge which of two sales led to a better profit (for example, 3 pieces of candy for $500 or 7 pieces for $1,000).

2   Inflation problems, where *the retail price of a box of candy was to be treated as a function of the wholesale price* in the context of an inflationary economy (for example, during Christmas last year the candy-sellers were buying this box for $3,000 and selling the candy for $6,000; now they have to pay $9,000 for the box; what should they try to sell all the candy for?). The use of one-to-many correspondence strategies in this case was not simple because the children were not told how many units there were inside the box.

According to our analysis of multiplicative reasoning, the first type of problem should be easier than the second because the correspondences are explicitly stated. The second problem type is expected to be harder because the youngsters themselves must come up with the relationship that connects the variables.

Saxe's results clearly support these predictions: approximately 80 per cent of the children in each of the groups solved the best-profit problems whereas the rates of success for the inflation problems were much more modest.

Saxe also described in detail some of the strategies that the street vendors used to solve these problems. The vendors typically turned to oral arithmetic for both types of problem. The non-vendor, schooled children, in contrast, used written computation algorithms. Here is an example of the procedure adopted by the vendors to solve the correspondence problems:

In comparing 3 lollies for $500 with 7 for $1,000, a 12 year old seller who had attended school up to grade 2 explained that the first sale would be better: 3 lollies for $500 meant selling 6 lollies for $1,000 and, in the second sale, he would be losing one lolly in each sale.

The vendors either equated the amount of money (as in the example above) and verified how many units would be sold for the same amount or made the number of units constant and calculated the income. It is easy to recognize these solutions as being obtained through replicating – i.e. 3 for $500 means 6 for $1,000.

Although the US children typically worked with paper and pencil, their reasoning seems to have involved the same concepts. They used written algorithms to calculate how much money would be spent if equal numbers of units were sold. Saxe offers two examples of this kind of solution for the problem which we have just presented. One child, for example, used the scalar factor and compared the income if 21 units were sold at each of the two price-rates; 21 units is obtained by using a scalar solution whereby 3 for £500 is multiplied by seven, whereas 7 for $1,000 is multiplied by 3. This is a rather sophisticated solution based on finding a common multiple. A second child calculated the price for 1 unit when 3 were being sold for $500 and then calculated the income that would be obtained if 7 lollies were sold at this same rate. In spite of the difference in the arithmetic procedures, the similarity of reasoning is quite clear. By replicating the sales (or its inverse) the students made the number of units (or amount of money) constant across sales and then carried out a direct comparison.

Saxe reported no examples in either group of a functional solution, obtained by calculating and then comparing the price-per-unit for each of the sales. This striking preference for the scalar solution cannot, in the case of the US children, be explained by a particular difficulty with the arithmetic involved in the functional solution: at least some of these schooled youngsters accurately carried out the long divisions required to find out the price of 1 unit when 3 were sold for $500, and this is much the same arithmetic as that involved in computing the price-per-unit when 7 were sold for $1,000.

In short, both groups of children used the reasoning typically developed in one-to-many correspondence situations to solve the best-profit problems. It must be stressed that this reasoning is adequate and both groups were equally successful in the best-profit problems.

In complete contrast, the inflation problem led to large differences between the two groups. This problem was presented in a manner that did not encourage replication solutions: the number of units in the boxes was not given and the youngsters had to calculate the retail price for a box as a function of the wholesale price without knowing how many items were inside the box. A well-known, additive error was observed in this problem: this consists of keeping the difference between the wholesale and the retail prices constant. Someone making this error would conclude that, if a box cost $3,000 at Christmas time and was then sold for $6,000, then later when the wholesale price was $9,000 the retail price would be $12,000.

Saxe found that more than half of the non-vendor, schooled children produced this kind of additive answer to the problem, while fewer than 10 per cent of the vendors did so – a highly significant difference. The non-vendors seem to have reasoned that the difference between wholesale and retail – that is, the profit – should be the same at any time. Of course this reasoning does not take into account the facts of an inflationary economy. At Christmas time, with the profit obtained, the youngsters would be able to buy a new box of candy to sell the next day and still take some money home. With the same profit when the wholesale price is $9,000, the purchase of another box to sell the next day would not be possible.

The vendors had different ideas about how the wholesale and the retail price should be related. In spite of the meagre instruction that they had been given in mathematics, they realized that the additive solution was not the right one and also that a proportional solution would not work either: they wouldn't sell as successfully if the prices shot up too much. Thus their knowledge of the facts of an inflationary economy led them to a solution which Saxe calls 'partial adjustment': the new value of profit must be larger than the old value but not necessarily as high as a proportional adjustment. Approximately 60 per cent of the vendors used this partial adjustment solution for inflation whereas only about 20 per cent of the non-vendors did so. If we consider together the proportional and the partial adjustments and look only at the performance of vendors in the age range 8 to 15 years (that is, selecting the group more comparable in age to the non-vendors), the difference is even more striking: whereas more than 80 per cent of the vendors produced either proportional or partial adjustment solutions, only about 30 per cent of the non-vendors did so (values are approximate because Saxe presented his results in graphical rather than numerical form).

We believe that Saxe's results indicate that the understanding of functions cannot be viewed simply as a mathematical issue. Even the simplest of functions, the linear one, should be viewed as *a model for situations*. If the child's assumptions about the situation are that the relations should not be proportional, then the proportional solution is inadequate. The non-schooled vendors, whose knowledge of school mathematics did not go beyond second grade, had a more sophisticated idea of the kind of relation to consider when dealing with inflation and offered more sensible solutions to the problem than the non-vendor, schooled subjects did. In other words, in order to use a good mathematical model for a situation, the facts about the situation need to be considered.

These results have important implications for instruction. The problems that are used at school in mathematics exercise books for teaching children about proportions are often more an excuse to use the arithmetic than a content for the youngsters to think about. Saxe's results indicate that it is fundamentally important that the youngsters should engage with the content of the problem. If they do not consider the content deeply enough, they will not treat the proportional calculations that they are given in school as a model for any situation, because they will not see why this particular model is more appropriate than another. Instruction about proportions, however carefully designed it is, will fail if it only takes mathematics into account: teachers must also take the content of the problem seriously.

So far we have looked at several different aspects of children's understanding of functions: at their ability to reason about functional relations in a non-quantified fashion, at their ability to solve quantitative problems, at the use of the one-to-many correspondence strategies when solving problems about the relationship between variables, and at the significance of the children's understanding of the content of the problem in order to choose an adequate mathematical model for it. In the next section, we will consider another sort of multiplicative relation between variables.

Different sorts of relations between variables We now turn from simple co-variation problems to another sort of situation which involves multiplicative reasoning but not simple co-variation. This sort of situation can most easily be described by analogy with one-to-many correspondence relations. We mentioned earlier that there is one type of one-to-many correspondence problem which is significantly more difficult than the others: this is the Cartesian product problem. As we pointed out, Cartesian product problems are more difficult because they involve two basic sets (for example, skirts and blouses) plus a third set (for example, the outfits) which is created by the systematic one-to-many correspondence between each element in one set and each element in the other set. There is no relationship between the number of skirts and the number of blouses to begin with, but they constitute the set of outfits when they are systematically placed in one-to-many correspondence. The product is the number of outfits, which is simultaneously influenced by the number of skirts and the number of blouses. Thus the correspondence between skirts and blouses is not part of the initial situation, but has to be constructed by the subject in order to solve the problem.

In the context of problems that involve relations between variables, there is an analogous sort of situation where the two initial variables do not have a fixed relation from the outset but their product creates a new variable. A simple example of this sort of situation is provided by the relations between length, width and area in a rectangle. Whereas length and width are independent from each other, their product defines the area of the rectangle, which is simultaneously influenced by its length and width. This class of problems is known as *product of measures* (Vergnaud, 1983).

Product of measures problems are more difficult for pupils than co-variation ones. Vergnaud (1983), for example, compared pupils' ability to solve a multiple proportions problem and a product of measures problem about volume. Three successive multiplications were required in both problems and so, in arithmetical terms, the problems were equally difficult. Yet the pupils did much better in the multiple proportions problem than in the product of measures (volume) problem.

Product of measures problems involve three extensive (or more) quantities, where the product of the first two gives origin to the third. In this last section, we will turn to another issue that concerns functional relations between variables: the relationship between intensive quantities and numbers. We commented earlier that, in problems where two variables are functionally related, it is often possible to speak of a third variable, an intensive quantity, which expresses the relationship between the two. This third variable poses interesting problems for children but unfortunately some of these have not yet been investigated frequently enough in the context of mathematics education. The next section will offer some indication of what pupils' difficulties with intensive quantities seem to be.

Understanding intensive quantities   When we discussed the new problems in understanding the relationship between variables, we introduced one example of intensive quantity: cost per kilo. We stressed that this value remains constant when the values in the other two variables, cost and amount, change. If you buy 5 kilos of potatoes, you spend more money and get more potatoes than if you buy 2 kilos but the cost-per-kilo is the same. The cost per kilo does not refer to a quantity, but to the relation between amount purchased and price; it applies to any amount in the same way.

Recently researchers have started to question whether children realize that intensive quantities are constant across amounts – in a sense, there is some doubt about children's understanding of the *conservation of intensive quantities*. In contrast to extensive quantities, where the parts are smaller than the whole, in the case of intensive quantities the part and the whole are equivalent; any amount of the same intensive quantity will have the same value. For example, if there is a particular mixture of water and concentrate in a container of orange juice any amount of juice poured from that container will have the same taste as the whole (and also the same taste as any other amount).

A group of US researchers (Harel et al., 1994) studied whether children understand this conservation of taste. They gave a written test to 16 sixth-grade pupils attending a private school (approximate ages should be about 12 years). The problem was presented through a drawing showing a container of orange juice that indicated on the label that it contained 40 ounces of water and 24 ounces of orange concentrate. Next to the container on the picture were two glasses, with the respective capacities indicating 7 ounces and 4 ounces. The children were asked whether the orange juice in the 7 ounces glass would taste the same as the orange juice in the 4 ounce glass and, if not, which would taste more orangey. They were also asked to explain their answer. Only 6 of the 16 pupils answered that the orange juice in the two glasses would taste the same. Half the pupils asserted that the orange juice in the two glasses would not taste the same and the other two were undecided. Some of those who decided that the orange juice would not taste the same thought that the juice in the larger glass would taste more orangey: others picked the smaller glass as the more orangey one.

The study suggests that most children did not understand the conservation of an intensive quantity across samples of this quantity. However some caution is needed about these results. The question about the orange juice was one item, among many, in a mathematics exercise. Pupils seem to believe – and rightly so, considering how they usually solve problems in mathematics lessons – that, in order to answer a question on a mathematics test, one must carry out calculations but this was not the case in the problem above. There were numbers on the picture of the carton of orange juice and on the glasses and, spurred on by these, some children tried to carry out calculations using these numbers. There is a need, therefore, for further investigations of pupils' understanding of conservation of intensive quantities in other contexts which do not encourage calculations. Some of the research which we are about to present also suggests that pupils do have difficulty with intensive quantities, but again most of this research is carried out with numbers attached to the quantities.

Comparing intensive quantities What do children know about numbers that refer to intensive quantities? We will consider evidence from young people's performance in two types of tasks involving intensive quantities: comparisons of such quantities and addition of them.

A considerable number of studies have investigated children's performance in tasks where intensive quantities are to be compared. Piaget and Inhelder's work on the quantification of probabilities (1975) was the starting-point for a great deal of this research. Probability is an intensive quantity which is measured by the ratio of favourable cases to total cases. For example, if there is a set of 6 cards where 3 are marked with a cross, the probability of choosing a card marked with a cross from this set of six cards is 0.5. Piaget and Inhelder suggested, that at the age of 7 or so, children start to deal systematically with the relation between favourable, unfavourable, and total number cases when they reason about probability, but they only do so to some extent. Piaget and Inhelder showed that they can judge correctly which of two decks of cards is the one from which we are more likely to pick a cross, provided that one of the variables is controlled. If both decks have the same number of cards marked with a cross but different total number of cards, children of this age understand that the deck with the smaller total number of cards gives them a better chance of picking a marked card. However, children of this age had much more difficulty when the value of both variables (the absolute number of crosses and the absolute number of cards) was different in the two decks.

It is only much later, at about the age of 11 or so, that young people can systematically solve these more difficult comparison problems. At this older age they can, for example, work out that the probability of getting a marked card in two decks, one with 2 marked cards out of 4 and the other with 3 marked cards out of 6, is the same.

We have already mentioned the possibility that the younger children's difficulty with intensive quantities might be due more to the difficulty of the concept of probability than to any problems with intensive quantities *per se*. However, Noelting's (1980b) work on the concentration of orange juice, for example, produced very similar results in spite of the great familiarity of the content of the task and in spite of the fact that it dealt with a completely different intensive quantity. We saw earlier that in problems where only one variable differed – either just the amount of water or just the amount of orange concentrate – young children aged 7 to 9 years were easily able to tell whether two mixtures of orange juice would taste the same or not. However, when the value in both variables differed, this same comparison of the intensive quantity was far too difficult for children of this age and the problem was mastered only by adolescents (aged 16 in this study). Thus in Piaget and Inhelder's probability study and in Noelting's orange juice study we find the identical pattern of an easy task in which one variable only differs between variables and a difficult task in which both variables differ. It is impossible to resist the conclusion that the similarity between the two studies is due to both being about judgements of intensive quantities.

Singer et al. (forthcoming) also report a study of children's and adults' performance in comparison tasks involving another intensive quantity: the density of flowers in a flower box. The density of flowers in this task was in effect a ratio between the number of flowers and the area in which they were planted. When the flowers were actually distributed inside the flower boxes and thus the distance between the flowers indicated their density, even kindergarten children had no difficulty in making a judgement about which of two flower boxes was more densely planted: they gave correct answers to comparison questions approximately 70 per cent of the time. However, in another condition this perceptual comparison of the density of flowers was no longer possible because the children were shown the flowers outside the areas in which they were to be planted. In this second task their performance was markedly worse and quite as bad as that described by Piaget and Inhelder in the probability task and by Noelting in the concentration of orange juice task: it was only at about age 11 that the level of success approached 70–80 per cent correct responses (see Singer et al., forthcoming, for a review of studies on comparisons of intensive quantities).

In short, children's performance in tasks that require them to compare intensive quantities undergoes striking changes during childhood. Even 7/8-year-olds can understand that two variables are concerned in the evaluation of intensive quantities: the amount of water and concentrate, the number of positive and negative cases, the number of flowers and the area of the flower box. But the understanding of how to take both variables systematically into account only seems to appear later.

These studies, however, do not tell us much about how children manage to take the step from considering one variable at a time to considering both in a genuinely multiplicative fashion. How do children view the relationship between an intensive quantity and the numbers used in its quantification? What is the role of operating with intensive quantities in the development of children's understanding of this type of quantity? There is much less research on operating with than on comparing intensive quantities and so it is not possible to answer this question at the moment. However, it is still possible to suggest some hypotheses about the answers. In the next section we will consider how children view the addition of intensive quantities and the possible pathways for development suggested by the research available so far.

Operating with intensive quantities   Science educators, as well as mathematics teachers, have an interest in the way in which children think of the addition of intensive quantities. Most of this interest has been in children's understanding of temperature. Temperature is an intensive quantity and it describes the state of, for example, a liquid; temperature 'expresses the state of agitation or disordered motion of particles' (Erickson and Tiberghien, 1985). The temperature of water, for example, has nothing to do with the amount of water: a small ice cube is the same temperature as a large one.

For over two decades science educators have studied how pupils think about intensive quantities in the context of questions about temperature. Two types of tasks have been given to children to investigate whether they understand that amount of substance and temperature are not related (for a review, see Erickson, 1985). In one type of task, the children are asked to estimate the temperature of ice blocks of different sizes and the temperature of boiling water when there are different amounts of water in a container. Young people up to about 10 years tend to indicate that a larger block of ice is colder than a smaller one; they also indicate that the boiling water in the larger container is hotter. Thus these young people seem to view temperature as an extensive rather than as an intensive quantity.

In the second type of task, children are asked about the results of putting together two intensive quantities. If they view temperature as an extensive quantity, they would have to answer that, for example, adding boiling water to water that is already boiling (that is, adding two amounts of water with the same temperature) increases the temperature of the water.

In these tasks, the children are shown pictures of two containers, A and B. that contain water at a certain temperature and they are asked to predict the temperature of the water in the second container when the water from the first one is poured into it. In some cases the actual temperature (in degrees) is not mentioned. The children are asked, for example: if we pour hot water from a container A into a container B that already has hot water at the same temperature, will the water in B continue to have the same temperature, become hotter, or become colder? In other cases the temperature is mentioned, and the question becomes, for example: container A has water at 80°: if it is poured into B which has the same amount of water at 80°, what will be the temperature of the water in container B?

These studies have produced two consistent results. One is that the task is a difficult one for young children, and substantially more difficult than the one-to-many tasks that we have already discussed. The second is that, in much the same way as in other studies that we have reviewed, the version of the task which involves no numbers and in which the children simply have to make judgements about relations is appreciably easier than the other version which does involve actual temperatures in degrees. In one study with Greek children, for example, Aidinis and Desli (1993) found that, for problems in which the temperature of the water in the two containers was the same, 33 per cent of the 10-year-old children were correct when they answered the question about relations but only 13 per cent were correct when they had to quantify their answers. Both in relational and in quantification problems, the children's predominant error was to think in terms of the addition of extensive quantities: they predicted that the water would get hotter in the relational problems or that the temperature would be 160° in the quantification problems. Erickson (1985) concluded from his review of this body of research that it is not until the age of 12 or 13 that questions such as these are solved by the majority of children.

It is important that we ask the same question about children's difficulties with judgements about temperature as we did with probability. Are these difficulties simply due to the children not understanding the concept of temperature, or is the problem genuinely a mathematical one?

Further evidence of children's difficulty with intensive quantities comes from research on their understanding of speed. These are illustrated in a teaching study carried out by Patrick Thompson 1994). Thompson used a computer environment in which animals could run at speeds determined by the subject. The screen displayed two animals, a rabbit and a turtle, and also the track which the animals would run along. This was a 100-foot track divided into ten sections. In the initial session, Thompson asked his subject, JJ, a 10-year-old fifth-grader, to explain what we mean when we say that 'the turtle ran at the speed of 40 feet per second'. JJ explained that it means that every second the turtle runs 40 feet. Thompson then posed to JJ a question of adding speeds: the rabbit ran over at 40 ft/sec and back at 20ft/sec, while the turtle ran at a constant speed; could JJ set the turtle at a speed that would make it tie with the rabbit? JJ decided that the speed would be 30 ft/sec because this is the number in-between 40 and 20. When answering other questions, JJ demonstrated the knowledge of the arithmetic needed to solve this problem: for example, JJ calculated the time it would take the rabbit to go over at 30 ft/sec correctly ($3\frac{1}{3}$ seconds). This means that JJ could have calculated the time needed to go over at 40 ft/sec and back at 20 ft/sec, and could have realized that the problem was then to figure out what 200 feet in 7.5 seconds meant when expressed in ft/sec. However, JJ's answer reflects an understanding of the relations in the problem without quantification: he knew that the answer was going to be a number between 20 and 40 and therefore understood the relations but did not know how to obtain a more precise quantitative answer. Even in a more familiar context, such as speed, operating with intensive quantities is not easy for children.

Thompson's subsequent work with JJ took the form of a series of sessions, in which JJ was asked to add speeds for going and coming back and was given feedback by the computer through running the simulated races with the speeds that had been chosen. Throughout the sessions, JJ was asked to add the speed of going and coming back (as in the example above), calculate how much time it took to go and how much to come back, how much time altogether for the 200 feet, and solve other similar problems that involved operating with these quantities. This gave JJ the opportunity to reconceptualize the relations between time, space and speed and eventually to master the question of average speed as the addition of two different speeds.

After mastering the average speed problem, JJ was able to apply the same reasoning to problems of average flow of water when two pumps working at different rates of flow were used to fill up one pool. JJ explicitly referred to the flow as being just the same as the speed in the races, and went on to solve the problems correctly in the same way.

To sum up: these studies indicate that intensive quantities do pose difficulties to children both in comparison and addition tasks.

Thompson's case study shows that it may be possible to promote young people's understanding of intensive quantities by giving them the chance to operate with these quantities in an environment where they can add, make predictions, and receive feedback about these predictions. But it must be noted that even in this case study, where a single child worked with the investigator and had the privilege of a special environment, the development did not come about easily. It appears that the relationships involved in understanding a particular intensive quantity must be very carefully considered over a series of problem situations that challenge the pupil's understanding.

If we risk a conclusion on the basis of Thompson's case study, this kind of investment in one situation might be well worth making: pupils may then be able to realize the similarity between this initial situation and other, new ones, where intensive quantities are also involved. The initial situation can perhaps provide a model for thinking about other situations encountered later on. Finally, we wish to point out that, in order to take advantage of pupils' ability to make an analogy from one situation to others, it is important to investigate the understanding of other types of intensive quantities – price per kilo, colours of mixtures of paint, concentration of substances etc. It might be the case that certain intensive quantities are mastered much earlier than others and could thus be used as the initial models on the basis of which children can come to understand other intensive quantities.

3 Systems of Signs and the Development of Multiplicative Reasoning

So far we have only discussed the invariants and the situations involved in multiplicative reasoning. We wish to turn now to issues which concern the impact of systems of signs and the development of multiplicative reasoning. In fact there are many issues here, but we will concentrate on two, which, we believe, are fundamental and can provide an example of how systems of signs may affect multiplicative reasoning.

The first of these relates to the fact that in multiplicative reasoning, variables are always represented through the specific systems of signs used in their measurement. For example, when we speak of the relationship between length, width and area, the problem is defined by a particular way of measuring these variables. The area of a rectangle in cm² is the product of the length in cm by the width in cm. If our original measurements take a different form, we might face a different sort of problem. Thus the first part in this section will briefly review one study which analyses the effects of varying systems of signs on understanding the same situation.

The second issue is the best way to teach children to recognize the differences between additive and multiplicative reasoning. We have seen that it is possible to solve many multiplicative problems through replication – a strategy that draws on the continuity between additive and multiplicative reasoning. We have also seen that children can go a long way in solving multiplicative reasoning problems through the replication strategy, but that they face difficulty when replicating would involve multiplying or dividing by fractions (see Hart's onion soup problem above) or when one-to-many correspondences are not given (see Saxe's inflation problem above). When children start to approach multiplicative reasoning problems it certainly might be useful for them to explore the continuities between additive and multiplicative reasoning, but it also seems worth while to ensure that they come to grips with the discontinuities too. We will examine below how computer environments have been used in this context.

3.1   *The effect of systems of signs on understanding*
   multiplicative problems

In order to analyse the impact of systems of signs on the understanding of multiplicative problems, we (Nunes et al., 1994) chose to work with the concept of area. Area can be measured directly with area units or it can be calculated from the linear measures of length and width. Let us take as an example a rectangle measured by area units of 1 cm²: if the rectangle is 8 units wide (8 columns) and 5 rows from top to bottom, the reasoning used in finding out how many squares cover the rectangle involves a one-to-many correspondence between the rows and the number of square centimetres in a row: 1 row, 8 cm²; 5 rows, 5×8 cm². This is not a product of measures problem because the units of measurement of area are there from the start and children can calculate the area on the basis of their number. In contrast, when the area must be calculated from the linear measures of the length and width, the problem is a product of measures one: 8 cm times 5 cm give as a product a new measure, 40 cm².

This analysis draws our attention to the possibility that a multiplicative situation might vary in difficulty depending on how the variables in the situation are measured. We wanted to know whether the system of sign used in measuring does have an impact on children's thinking about this particular multiplicative situation.

We asked pupils whose ages ranged from 8 to 11 years to compare the areas of two figures and to say which was larger. The pupils were given the problems in pairs, in order to promote discussion. The context for the problems was the following: the pupils were told that the two figures represented walls that had been painted by two friends – each one had painted one wall. When the friends got paid for their job, they decided that, if one had done more work than the other, he should get more money. The pupils' task was to decide whether the friends had done the same amount of painting work and, if not, who had worked more. The two figures were always designed in a way that prevented the children from solving the problem simply by visual inspection. For example, when the comparison was between two rectangles, one was longer and the other was wider, which made it difficult to tell whether they had the same area or not.

In order to study the effect of the system of signs on the children's problem-solving, half of the pairs of pupils were given a small number of blocks as their measuring instrument whereas the other half were given rulers. There were not enough blocks for the pupils simply to cover the figures and count the blocks; they had to find a way of calculating the total from partial tiling of the figures. The pupils were randomly distributed across these conditions so that differences between their performance could not result from differences in their previous mathematical ability.

Two questions were central in this study: (1) does the system of measurement used influence the way the problem is represented by the pupils and, consequently, their success? and (2) do the pupils who work with different measurement tools come up with different formulae for the area of rectangles and adjust them differently when they have to solve new problems, such as finding the area of a parallelogram?

This study showed that pupils who were given the bricks as their measurement tool were significantly more successful than the others, who worked with rulers. The rate of correct responses was 80 per cent for the pupils working with bricks and 30 per cent for those working with rulers in the problems of comparing rectangles. In the more difficult problems, where a rectangle had to be compared with a straight-sided U-shaped figure or with a parallelogram, the rate of success was 50 per cent for the pupils working with bricks and 30 per cent for those working with rulers.

An analysis of the pupils' explanations of their reasoning clearly indicated that they had different reasons for solving the problems in the way that they did, even when they gave a multiplicative solution. The pupils using bricks worked with a '1 row – x bricks' representation of the situation and were able to discover a formula, the number of bricks in a row times number of rows, that they used in solving new problems.

The reasoning of the pupils working with rulers was not always so clear. Some pupils said that they knew how to calculate the area of the rectangle and they simply multiplied the measures. However, we did not observe pairs of pupils developing the height × width formula during the interview. Area as a product of measures, resulting from the multiplication of two linear measures, seems to have been much too complicated a problem for the pupils whom we interviewed. Either they had learned it before or, if not, they could not construct it on the spot.

Thus this study indicates that the system of signs that is available to pupils when they solve multiplicative reasoning problems has a significant impact on their thinking. We have already discussed the evidence for the effect of the systems of signs on children's ability to solve additive reasoning problems. The discovery of a similar effect when pupils are solving multiplicative reasoning problems emphasizes the central importance of systems of signs. What may seem at first to be 'the same problem' might in fact become a very different one when the resources the children have at their disposal to solve the problem are different. This means that, when we propose problems to children, we need to consider what systems of signs we are asking them to use. Their problem-solving capacity is not fixed, but can be enhanced or constrained by the representational environment in which they are solving the problems. When children are developing their understanding of situations, we may want to enhance their problem-solving ability so that they can construct clear representations of the situation for themselves. But we may also want to constrain their choices at a later point in instruction if we wish to lead them to think about a situation in a particular way. This may be the case with the concept of area: we may initially want pupils to build a multiplicative understanding of area on the basis of area units but we may later want them to connect this understanding with a product of measures view of area.

3.2   Getting to grips with the discontinuity between addition and multiplication in a computer environment

We have argued that children's first steps in multiplicative reasoning follow directly from their experiences with additive reasoning, but we have also tried to show that children who rely entirely on the continuity between the two types of reasoning will begin to make serious blunders in multiplicative tasks. So they must at some stage come to grips with the differences between the two kinds of reasoning.

Some recent evidence suggests that an effective way of doing so is to introduce children to a computer environment which constrains their choices in order to encourage particular representations of the relations in multiplicative problems. In an ingenious study Celia Hoyles, Richard Noss and Rosamund Sutherland (Hoyles and Noss, 1992; Hoyles et al., 1991) worked on multiplication games and on enlargement problems which, as we have seen, are rather difficult for young children (see, for example, Hart, 1988; Kaput and Maxwell West, 1994). The aim of the study was to engage pupils in solving ratio and proportions problems in an environment where they were at times constrained to represent certain relations by multiplication.

The pupils who took part in the study were 13-year-olds from a London comprehensive school, described as of average ability in mathematics, who had a fair amount of experience with LOGO, the computer environment in which the project was carried out, and regularly used calculators in the classroom. Only some of the tasks solved by the pupils in this study will be discussed here – namely, those that aimed at stressing the discontinuities between addition and multiplication.

In one of the tasks, the pupils were asked to reach a target number (for example, 100) from a starting-point (for example, 13) through successive multiplications. The game was played in pairs and the pupils took turns. Each turn (except for the first one) involved multiplying the result of the preceding multiplication by a new number that would bring the next product as close as possible to the target.

Because pupils easily overshoot the target, the game makes the pupils face the question: how do you make a number smaller by multiplying it? This is a significant question because it helps pupils see some of the discontinuities between addition and multiplication.

Whereas the addition of positive numbers always results in a larger number, the multiplication of a positive number by a number between 0 and 1 results in a smaller number. The question is of even greater interest because it has been shown (Bell et al., 1989) that many pupils think that 'multiplication makes bigger' which is probably a consequence of their not appreciating the discontinuity between multiplication and addition. Hoyles and Noss report that some students who, at first, only multiplied by integers and could not therefore get any closer to the target if they had gone beyond it, would eventually multiply by numbers between 0 and 1 to obtain a smaller value. However, not all the pupils were able to come up with this idea.

A second exercise of interest involved enlarging a house that had been predesigned through a LOGO procedure. The inputs to draw the first house were already in the procedure (see figure 7.6) and the pupils were asked:

1   to make a DOUBLEHOUSE, that is, a house twice as big, by multiplying all the sides by 2 (nothing should be altered in the angles), which could be accomplished by entering an explicit multiplication rule into the procedure;
2   to go through a series of houses where the original inputs to the HOUSE procedure were to be multiplied by 3, 0.5, 1.5 and so on, always using the same rule;
3   to find out the rule that had produced a particular house, when they were only told the value of one of its sides;
4   to create new houses from the same procedure themselves and to challenge other pupils to identify their rule.

The children carried out some of these tasks at the computer and others as homework. The first two tasks were exploratory and allowed pupils to observe what happened to the houses when the sides are all multiplied by the same number. They had the opportunity to find out that the houses 'looked the same shape' or 'were in proportion' when the sides were multiplied by the same number. They also had the opportunity to notice that the procedures worked: there would be no gaps at the end, when the base was drawn. The third task was carried out away from the computer as homework. Part of the fourth task was carried out on the computer and part of it away from the computer. When the pupils were trying to figure out how another group had constructed their house in this task, they ended up with a gap, if they did not use a multiplicative solution.

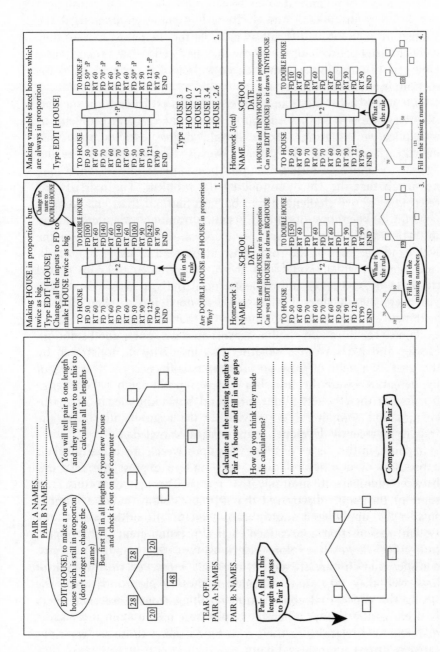

Figure 7.6 Exercise of enlarging a house predesigned using a LOGO procedure

Hoyles and Noss indicate that some pupils adopted the multiplication strategy in tasks 3 and 4. In task 4 these children used the strategy to make it as difficult as possible for the pupils, whom they were challenging, to figure out how they had constructed their house. One pair of girls, for example, chose a decimal input of 2.6075 for their multiplication rule.

The pupil's behaviour can be interpreted as evidence for a successful intervention in leading the pupils to see enlargement problems as multiplicative situations. To a certain degree, Hoyles and Noss indicate that this was the case. However, they caution the reader against too much enthusiasm. Pupils' behaviour in one situation may not mean that they have conquered the problem. The pair of girls referred to above challenged two boys to find out their enlargement procedure. The boys obtained a similar (but not identical) house through additive procedures: they kept the *difference* between the walls and the lines of the roof constant (instead of using a multiplication factor, which would keep the ratio constant), and constructed the base by successive adjustments, until the gap was closed. The girls were then unsure of what they had done and checked all their arithmetic. It was only after this check that they could confidently explain to the boys why the boys' procedure was not a good solution. Hoyles and Noss wonder whether this insecurity demonstrated by the girls is a sign of how social aspects influence the learning of mathematics – were the girls simply shaken up by the boys' challenge because of their beliefs about girls' and boys' knowledge of mathematics and computers? – or whether the example illustrates the fragility of recently developed mathematical knowledge.

In short, in this series of tasks the pupils were constrained in their expression of number relations: they had to express the relations between numbers in multiplicative terms. Through this constraint some of the pupils discovered that it is possible to make a number smaller by applying a multiplicative factor. In other words, the system of signs that constrained their expression created the opportunity for them to explore relations that they might not have considered in an unrestricted environment. However, the question of how well they take in the results of these explorations and how strong the conceptual construction resulting from these encounters is, needs further study. When the pupils were free to express the same mathematical relations in their own terms, some chose the multiplicative relations and others did not.

4 Conclusions

After this overview of work on multiplicative reasoning, it seems quite easy to make the case that multiplication and division are not simply two new arithmetic operations which children learn after addition and subtraction. There is a host of new number meanings to be learned and new situations to be understood. In a sense, it is easy to overlook the great shifts that take place from additive to multiplicative reasoning because there is not a new system of signs to be mastered when we only consider the two types of multiplicative situations described in this chapter. Another reason why it is easy to overlook the gap between additive and multiplicative reasoning is that the strategy of replicating, which can be used effectively to solve a variety of multiplicative reasoning problems, is clearly connected to addition and subtraction. However, as we saw, there are new number meanings to be mastered – ratio, scalar and functional factors – and new sorts of relations represented by numbers, such as those that emerge in the context of intensive quantities.

Much of the work on multiplicative reasoning has explored the understanding of invariants and situations. It is surprising that children as young as 5/6 years already understand much about multiplicative relations: they can order sets on the basis of one-to-many correspondences, they can build sets with the same total of units when the pieces in the sets contain different units, and they can make proportional judgements to evaluate whether a picture adequately represents a scene or an object. Even if these early competencies are restricted to the domain of relations and do not involve quantification, it is clear that children do not have to master addition and subtraction before they start to reason multiplicatively. Mathematics teaching has often overlooked young children's understanding of multiplicative relations. It is possible that, if children were to explore their early understanding of multiplicative relations, the progress from understanding relations to solving quantification problems might be different.

Children's strategies to deal with quantification problems are often based on their understanding of one-to-many correspondence situations. These strategies, although powerful, have limitations: for example, they cannot be used when the one-to-many correspondences are not known. What this means is that instruction needs to concentrate on creating situations that will bridge the children's understanding to new strategies using functional or scalar factors expressed multiplicatively. Computer environments may be powerful tools for such an instructional task. Pupils can be constrained to express relations in multiplicative terms in playful, non-threatening contexts, using particular systems of signs that allow them to connect number relations and meanings in multiplicative situations. The work by Hoyles and colleagues offers provocative suggestions in this context.

The role of systems of signs in multiplicative reasoning, especially in the problems that involve relations between variables, is much more significant than has been acknowledged so far. Variables are measured by particular systems of signs that pupils need to reflect about. Their understanding of the systems of signs and the variables they work with in these problems is intricately interwoven. The same situation measured with different systems of signs can be a completely different problem. The consequence of this participation of systems of signs in concept learning for teaching is that much more attention must be paid in the future to how a problem is presented, which systems of signs are used in the description of the problem. Mathematics educators have for a long time concentrated on the invariants of concepts and overlooked the fact that many concepts used in mathematics are considered basically in terms of their operational definition – that is, in terms of the way they are measured. This means that measurement becomes an important issue in their understanding.

Another aspect to be considered when analysing children's multiplicative reasoning is their understanding of intensive quantities. Studies so far indicate that the way in which numbers represent intensive quantities poses a considerable problem for children. Although this work is still scarce, there is evidence that pupils may understand this relationship better in some contexts than in others and that, if they master the connection between the intensive quantity and numbers in one situation, they may be able to use this understanding as a model for other situations where intensive quantities are concerned. The paucity of studies on the development of children's understanding of how numbers and intensive quantities are connected is a problem for mathematics but also for scientific instruction: many of the concepts pupils need to learn in science refer to intensive quantities.

Finally, the analysis of multiplicative reasoning developed in practice exemplified in the study of vendors' and non-vendors' solutions to inflation problems indicates that much more attention needs to be dedicated in mathematics teaching to the understanding of the situations pupils have to deal with. The practice of using word problems as examples for the mathematics to be carried out, without a genuine analysis of the relations in the situations, does not seem to suffice. In the study of functions, that starts with proportional relations, one of the goals of instruction should be to develop pupils' awareness of mathematics as a source of models for situations. This is what allows us to manipulate the mathematical symbols in order to come up with conclusions about the situations. In order to understand the relationship between a model and a situation, both the model and the situation need to be objects of reflection. If we concentrate in mathematics instruction on teaching techniques, and pay only token attention to the relationship between the model and the situation it mathematizes, we will create a divorce between the knowledge of techniques and the awareness of the meaning. This divorce has been amply documented in the context of multiplicative reasoning.

8

Understanding Rational Numbers

With fractions appearances are deceptive. Sometimes children appear to have a full understanding of fractions, and yet they do not. They use the right fractional terms; they talk about fractions coherently; they solve some fractional problems; but several crucial aspects of fractions still escape them. In fact appearances can be so deceptive that it is possible for some pupils to go through school not mastering the difficulties of fractions, with no one realizing it.

One common way of introducing children to fractions for the first time is to show them wholes divided into parts, some of which are distinguished from the rest, for example, by being painted. The children are told that the total number of parts is the denominator, whereas the number of painted parts is the numerator. This introduction, together with some instruction about a few rules for calculating, allows children to convey the impression that they know a great deal about fractions.

Kerslake's (1986) interesting work with children aged 12–14 shows as much. These children did very well in judgements about the equivalence of fractions in the items depicted in figure 8.1. In these, all the pupils interviewed produced equivalent fractions for the diagrams and appeared very familiar with the problem; some pupils added that, if you remove the line, the diagrams look the same, and that was how they knew that the fractions were the same.

However, several pieces of research have demonstrated that the impression of children reasoning successfully about fractions might be false. For example, in Brazil, Campos et al. (1995) have been able to show quite clearly that this way of introducing fractions can actually lead children into error. The teaching method, they claim,

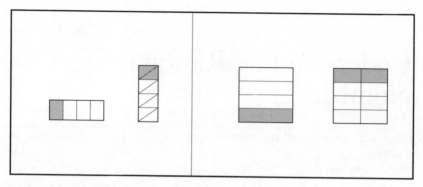

Figure 8.1   Sample items from the equivalence questions
SOURCE: Kerslake (1986)

simply encourages pupils to employ a sort of double-counting procedure – that is, to count the total number of parts and then the
painted parts – without understanding the significance of this new
sort of number. The test of this hypothesis is to ask children to
identify fractions in diagrams that cannot be solved by double-
counting and to require that they reason in terms of part–whole
relations.

As a test of their hypothesis, Tania Campos and her colleagues
gave three types of item to pupils (fifth-graders, approximate age 12
years or older) who had been taught the double-counting procedure
and asked them to name the fractions depicted in each case. The first
type was a straightforward example of what the children had learned
in their classroom exercises: the whole was divided into equal parts
and the painted parts were contiguous. The second type of item was
less typical but could be solved through the same process of double-
counting: the whole was divided into equal parts but the painted
parts were not contiguous in the picture. The third type of item was
not typical and could not be solved through the double-counting
procedure: the whole was not explicitly divided into equal parts, and
the number of parts had to be figured out by the pupils through an
analysis of the part–whole relations. Figure 8.2 presents an example
of each of these types of item; these should be contrasted with the
items contained in figure 8.1, where there is an explicit division of
the wholes in equal parts.

Campos and her colleagues made three predictions: (1) items of
type 1 and 2 would not differ significantly in their difficulty because

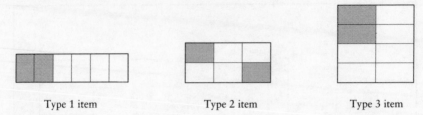

Type 1 item   Type 2 item   Type 3 item

Figure 8.2 Examples of the items used to study children's understanding of fractions
SOURCE: Campos et al. (1995)

both types could be solved through the double-counting procedure; (2) type 3 items would be significantly more difficult than type 1 and 2 because these could not be solved by double-counting; and (3) the most frequent error in type 3 items would result from double-counting the number of parts in the drawing and the number of painted parts, without any adjustment for the inequality of the explicitly indicated parts.

The results of the study supported these predictions. The pupils did well, and equally well, with the type 1 and 2 items; their performance with these items was close to ceiling, though not perfect because some students used double-counting in a different way, counting the painted parts for the numerator and the not-painted parts for the denominator. Type 3 items were much more difficult than the other two, and in these items the most frequent error was to indicate the fraction that corresponded to the double-counting procedure. In the item depicted in figure 8.2, 56 per cent of the pupils chose 1/7 as the corresponding fraction; 12 per cent chose 2/8 and 4 per cent indicated both 1/4 and 2/8 as correct responses.

These results confirm the suspicion that children can use the language of fractions, without fully understanding their nature. Kerslake's study also contains further evidence of pupils' lack of understanding of equivalence of fractions, even if they succeeded in the test items about equivalence. Although her subjects did well in the equivalence items she presented, they did not necessarily find equivalent fractions in order to carry out addition, and added fractions with different denominators (for example, 2/3 + 3/4 was calculated as 5/7). Even the children who first transformed the fractions into equivalent ones with the same denominator did not seem to see the connection between equivalence of fractions and addition. Five (of 15) children solved correctly 2/3 + 3/4 but none could explain why they had changed the fractions and used the common denominator 12 before adding the fractions. They were simply 'repeating a routine' used many times in the classroom (Kerslake, 1986, p. 21).

These studies stand as a warning of the dangers of overlooking the complexity and the diversity of the concepts involved in fractions and rational numbers. (We will use the expression 'rational numbers' in a more general way and fractions only when referring to part–whole problems.) In fact, this diversity has been recognized by several researchers. For example, Behr et al. (1993), Kieren (1988; 1994) and Vergnaud (1983) have all proposed ways of classifying different constructs that are related to rational numbers. Carpenter et al. (1993) attempted a synthesis of these different views, but they concluded that it is still not clear what level of detail these classifications should include because there is not enough research yet for us to decide which distinctions are central and which are not.

We will not attempt a classification of situations that involve rational numbers, because we agree that the facts that are needed are not yet in. Instead we will pursue two themes; children's understanding of rational numbers as extensive quantities on the one hand, and as intensive quantities on the other. These themes do not cover the whole gamut of problems that can be posed about rational numbers, but we believe that they involve the most fundamental issues that children must deal with in order to understand this new kind of number.

At this point, it seems important to point out the connection between rational numbers and multiplicative reasoning which we have already mentioned in chapter 7. In the first section of that chapter we introduced the general idea of division and splits and so we will not repeat it here. We will proceed directly to the empirical work on the question of children's understanding of division and splits.

The first section in this chapter deals with children's understanding of the relations involved in the simple division of discontinuous and continuous quantities. It examines the evidence on children's understanding of relations in division situations and the beginnings of quantification. Only the extensive aspects of rational number are considered in this first section. The second section examines children's understanding of the extensive and intensive aspects of rational numbers in the context of their understanding of equivalences and successive splits. The third section discusses questions related to the understanding and the representation of rational numbers. The final section presents our conclusions and indicates further questions for research.

1 Understanding Division and Simple n-Splits

1.1 *Dividing sets*

It has often been proposed that the understanding of division starts with children's understanding of sharing. Even children as young as 5 years of age can divide sets into equal amounts by using the one-for-me one-for-you procedure without error. Most 5-year-olds go on to make inferences about the equality of the sets obtained in this fashion, as we saw earlier (Frydman and Bryant, 1988). But one must make a distinction between sharing and division. When children are concerned with sharing, they concentrate on giving equal amounts to each recipient. The invariant in sharing is one-to-one correspondence between the shared sets. In division the invariants are more complex: they concern the relationships between the dividend (the number that is being divided), the divisor (the number into which the dividend is divided), and the quotient (the result of the division). (In the division $72 \div 8 = 9$, 72 is the dividend, 8 is the divisor, and 9 is the quotient.) In a sharing situation, focusing on division problems involves considering the relationships, for example, between the number of sweets to be shared, the number of children who will receive sweets, and the number of sweets that each child will receive. If we want to test children's understanding of these relations, we need to know whether they realize that there is an inverse relation between the number of recipients and the size of the quota. In other words, we need to know whether children understand the consequences of the size of n in an n-split.

The first question that we will consider in analysing children's understanding of division is whether young children can understand these relations in a division situation before they can actually compute division sums. So far in this book, we have repeatedly found that children understand about relations before they can deal with absolute values: this was true of measurement, comparisons in additive situations, one-to-many correspondence, and intensive quantities. Lauren Resnick and Janice Singer (1993) have also suggested the possibility that children reason about relations both in the domain of whole numbers and in the domain of rational numbers before they can quantify these relations. Thus, we will start the review of empirical studies by considering how young children perform in tasks that involve the division of discontinuous and continuous quantities before they have learned how to solve these sorts of problem in school.

Jane Correa (1995) carried out a series of studies about young children's understanding of the consequences of the size of n in an n-split where the results of sharing sweets among different numbers of recipients were to be anticipated by the children. The children were in three age groups (5, 6 and 7 years) and were interviewed individually in their schools in Oxford. They were presented with a series of situations where the same number of sweets was to be shared independently to the rabbits attending each of two different parties. The question posed to the children was: are the rabbits in one party going to receive the same number of sweets as the rabbits in the other party? Correa used small rabbits with little baskets on their backs into which she put the sweets. She carried this distribution out behind a screen, so that the children could not see how many she was giving to each rabbit. Considering these methodological precautions, there was no ambiguity about what the questions referred to; the children's responses could not be based on perceptual information. They had to anticipate the results of the distribution.

Two types of problem were given to the children. In one, the number of rabbits was the same in both parties; in the other, the number was different. For each of the items the children were asked to indicate whether the rabbits in both parties got the same number of sweets, and if not, in which party the rabbits would be given more sweets.

Correa's prediction was that the second type of problem would be significantly more difficult because it requires an understanding of the inverse relation between the divisor and the quotient. Her results confirmed her expectation: there was a significant difference in the level of difficulty of the two problems. The children made very few mistakes when the number of rabbits in the two parties was the same. In contrast, the percentages of children performing above chance level (that is, giving 5 or 6 correct responses out of 6) in the situations where the number of rabbits was different were 30, 55 and 85 per cent, respectively, for the 5, 6 and 7-year-olds. Thus, the younger children had great difficulty with this problem, but half of the 6-year-olds and most of the 7-year olds did get it right most of the time.

Correa also analysed the children's errors. It might be thought that the children who made errors simply answered that, because the number of sweets to be distributed in the party was the same, the rabbits in both parties would receive the same number of sweets. This is in fact what most of the 5- and 6-year-olds said, when they made mistakes. Among the 7-year-olds, however, there was a different type of error: the great majority of the wrong answers indicated that the greater the number of rabbits in the party, the more sweets they would receive. This answer could be viewed, in a sense, as a worsening in performance with age because this response seems less sensible than to say that the rabbits get the same number of sweets. On the other hand, this answer might reflect the children's attempt to take into account the number of recipients in the sharing situation, which seems to be completely ignored by the younger children. In doing so, they come up with the wrong conclusion about how the number of recipients and the size of quota relate to each other. If this interpretation of the errors of 7-year-olds is correct, this apparent worsening in performance is likely not to be a peculiar finding about the children interviewed by Correa.

In short, about half of the 6-year-olds and the majority of the 7-year-old children could understand the effect of the size of n in an n-split situation and could reason about the inverse relation between quotient and divisor, even though they did not know how to calculate division sums.

1.2   *Dividing continuous quantities*

The connection between division and fractions is immediately clear when we think of the kind of problem that we have just described above but replace the sets of sweets with continuous quantities, such as bars of chocolate, as the objects to be distributed at the parties. The result of splitting continuous quantities, instead of being subsets, would be fractions. The connection that we are making between problems with discontinuous and continuous material is, of course, not accidental. Thomas Kieren (1988; 1994), on the basis of a mathematical analysis of rational numbers, has suggested that fractions are numbers produced by divisions (rather than by joining, as whole numbers); they are numbers in the field of quotients. The fundamental new properties or invariants that distinguish rational numbers from whole numbers are identified when rational numbers are placed in the field of quotients.

If this is right, we should seek the origin of children's understanding of rational numbers in division situations. The action of dividing or 'splitting' (a term that emphasizes the symmetry of the resulting parts) makes it possible to answer the question 'how much?' in a new way. When we obtain a number through division, there is always a double relation to be considered: there is a reference to a unit, which is taken as the whole, and a reference to the size of n in the n-split: the larger the size of n, the smaller is the answer to the 'how much?' question.

Let us consider what happens when young children are asked to consider bars of chocolates rather than sets of sweets being shared out: are they able to understand the inverse relation between the size of n in the n-split with continuous quantities as well as they do in the context of the division of sets?

There is little evidence on this question, unfortunately, and none, so far as we know, that directly compares children's understanding of the relations in division with discontinuous and continuous quantities. However, one study (carried out for other purposes and discussed later in greater detail) provides an initial answer to the question, and a rather encouraging one. Despina Desli (1994) carried out an investigation with 6-, 7-, and 8-year-old Greek children from state schools in Thessaloniki. The problem situations in her study were parallel to those in Correa's (1995) study but the parties were for children and the distribution was of chocolate bars. The children were asked to say whether the children in the two parties would get the same amount of chocolate or whether the children in one party would receive more than those in the other, holding the number of chocolates constant and varying the number of children across the parties or vice versa.

The percentages of correct responses for the 6-, 7- and 8- year-old children, respectively, were 75, 85 and 95 per cent. Thus as a group the children in this study seem to have done as well with continuous quantities as the children in the previous study did when solving problems with discontinuous quantities.

Like Correa, Desli also observed a number of children who indicated that the children in the party with more children would receive more chocolate. This sort of error, as in Correa's study, was observed more frequently among the 7-year-olds than the 6-year-olds. Thus again the apparent deterioration in reasoning at around this age level is probably related to the children's attempts to consider both variables, the number of chocolates and the number of children invited to the party. As they do so, they misconstrue the inverse relation between quotient and divisor as a direct one.

However, no direct comparison between the studies is possible for two reasons. First, they were carried out with two groups of children that might differ: one group of children was from Oxford and the other from Thessaloniki. Second, Desli's study only includes two items that are directly comparable to those in the work by Correa and thus she cannot investigate whether the performance of individual children was significantly above chance level. More research is clearly needed but we can reasonably expect that a good number of 6-year-olds and perhaps the majority of 7-year-olds will be able to understand the effect of the size of n on the n-split when continuous quantities are involved. These abilities clearly precede children's knowledge of fractional representations and their ability to calculate with fractions.

1.3   *Inverting splits*

In a division situation, the children can be told how many sweets there are and how many rabbits will be invited to the party and asked about what happens to the size of the portions when the number of rabbits is changed. This is the most usual way in which children will consider questions about division in everyday life; these problems are called *partitive problems*.

There is a second type of problem which can be presented to children about the same divisions: if you have a certain number of sweets and establish the quotas beforehand, what happens to the number of rabbits that can be invited to the parties as you change the size of the quotas? This second type of problem, often termed the *quotitive* (or *measure*) *problem*, involves the same invariant in division: the inverse relation between the quotient and the divisor. However, we believe that, as far as young children are concerned, partitive and quotitive problems are different from the psychological perspective.

If we consider how children might solve these two types of problems with concrete materials, it becomes clear that the actions to be carried out are different in the two situations. In the partitive problems, the children can share out the sweets in a one-to-one correspondence fashion, and can then count one of the sets in order to find out how many sweets the rabbits received. Little anticipation is involved as the actions are carried out as if the rabbits are present;

all the children need to do is distribute the sweets accurately. In the quotitive situation, the children need to build each quota in succession – for example, take 4 sweets and then another 4 and so on – and establish a one-to-many correspondence between the quotas and the rabbits as they use up the sweets. Quotative problems can be viewed as inverting the *n*-split: given a certain result, what was the size of *n* in this split? This analysis leads us to expect that understanding the inverse relation between quotient and divisor in quotative problems is a later achievement than the understanding of the same relations in partitive problems. We can also expect the difference in rates of success to disappear as children reach 7 or 8 years because they will be able to invert the *n*-split.

Correa (1995) compared children's understanding of the inverse relations between quotient and divisor in partitive and quotitive situations without quantification. The scenario used in the study was the same one of rabbits and parties described above. The partitive problems have already been described in section 1.1. In the quotitive problems the children were told that they were going to organize two parties, one for the pink and one for the blue rabbits, and they had to decide how many rabbits to invite. For the pink rabbits' party, they would prepare little plates with, for example, three sweets in each plate; for the blue rabbits' party, they would prepare plates with four sweets in each plate. The children were also shown for each party a drawing of a plate with the correct number of sweets as a memory support. The total number of sweets to be used in both parties was the same. The children were asked whether they could invite the same number of rabbits to come to each party and, if not, which party could have more rabbits coming to it. The subjects were, like those who answered the partitive problems, 5-, 6- and 7-year-olds from schools in Oxford. Similarly to the procedure used in the partitive problems, half of the items had the same quotas on the plates (seen as control tasks) and half had different quotas.

The children performed significantly better in the same-quota than in the different-quotas problems. Performance was at or close to ceiling level on the same-quota problems, indicating that the children understood the problem situation. In the different-quotas problems, the percentages of children performing above chance level were 15, 38 and 40 per cent, respectively for the 5-, 6- and 7-year-old children. These percentages are considerably lower than those observed in the partitive problems. Whereas in the partitive problems the majority of the 7-year-olds performed above chance level, in the quotitive problems the number of children performing above chance level was less than half. Thus understanding the relations in problems that required inverting an *n*-split (quotative problems) is more difficult for young children than understanding the same relations when the value of *n* in the split is known (partitive problems).

So far we have only been concerned with children's understanding of relations. How does this understanding tie in with the quantification of splits? In the section that follows, we will look at how children begin to quantify relations in division situations.

1.4   *The beginnings of quantification*

Quantifying division with discontinuous quantities   The situations described in the studies by Correa (1995) appear so simple to an adult that one could expect young children to be able to solve division problems with concrete materials long before they need to understand relations. This might be so if the children have the rabbits and the sweets in front of them so that all that they need to do is to carry out the distribution. But that would not be solving a problem at all: there is no need to reason about or anticipate anything in such a situation. On the other hand, if the rabbits are not present and the children need to conceive of the correspondence between rabbits and sweets mentally, then the children would have a genuine division problem to solve. How well can young children solve this sort of problem? We have seen that many children of about 6 years successfully solve additive reasoning problems with concrete materials, at least if they can directly model the situations. The same is true of one-to-many correspondence problems. Is it possible that such young children can also solve division problems with concrete materials?

Correa (1995) studied children's ability to solve quantitative division problems using concrete materials in tasks where the rabbits, although visible, were piled up in a corner so that the children could not just distribute the sweets in a mechanical fashion. She devised partitive and also quotitive problems which she gave to children aged 5 and 6 years from state schools in Oxford.

In the partitive problems, the question was how many sweets would each rabbit receive. The children were initially shown the rabbits that were coming to the party and allowed to play with them. After a while, the experimenter said that the rabbits were tired and had to go to sleep. The rabbits were then piled in a corner of the table and the children were asked to prepare the party for the rabbits while they were sleeping. The pretend-sweets would have to be shared without recourse to the perceptual correspondence between sweets and rabbits. The children had to anticipate that each location, in which sweets were placed, represented a rabbit.

In the quotative problems, the question was how many rabbits would be invited to the party. The children played with the rabbits, put them to sleep, and were then asked to prepare the party by organizing groups of, for example, three sweets for each rabbit. They could then decide how many rabbits would be invited to the party. Thus the children had to reason that for each quota that was established, one rabbit could be invited.

The results (presented in figure 8.3) were that 5-year-olds had considerable difficulty in solving quotative problems although they could succeed in some partitive problems. By 6 years the children were able to solve quotative problems reasonably well but the difference between partitive and quotative problems was still significant.

Correa also analysed the children's strategies when solving these problems. Among the 5-year-olds, success was most likely in the partitive problems, especially those problems that only involved two rabbits; in these, the children could simply use a one-for-you and one-for-me strategy, and then count the blocks in one of the subsets. Even in this situation, however, some 5-year-olds went on to count the whole lot of blocks and gave the wrong answer. This sort of counting should not surprise us: we have seen in chapter 2 that some 5-year-olds still do not appear to grasp the significance of counting and do not change the way that they count depending on the kind of question they have to answer.

In contrast, the majority of the 6-year-olds (70 per cent) showed clearly distinct strategies for solving partitive and quotative problems. In partitive problems they placed blocks one at a time at different locations on the table, with the number of locations corresponding to the number of rabbits that were going to the party, repeated the sharing operation until they ran out of blocks, and then counted the subsets. In the quotative problems, the preferred strategy was to take repeatedly a group of blocks with the same number as the quota, place these groups at different locations on the table until there were no blocks left, and then count the number of groups formed.

Thus their strategies directly modelled the problem situation and they could succeed even when the correspondences between rabbits

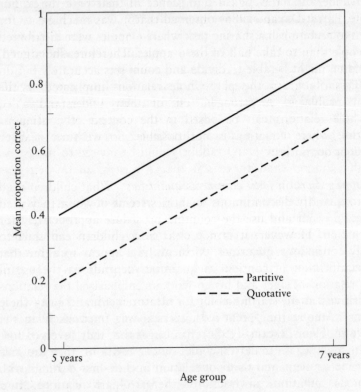

Figure 8.3   Correct responses in the partitive and quotative tasks
SOURCE: Correa and Bryant (1994)

and sweets had to be represented mentally. But Correa also notes that some of the children who had adequately carried out the modelling of the situation with blocks in the quotative situation might have made mistakes and named the number of blocks in a set rather than the number of sets as the answer. This confusion, also noted by Gravemeijer (forthcoming), might result from the use of only one sort of representation – blocks – to deal with two variable problems – rabbits and sweets.

The results of this study are rather encouraging in that they suggest that 6-year-olds can already organize their actions and reason about division well enough to solve problems with concrete materials. But we must be cautious about the meaning of this success. As Parrat-Dayan and Vonèche (1992) pointed out, when children solve problems in distribution situations like those described above, they might not yet understand the logical significance of their procedures. For example, Parrat-Dayan (1985) observed that it was much easier for children to accomplish a sharing task where 6 apples were distributed to 2 people than to take half of the 6 apples. Therefore, she argued, the children might be able to divide and count sets accurately but do not necessarily grasp the part–whole relations implicated in the division problems. A stronger test of their understanding of part–whole relations can be posed in the context of continuous quantities, where counting is not possible. So we turn next to continuous quantities.

Quantifying division with continous quantities What children need to do to quantify discontinuous quantities seems obvious: they need to learn to count and use the counting procedure appropriately for the situation. However, it is not clear how children can start to quantify continuous quantities. Most authors appear to agree that the quantification of continuous quantities depends on the use of logical relations. Piaget and his co-workers emphasized the relations of transitivity as the starting-point for measurement, and part–whole relations as the starting-point for understanding fractions (Piaget et al., 1960). Peter Bryant (1974) has suggested that, even before children can start to understand part–whole relations, they are able to use a more elementary sort of relation in their first dealings with continuous quantities in fractions: the part–part relations. If a continuous quantity is divided in only two parts, one can often judge quite easily whether one part is greater than the other. The relations 'greater/smaller than' and 'equal to', he suggested, could be the first logical relations used in the very beginning of the quantification of fractions. Because they must be used in situations where the whole is divided in two parts, then 'half' has a special status in the origins of quantification of fractions: the half-boundary defines whether the two parts are equal or one is greater than the other.

In order to verify this hypothesis, Spinillo and Bryant (1991) devised a series of experiments to analyse children's use of the half–boundary in equivalence judgements. The task, already described in chapter 7, required the children to match a picture to a box, by indicating which of two boxes was represented in the picture. The boxes were divided in two parts corresponding to the amounts of blue and of white bricks. The picture was much smaller than the boxes so that direct perceptual matches were not possible. Furthermore, the bricks were said to have been re-arranged after the picture was taken so that they formed horizontal stripes in the boxes and vertical stripes in the picture or vice-versa.

In order to investigate the role of the half-boundary in children's performance, three experimental conditions were created. In one condition (the half tasks), half of the bricks in one of the boxes were blue and the other half white, whereas in the other box there were more blue than white bricks. In the second condition (the cross-half tasks), the values crossed the half-boundary: one box had more blue bricks than white bricks and the other had more white than blue bricks. In the third condition (the within-half tasks), both boxes had more blue bricks than white bricks (see figure 8.4). The children, in the age range of 4 to 7 years, were attending preschool and state schools in Oxford. Spinillo and Bryant predicted that children would perform significantly better in tasks that involved the half-boundary (first condition) or crossed the half-boundary (second condition) than in those tasks where the half-boundary could not be used as the basis for the judgement.

Their results can be summarized as follows (for a complete description of the three studies, see Spinillo and Bryant, 1991):

1   there was a clear progression in the mean number of correct responses by age level and this progression was statistically significant;
2   the children performed better in the tasks where they could use the half-boundary to make their judgements and this difference was also statistically significant;
3   less than half of the 5-year-olds, about half of the 6-year-olds, and the majority of the 7- and 8-year-olds performed significantly above chance level in the tasks where the half-boundary could be used as a reference for matching the picture with one of the boxes.

These results strongly suggest that the half-boundary might represent the first step in children's use of relations to quantify fractions.

In the studies by Spinillo and Bryant, the relations concerned were part–part relations. The children were concerned with whether the parts where the same size or one was greater than the other when making their picture-to-box matches. In a later study, Despina Desli (1994) investigated further the role of the half-boundary in quantifying fractions by examining part–whole situations. Her study was carried out in Thessaloniki with children in the age range 6 to 8

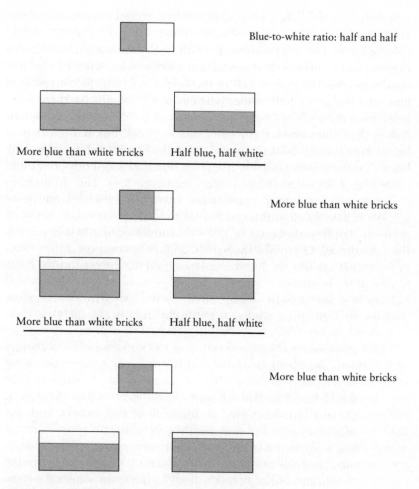

Figure 8.4 The material used to test the importance of the half-boundary in children's judgements about proportions
SOURCE: Spinillo and Bryant (1991)

years, all attending state schools. The children solved a series of items in a new task involving part–whole relations. In this task (briefly described earlier in this chapter, section 1.2), the subjects were told that there were two parties being organized and, in each of the parties, a certain number of chocolate bars would be equally divided among the children attending the party. The task involved judging whether the children in the two parties would receive the same amount of chocolate and, if not, in which party the children would receive more. Three conditions, parallel to those used by Spinillo and Bryant, were created: two conditions where the children could use the half-boundary as a reference to make their judgements (the half and the cross-half items) and one condition where the half-boundary was not a good reference for a correct judgement (the within-half items). A sample item from each of the conditions is presented in figure 8.5; the children in the different parties were represented by cut-out dolls colour-coded by party to facilitate communication and recording of the answers.

The results are briefly summarized here. First, the children at all age levels performed at ceiling level when the half-boundary could be used as a reference for their judgements and made no mistakes. When the half-boundary could not be used as a reference, the percentages of correct responses for the 6-, 7- and 8-year-olds were, respectively, 40, 60 and 75 per cent. Only the 8-year-olds, as a group, performed significantly better than chance level. Thus Desli was able to show that the half-boundary plays an important role in the quantification of part–whole relations, as it does in part–part relations.

These positive results should not lead us to overlook the difficulty of the questions posed to the children: they had to consider what fraction of a chocolate bar would be given to the children in each party and had to do so without any explicitly presented division of the wholes. In all of the problems discussed in this section, both the number of chocolates and the number of children were different across parties. When these two-variable problems were compared to the one-variable problems presented in section 1.2, where either the number of children or the number of chocolates was constant across the parties, the two-variable problems were found to be significantly more difficult as a group, but those involving the half-boundary were not more difficult than the one-variable problems.

An analysis of the pupils' justifications gave further support to the hypothesis that *half* plays a significant role in quantification. This was so *even in the within-half problems* where the children in both parties received more than half a chocolate each – for example, one party had 4 children and 3 chocolate bars and the other party had 8 children and 6 chocolate bars. In these items, two types of reasoning emerged: (1) the mental distribution of half a chocolate to all the children without exhaustive quantification; and (2) the mental distribution of half followed by exhaustive quantification of what had

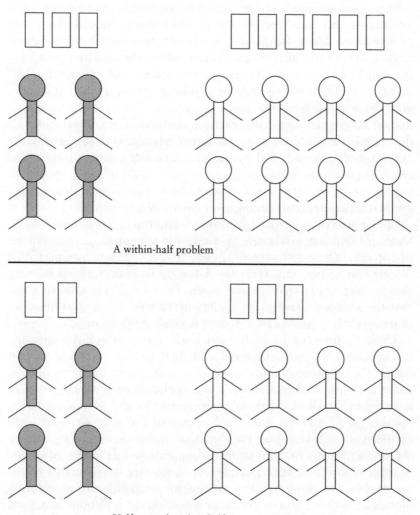

A within-half problem

Half versus less than half

Figure 8.5   The material used to study part–part and part–whole judgements
SOURCE: Desli (1994)

remained. The first of these strategies – distribution of half without exhaustive quantification of the remainder – resulted in wrong conclusions. For example, in an item where 3 chocolates were to be divided among 4 children in the blue party and 6 chocolates would be divided among 8 children in the yellow party, one pupil suggested:

'The yellow group will get more because they will divide each chocolate into two pieces and there will be two remaining chocolates to be divided again. Doing the same in the blue group, there will be only one chocolate left.' The quantification attempted by the child is in terms of half; the remaining portion, which is not enough for half for each child, is not quantified. The second strategy, where the pupils first mentally distributed half and then exhaustively quantified the remainder, led to success. One pupil, for example, suggested: 'All the children will get the same amount of chocolate. They will divide each chocolate in two pieces, and each one will get half. In the blue group there will be one chocolate and in the yellow group there will be two remaining chocolates (to be divided again) because the yellow group has two times more children than the blue group.'

Similar findings for the significance of half in children's reasoning, with and without exhaustive quantification, have been reported by Ball (1993), Kieren (1994) and Lamon (1993).

Summing up: the studies reported in these first two sections indicate that 6- and 7-year-olds start to develop an understanding of the inverse relations between the quotient and the divisor in division situations. They can make judgements using these relations when the dividend consists of both discontinuous and continuous materials, thus showing an emerging knowledge of relations among unit fractions. They can also solve simple quantitative division problems about discontinuous quantities by manipulating concrete materials in ways that require anticipation or structuring of the situation, and go beyond the simple carrying out of routines that may have been observed in everyday life. Finally, these studies indicate a pathway that allows for the first attempts at quantifying splits with continuous quantities: the division of the whole in two parts. When the parts are equal, they can think in terms of equality; when they are different, they can use their understanding of 'greater/smaller than' relations to solve part–part problems. In part–whole problems, not only are children much more successful in solving problems when they can rely on the notion of half but they can also use half to simplify within-half problems and obtain a correct solution through the exhaustive quantification of what remains after half has already been dished out.

In the studies reported so far, we were concerned only with extensive quantities – with sets (that is, whole numbers) and with the extensive aspect of fractions – or, as Kieren (1994) explains, the 'how muchness' of rational numbers. But, as Piaget et al. (1960) pointed out a long time ago, understanding rational numbers depends on coordinating two types of relation: the part–part relations, which are extensive, and the part–whole relations, which are intensive. In the next section, we will turn to the intensive aspect of rational numbers and investigate how the extensive and intensive aspects are related during children's development.

2 Coordinating Extensive and Intensive Aspects of Rational Number: The Understanding of Equivalences in Successive Splits

Piaget et al. (1960) started the investigations about children's understanding of fractions, asking children to divide wholes into equal parts – two, three, four, five and six – and then make judgements about the equivalence of: (1) the whole and the sum of the parts; or (2) two identical wholes that had been divided in different parts. Their hypothesis was that, in order to achieve a division of the whole in equal parts (the extensive aspect of fractions), children need to anticipate what the relation between the parts and the whole will be (the intensive aspect of fractions), and that this anticipation is intrinsically connected to the conservation of the whole irrespective of the divisions it had gone through. These tasks were carried out in the context of giving equal parts of a pretend-chocolate cake to dolls and comparing the sum of the parts to an identical, undivided whole. In the Piagetian studies therefore, the idea of sharing and how much is received by each doll represents the extensive aspect of rational number and the reconstruction of the whole or unit in relation to the parts represents the intensive aspects.

Their findings can be summarized briefly. First, they observed that young children of about 4 and 5 years of age failed in their attempts to divide a whole equally into a prespecified number of parts. They either took two pieces, for example, when asked to divide the whole in two equal parts, and ignored the remainder, or only achieved the division by successive approximations. This failure Piaget et al. attribute to the children's lack of anticipation of the relationship between the parts and the whole. Second, the young children did not show conservation of the whole. When asked whether there was more to eat in the cake that had not been cut, or in the one that had been cut up, or whether there was the same amount to eat in both, the children would deny the equivalence of the wholes. It was only when they achieved the conservation of the whole, at about 6 or 7 years, that they also became able to anticipate the relationship between the parts and the whole and accomplished its division into a predetermined number of parts that were approximately equal. These findings led Piaget and his colleagues to conclude that the understanding of fractions is intimately connected with the understanding of the conservation of the whole.

Piaget's work dealt only with continuous quantities. Mauricio Lima (1982), working with Brazilian children, replicated and expanded Piaget's investigations by having children work both with discontinuous and with continuous quantities, and asking them equivalence questions in which the researcher himself split the sets or areas in order to ensure that an accurate division had been carried out. Lima had three goals in his study: (1) to investigate the children's ability to compare parts of the same whole (extensive aspect) without perceptual support, based only on the process of division (intensive aspect); (2) to investigate children's understanding of equivalences when the parts were different in size and in number (for example, 1/2 and 2/4); and (3) to contrast the children's performance in the division of sets with their performance in tasks about fractions of continuous quantities.

The division of discontinuous quantities involved a series of comparisons starting from two sets of marbles with the same number of elements that were put into small white cups by the children. The children knew the number of elements in the cups at the start; they could not see the marbles after they had been put into the cups but were allowed to look in if they wished. After the children had verified that the number of elements was the same in the two cups, one set was divided into two, with the marbles being placed in two blue cups. The children were then asked to compare the marbles in both blue cups with those in the white cup which contained the undivided set. In the next task, the undivided set was now divided into two cups, and then these sets divided again into two, each of the fourths being placed in a red cup. Finally, the children were asked to compare the subsets contained in one blue and one red cup, and then one blue and two red cups. After the comparison questions, the children were asked to justify their answers and also asked how many cups of each of the colours under consideration were needed to form a whole collection.

A similar set of tasks was posed in the context of continuous

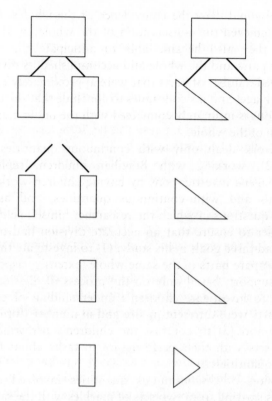

Figure 8.6   The material used to study division of continuous quantity
SOURCE: Lima (1982)

quantities. There were two initial, identical wholes, which were subsequently divided according to the schema presented in figure 8.6. In contrast to the discontinuous quantities, the continuous quantities were always visually presented to the children, but this did not make the situation easier because the parts, although representing the result of the same process of division, were perceptually distinct. The questions posed to the children were formally parallel across the contents being divided so that any differences in performance could be attributed to the difference between discontinuous and continuous quantities.

Lima presented the children also with further 2-splits of the original sets/wholes and another series of situations where 2-splits and 3-splits were the original splits; the 3-split was followed by a 2-split so that comparisons between 1/2 and 1/3 and then between 1/2 and 3/6 were carried out (other divisions were also used; for a complete description, see Lima, 1982).

Lima worked with Brazilian children in the approximate age range 7 to 13 years. The use of fractional language is introduced in grades 3 or 4 in school (ages 10 to 11); equivalence of fractions is taught in grades 5 or 6 (ages 12 to 13). Results in terms of age levels, therefore, will not be comparable to those obtained in Geneva by Piaget and his collaborators; the focus of interest will be in the processes leading to the understanding of equivalences.

With respect to comparisons involving the same fractions of the whole, Lima observed the following:

1   younger children (7/8 years) were easily misled by the appearance of the parts of the continuous quantities and denied the equivalence of different-looking halves of the same whole;

2   these children did not show conservation of the whole when it had been divided into different parts, and denied that two halves and four quarters would form the same whole.

Slightly older children already succeeded in judging the equivalence of two halves that looked different and of two wholes divided into a different number of parts. They justified their judgements of the equality of two different looking halves through reference to the whole (for example, Germana said: 'You cut both in two and you didn't take anything away').

With respect to equivalence of different fractions of the whole, the results were the following:

1   younger children were impressed by the number of parts or the number of cups (with discontinuous quantities) and denied the equivalences;

2   slightly older children (8/9 years) were able to overcome these difficulties in the simpler equivalence tasks (1/2 and 2/4) where the original splits were a 2- and a 4-split (a 4-split was easily converted into two 2-splits by children); they clearly justified their answers by relating the parts to the original whole, but they had difficulty when the original splits were unrelated to each other (that is, when the original splits were a 2- and a 3-split, respectively);

3   the oldest children in the study (11/12 years) were able to deal with complex equivalences where the original splits were not multiplicatively related; they justified their responses in terms of the relations between the parts and the wholes and were systematically correct in indicating how many parts were needed to form the whole.

Thus, Lima's results confirmed and extended the Piagetian work by showing that the equivalence of perceptually dissimilar parts and of different fractions – the extensive aspect of fractions – was understood by the children in connection with their analysis of the part–whole relations – the intensive aspect.

Finally, Lima also found that the division of discontinuous quantities was understood earlier than the division of continuous wholes. These results could reflect a genuine difference across contents but could also be an artefact of Lima's method. The methodological problem was the following: when the children worked with sets, the use of colours to code how many parts the whole had been divided into might have helped the children in reconstructing the part–whole relations. However, this interpretation seems unlikely because Lima indicated that the younger children, who did not succeed, paid no attention to the colour of the cups. It was only the children who were seeking to understand the part–whole relations who were able to use the colour of the cups to relate the subset to the whole; for these children, the colour of the cups was significant, whereas for the younger children it was meaningless.

The genuine difference between discontinuous and continuous quantities that we expect to have an effect on performance in these tasks is as follows: the children in the study were already quite familiar with numbers and could use numbers to support their conclusions about the part–part and part–whole comparisons, especially because the number of elements in the original sets was small (12, 24, 32 and 40 in different situations). Lima's examples of the justifications offered by children in the discontinuous quantities tasks often include references to numbers. For example, Jadilson (7 years) correctly compares half-to-half answering that they are the same because each cup has 6 marbles; one of the half-cups is then divided into two quarters and Jadilson correctly compares 1/2 and 2/4; when asked to justify his answer, he indicates 'I have 6 and you have 6'. He persists on his judgement of equality even after the interviewer makes a counter-suggestion by reference to the number of cups. Thus the use of the number of marbles in discontinuous quantities allows for the solution in this case of simple equivalence whereas in the context of continuous quantities no such support is available.

To sum up, the results we have reviewed so far are quite consistent in terms of the developmental pathway they indicate for the understanding of rational numbers. Rational numbers seem to be understood as the result of splitting wholes that are made up of continuous quantities. Children's understanding of relations in rational numbers – such as the inverse relation between the number of parts and their size – appears to be developed in parallel with their understanding of the inverse relation between the divisor and the quotient in the division of whole numbers (although studies with direct comparisons are still lacking). These are rather early accomplishments and seem to emerge at about the age of 6 or 7 years.

Another logical relation understood by young children appears to be used at about the same time in the beginnings of quantification of rational numbers: the part–part relations expressed by 'equal to' and 'greater than'. By establishing part–part comparisons, children can build an initial understanding of half on the basis of these relations. The notion of half appears to offer the opportunity for the development of an initial connection between the extensive and the intensive aspects that characterize rational numbers.

Subsequent developments consist of a progressive strengthening of this coordination between extensive and intensive aspects, which allows older children to define fractions in terms of the divisions of the whole through which they were produced and recognize complex equivalences.

We have painted a rather optimistic picture of pupils' understanding of rational numbers in light of the work reviewed in the two previous sections. However, this contrasts strongly with what we wrote in the beginning of this chapter, when we pointed out weaknesses in the knowledge of equivalence and use of fractional language of 12-year-olds. A rather negative picture was also painted, for example, by Hart (1986) with respect to equivalence of fractions, and Kerslake (1986), with respect to the ordering of fractions. Hart described how pupils could only produce their own diagrams to study the equivalence of fractions if they had already realized that the fractions were equivalent before producing the diagram. Kerslake pointed out 12/14-year-old pupils' difficulties in ordering fractions and indicating their position on a number line: in the latter task, only one of the 15 pupils interviewed could correctly place 2/3 and three of 15 could correctly place 1/2 on a number line.

How can these two series of contradictory findings be reconciled? In the next section, we will discuss the role of systems of signs in children's problem-solving activity with rational numbers; we believe that these contradictions involve the disconnection between children's understanding of situations and their learning of fractions in school.

3   Connecting Rational Numbers with Their Representation: Knowledge of Rational Numbers Developed In and Out of School

There is clearly a gap between children's understanding of basic properties of rational numbers in the studies described above and children's success in rational number tasks solved in the context of educational assessments. One possible explanation for this gap would be sampling: perhaps studies such as those described above were carried out with selected samples which do not cover the whole gamut of levels of mathematical understanding of pupils in the age levels described. We find this explanation implausible because the studies reviewed above included samples from state schools in Oxford, Greece and in north-eastern Brazil (a rather poor region of the country).

A second explanation is that, when the children solve experimental tasks about division and rational numbers, they engage in reasoning about the situations. In contrast, when they solve mathematical tasks in educational assessments, they view the situation as one in which they need to think of what operations to do with numbers, how to use what they have been taught in school; by concentrating on symbol manipulations, the pupils might perform at a lower level than they would have performed if they had focused more on the problem situation. It is thus possible that the same pupils engaged in reasoning tasks similar to those described previously, where they can focus well on the problem situation, perform rather differently when they are solving problems in written educational assessments: their perform-ance shows a gap between what they understand and what they can do with the symbols after these have been learned in a particular way.

This second hypothesis is supported in a study by Nancy Mack (1993) with sixth grade students in the United States. Her technique consisted of presenting the same problems to the children alternately as situations that they might encounter in everyday life and then as symbolic problems, or vice versa. For example, a question like 'suppose you have two pizzas of the same size, and you cut one of them into six equal-size pieces and you cut the other one into eight equal-size pieces. If you get one piece from each pizza, which one do you get more from?' was followed by the question 'tell me which fraction is bigger, 1/6 or 1/8?' Mack observed that, although the everyday life problems did not appear to cause difficulty, the students could not solve many of the problems presented symbolically, and justified their responses through faulty algorithms or inadequate comparisons. For example, in the problem above, all but one student said that 1/8 was bigger because eight is a bigger number.

But how is this curious gap produced between children's understanding of rational numbers and their performance in the symbolic tasks? One possibility is that symbolic tasks somehow require a different sort of knowledge, more abstract than the sort mastered by the pupils. But an alternative hypothesis, which we take to be more plausible, is that this gap is a consequence of the pupils' learning of fractional language in school simply through the double-counting procedure we described earlier. The disconnection between pupils' understanding of division of discontinuous and continuous quantities developed out of school and their learning of fractions might come about exactly because pupils do not think of fractions as having anything to do with division, and only relate fractions with part–whole language. Evidence supporting this idea was found by Kerslake (1986), who summarized her findings in the assessment of pupils' performance in fractions tasks thus (1986, p. 41):

> There was considerable evidence to suggest that the only model of fraction with which children felt comfortable was that of fraction as part of a whole. In particular, they found it difficult even to extend this view to indicate the division or sharing aspect: that is, for example, that the fraction a/b can be interpreted as 'a' things shared between 'b' people. Although this aspect appears in textbooks or work-card-based courses, and is the basis for the method commonly used to turn fractions to decimals, pupils were very reluctant to acknowledge any connections between a/b and a ÷ b.

Further evidence supporting this hypothesis is provided by Mack (1993). If the disconnection between children's understanding of division and fraction developed outside school and the symbolic representations learned in school is due to the way in which the school learning was implemented, it should be possible to bridge this gap: by moving back and forth between their knowledge developed outside school and the symbolic representations, pupils should come to realize what connections have to be made. This is exactly what Mack reports (1993, p. 96):

> I found that by moving back and forth between problems represented symbolically and similar problems presented in familiar contexts, students began to relate fraction symbols and procedures to their informal knowledge. At times students required that we move back and forth between problems presented in different contexts several times before they recognized the connections, whereas at other times the connections were readily recognized. After a relatively short period of instruction in this manner, students were drawing on their informal knowledge on their own initiative to solve more complex but closely related problems.

Mack's results are significant – but could the gap not be avoided in the first place? And how should instruction proceed so that pupils' learning of the symbolic representations of rational numbers is connected from the start with their understanding of situations?

There are currently several voices in the mathematics education community which suggest that we need to avoid this gap by choosing the right instruction situations. Streefland (1990b; forthcoming) and Gravemeijer (forthcoming) have suggested that the key to the development of symbolic representations in close connection with the children's understanding of division situations and fractions is to work clearly with situations that involve *two variables* and offer the children the means of representing both of them. Instead of simply depicting one pizza that is cut into pieces and then teaching the pupils the fractional language, it is necessary to pose problems where two variables are concerned and must be represented.

Gravemeijer (1990; forthcoming) offers some examples of how this can be accomplished in the division of discontinuous quantities into subsets. In one of his problems, the children have to figure out how many tables will be needed so that all the parents can sit down at a meeting; 86 parents are expected and 6 parents can be seated around each table. The pupils who solved his problem were clearly used to working with diagrams in order to depict the situation; they represented both the tables (for example, with small rectangles) and the parents in order to solve the problem.

Streefland (1990a and b; forthcoming) offers an example in the context of the division of continuous quantities: 4 children have to share 3 bars of chocolate; how much will each child get? The children and the bars of chocolate are schematically presented (as in the study by Desli (1994) described in section 1 of this chapter but through drawings rather than cut-out figures). Different solutions are reported for the problem 3 ÷ 4 – that is, 3/4. One pupil might divide each chocolate bar in 4 pieces and give 3 of these pieces to each child (that is, each child gets 1/4 + 1/4 + 1/4). Another pupil might divide two chocolate bars in half and give a half to each child and then divide the third bar in quarters, giving one quarter to each child (that is, each child get 1/2 + 1/4). Streefland suggests that, if the children are encouraged to discuss and compare their solutions, they will come to recognize the equivalence of their procedures and connect their understanding with the teacher-introduced fractional language representations.

Streefland further suggests that successive splits can be used to help the pupils coordinate the extensive and intensive aspect of rational numbers. For example, the following problem is suggested: 24 children go into a pizzeria together for a party and order 18 pizzas; however, they cannot all sit around the same table; how should the children and the pizzas be re-arranged so that the distribution of pizzas is fair? The pupils can try different arrangements: if they used 2 tables, there will be 12 children and 9 pizzas on each; if they use 3 tables, there should be 8 children and 6 pizzas on each; if they use 4 tables, with 6 children at each, they will need to cut some of the pizzas in half to have $4\frac{1}{2}$ pizzas on each table. When the pupils try to figure out what portion each child will get, they have further interesting problems to confront to see whether they had in fact carried out a fair distribution.

These are clearly important suggestions and seem worth pursuing in view of all the research that we have reviewed. However, there is still a need for more systematic research before it is possible to reach empirically supported conclusions on the significance of the different changes that can be made to the instructional processes. For example, we need to find out how crucial the systems of representation offered to children during problem-solving in division and rational number situations are in terms of their effects on pupils' performance.

Gravemeijer (1990) suggested that if pupils are offered concrete materials in order to solve division problems, it may be crucial to consider what materials are offered and their use in problem-solving. Division problems involve two variables and a relation between them. If the children are offered only one type of concrete material – for example, Dienes blocks – the links between the materials and the results might be confusing for the children. In a quotative problem, for example, where the children are asked 'How many crates are necessary to hold 89 bottles if each crate can hold 16 bottles?', the children may count out 89 blocks, each block standing for a bottle. They will then make groups of 16, and find out that they can make 5 groups. Each group of blocks now represents one crate and the remaining 8 blocks represent 8 bottles. He suggests that this might confuse the children: if we want to support the children's reasoning, a two-variable problem must be solved with the support of materials that allow the children to keep both variables in mind.

Some evidence to support this claim was found by Marilyn Zweng (1964), working with second-grade children in California. She gave the children both partitive and quotative problems (which she refers to as 'measurement'). For some problems, the children only had one set of objects to represent the variable on which computations were required; for a second set of problems, they had two sets of objects so that they could represent both variables when solving the problems. In the case of both sets, each set could be randomly spread on the table (random arrays) or they were patterned, organized in rows with rough correspondences across sets. For example, a problem might involve dividing a set of 15 pencils in groups of three, and each group of three was to be placed into a box. For a one variable representation, Zweng only gave the children some pencils to use when working out the answer. For a two variable representation, the children had both pencils and boxes. In the random array, both sets were just spread about on the table; for the patterned array, the pencils were placed in a row and the boxes in another, parallel row. Zweng observed a significant association between success in the task and type of material available to the children during problem solving: the problems for which the children had two sets of materials were solved by a significantly higher percentage of children. However, this was only true for the partitive problems. The difference between the random and the patterned arrays did not affect the children's performance: they were just as successful with random as with patterned arrays. However, it must be noted that the numbers used in the problem situations were rather small. Although this is an important result, further research is needed for the investigation of the consequences of using one or two variable representations for children's success in problem solving about division and rational number situation.

4   Conclusions

Carpenter et al. (1993) suggested that there are (at least) two unifying elements that provide coherence to the great variety of uses of rational number: they are the notions of unit and partitioning. The research reviewed in this chapter reinforces their conclusion in a new way. We suggest that these two elements are not independent in the development of children's understanding: they involve the extensive and intensive aspects of rational numbers. Whereas the reasoning related to partitioning allows the children to approach the 'how muchness' of rational number – that is, the extensive aspect – the understanding of the equivalence of different splits can only be accomplished in reference to the whole or a unit – that is, by considering the intensive aspects.

In this chapter we saw how quite young children can already deal successfully with some aspects of the extensive aspects of partitioning: 6/7-year-old children understand the effect of the size of n on an n-split. They can succeed in problems that involve discontinuous or continuous quantities.

We also saw how the first quantifications they accomplish in this domain seem to emerge in tasks where the notion of half can be used. Half plays a central role in the process of quantification because it offers the children the opportunity to use logical relations that they already understand in part–part comparisons ('equal to' or 'greater than') in the new domain of part–whole: they can easily distinguish between half, more than half, and less than half. But young children can also be misled in their extensive comparisons by perceptual aspects: if confronted with two different-looking halves, they might not realize their equivalence. It is only by referring back to the whole through the reconstruction of the splitting process that they will understand the equivalence of these different-looking halves.

Finally, the discrepancy between children's understanding of division and rational numbers outside school and their knowledge of school-taught representations was considered. At present, a plausible explanation for this gap is that it might stem from the way in which fractional language is introduced: as a simple double-counting procedure in part–whole static situations. When pupils are brought to solve problems successfully using their everyday knowledge and symbolic representations, they can make the adequate connections spontaneously over a relatively short period of instruction and can use their everyday knowledge in solving more complex problems. Current approaches to establishing a connection between everyday and school knowledge of fractions indicate a different starting-point for instruction: rather than learning fractional language in connection with static part–whole representations, pupils should be engaged in solving division problems with continuous quantities, where both variables are explicitly represented, the quantity to be shared and the number of recipients. If fractional representation is introduced in this way, it is expected that the children will come to see the connection between their knowledge from outside school and the symbols they learn in school. This seems a rather promising route but one which needs to be verified through further research in the future.

9
Conclusions

Children's mathematical development is a rich subject and full of all kinds of interesting, but at times quite complex, puzzles and surprises. One should expect this: after all children have to come to terms with a large number of new concepts and new symbols and have to learn how and when to use them in a wide range of very different situations. So books about children's mathematics are bound to have their complexities, and readers always run the risk of being overwhelmed by detail.

But this is a problem that disappears when a simple theoretical framework can be found to organize and explain all these details. The main aim of our book has been to present a framework of this sort. We have tried to show how an extraordinary range of facts about children's growing mathematical knowledge can be explained by a theory which has just three main parts to it.

One is that children's understanding of mathematical concepts is generative and changes time and time again during childhood. These are basic premises of Piaget's theory and we believe that there is much evidence to support them. To say that knowledge is generative means that children do not need to learn every single bit of mathematics that they will need to know. If they understand how mathematical knowledge is structured, they can generate knowledge that they have not learned. To say that children's understanding of each mathematical concept changes many times during childhood means that the acquisition of mathematical knowledge is never an all-or-none affair. In every mathematical concept that we have looked at it has been possible to point to evidence that children have some understanding of it at an early age – often long before they go to school – and also that this understanding changes many times in many ways as they grow older.

The second part of our theory, which follows the pioneering ideas of Gerard Vergnaud, is that there are three quite different facets of mathematical concepts, and that all of mathematical development is the product of changes in one, or two or of all three of them. Children learn about logical invariants in mathematics: they learn about conventional mathematical systems: they learn about the mathematical demands of different situations. Although these facets of mathematical concepts are independent of each other, they do not exist on their own. Children come to understand invariants in situations and use symbols to represent the situations and the invariants to themselves so that they can reason about them. In order to solve problems, the problem situations must be represented. The representations may vary – they may be manipulatives, oral or written symbols, diagrams or graphs – but some system of signs is used as a tool for thinking. The representation of invariants may be implicit – as in theorems in action, which are implicit in the way that we organize our problem-solving activities – or they may be explicit and possible to state in words. These variations show that representations are an independent facet in concepts, but invariants and problem situations must be represented. Similarly, invariants and situations cannot be reduced to each other: one invariant may be central to many situations and the same situation may include different invariants. Thus in our efforts to understand conceptual change in mathematics we will always need to consider these three facets of mathematical concepts.

The third part of our theory is that mathematics is a socially defined activity and that children's social representations of mathematics have a significant impact on the way that they approach problems. The way in which we behave in a socially defined situation is intrinsically related to how we define the situation and ourselves in that situation in the first place (note that the word situations here refers to social situations; we follow the usage of terms although we recognize the possibility of confusion). We saw that children may define situations which involve the same mathematical reasoning so differently that they may not look like the same children across the different social situations: in one they will not engage in thinking but try to remember rules whereas in the other situation they may use their reasoning fully. The street vendors in our studies (Nunes, Schliemann and Carraher, 1993), just as the Pittsburgh youngsters in the study about rational numbers by Mack (1993), clearly had developed social definitions of mathematics in the classroom that interfered with their use of their own good sense when solving problems presented as mathematical tasks. People's ideas (or, more technically speaking, social representations) of what mathematics is include notions about which system of signs to use and what form the solution should have. Children's ideas about what mathematics is, like mathematical understanding, develop as children grow up. As they learn mathematics in school, some forms of mathematical knowledge are validated, others are excluded. Pupils seem to form ideas about how good they are in maths not solely (or perhaps not mostly) on the basis of what they can do in maths but on their ability to use the socially approved solutions. They can solve problems and at the same time deny their own ability to solve those same problems.

The three parts of our theory are not at all separate. In fact it is fair to say that the first two parts are clearly interconnected: the second part largely accounts for the first. Each of the many changes in children's understanding of particular mathematical concepts is due to changes in one or other of the three facets of mathematical concepts that we discussed or to some interactions between them. We have tried to show in the preceding chapters how this is so, and in this chapter we will bring the evidence together in an overview of the studies we reviewed. The third part of the theory offers a great challenge: if we want to understand *children doing mathematics* we have to understand what it is that children think mathematics is and how they solve problems that we think are mathematical. The challenge is to put it all together because what we define as mathematical knowledge is not the same thing that children define as mathematical knowledge. We are trying to work from a somewhat fixed conception of mathematical knowledge developed in interaction with one community – namely that of psychologists – and children are developing their conception of mathematics under the strong (but not exclusive) influence of teachers and schools. While we recognize the limitations of what can be accomplished, we still want to try to integrate the three aspects by pointing out examples of situations where children's representations of mathematics lead them astray.

1   Starting with the Beginning

We start with the beginning of children's understanding of mathematical concepts. The first point to make about these beginnings is that they are early: take any mathematical concept taught in primary school, and you will find that children have some understanding of this concept before they are taught about it formally. This understanding is often fragmentary and limited, and it can lead children into error in some situations. Nevertheless it is genuine in the sense that in every case the child understands something about the relations involved in the concept and can apply this understanding logically. We suggest that these early understandings should be viewed as a basis for children to learn more about mathematical concepts. We will recall four examples.

The first is about comparing the amount of objects in different sets. Before children are able to count out two sets of objects in order to compare them, they already have a logical way of constructing two equal sets by sharing. The use of one-to-one correspondence by 4-year-olds in sharing might be restricted to building equal sets – they may not be very good at comparing sets, for example – but they can build equal sets if they themselves construct the two sets from the beginning. They can accomplish this without counting and a long time before they are able to use the number system to compare sets. Of course, they will be able to make more comparisons, and to make them more reliably, once they realize that number can be used as a measure. But the point that we are making here is that children already have some understanding of the components that are needed to compare number when they begin to learn how to use number as an intervening measure. They do not learn to count in a vacuum, and their eventual success in using number as a measure is not just the result of their being taught to count. There is something there to start with – in this case some understanding of one-to-one correspondence in sharing.

Our second example is about inferences and measurement. In order to use a ruler, children must understand and must be able to make transitive inferences (A = B, B = C : A = C). Otherwise they will have no idea of the role of an intervening measure (B, in this example) and will not know why rulers and other measures can be used to compare different quantities. Of course, there is more to understand about measurement than this basic logical relation: children also have to come to grips with the nature of conventional measurement systems. But the logic is important and the data that we discussed in chapter 4 demonstrate quite clearly that young children do understand it well and can use it to advantage to solve simple measurement problems some time before they are formally taught about measurement.

For our third example of some early but incomplete understanding of mathematical concepts, we turn to division. Division is certainly difficult for young children. Yet our work has shown that even quite young children have a reasonable idea of the relations involved in dividing. At the age of about 7 years, before they have received any systematic teaching about division, they already have a clear idea of the relations that are involved in dividing. They understand, for example, that there is an inverse relationship between the number of divisors and the size of the quotient. Our evidence suggests that this understanding cannot be taken as obvious. Younger children do not seem to know about this inverse relationship, and many of them will actually tell you that the opposite is true: the greater the number of divisors, the larger the quotient. So children acquire the inverse principle apparently without the help of formal instruction, and this new knowledge should, in principle, help them to understand what is going on when they are formally taught how to divide.

Our fourth and final example (although we could cite many others) concerns multiplication. Multiplicative reasoning, as we have seen, poses some formidable problems for children. Yet here too, quite early on, children possess and use a form of thinking about multiplicative problems which is actually quite effective in solving some, though not all, such problems. They understand one-to-many correspondence quite well and they often use it effectively to solve multiplicative problems. In fact whether or not children succeed in multiplicative problems usually depends directly on the extent to which the problem is amenable to the strategies connected with one-to-many correspondence situations. For example, 9-year-olds were likely to be able to answer how many different outfits can be made by changing around four different t-shirts and six different shorts *if they realized that a one-to-many correspondence strategy could be used here*. Each t-shirt can be combined with six shorts, resulting in six different outfits (1-to-6 correspondence): therefore 4 t-shirts will allow for 4×6 different outfits.

Our main point about these early forms of knowledge is that they are there and should be respected. It is probably not an overstatement to say that whenever children are taught a mathematical concept, they already know something about it before the teaching starts. The teacher should surely take this early knowledge into account and build on it, and that is one reason why it is important to know exactly what children already understand about mathematical concepts at the time that they start being taught about them.

But there is another reason for paying particular attention to the beginnings of mathematical knowledge. Once we have established these starting-points we will be in a much better position to describe the actual form of mathematical development. We have already mentioned our conclusion that the knowledge that children start out with is impressive, but incomplete. We do not hold with the extreme view that all mathematical principles are understood by children from the outset and they just need to learn the skills to put the principles into practice. The evidence that we have reviewed in this book shows that young children start with an understanding of some principles but not of others. They start with fragments, but can we say anything else about this beginning knowledge except that it is fragmentary?

The four examples that we have given do suggest a pattern to this early mathematical knowledge. In each of the four cases the children show an impressive understanding of simple relations, and yet seem to be quickly thrown off their balance when numerical values are introduced. Sharing on a 'one-for-you, one-for-me' basis is a relational strategy *par excellence*. If that is all you do, you will end up knowing that the two recipients have the same number of objects as each other, but you will have no way of knowing the actual number in each set. In fact, as we have seen, children are in difficulty as soon as comparisons between sets do involve actual numbers. It takes them a surprisingly long time to understand how numbers can be used to make comparisons.

The same point can be made about inferences and measurement. Transitive inferences tell you about the relations between three quantities, but nothing about their absolute values. You can be sure in the end that A = C even when you have never been able to compare the two directly, but that says nothing about how large these two quantities are. Once again young children are proficient at making judgements about logical relations, but fall into error when these have to be translated into units of measurement, as the data that we reviewed in chapter 4 demonstrate quite dramatically.

With division, too, we found that children do have an initial understanding of the relations involved before they have learned how to solve division sums. Their understanding of the inverse relation between the divisor and the quotient initially seems to be quite specific: it is much easier for them to apply it to partitive than to quotative tasks. We shall return to this particular difference later in this chapter, but we mention it in a preliminary way here as a reminder that the subsequent development of children's mathematical knowledge does not always take the form of learning how to apply relational knowledge to the number system. Young children's reasoning about division does change in this way, but it also changes when children apply this reasoning to a wider range of situations.

The observation that mathematical development does not just take the form of initial relational understanding followed by learning how to cope with absolute values applies even more strongly to the question of multiplication. Here we can see that young children's initial reasoning is based on relations, but that they start with a good understanding of some relations but not of others.

The relation which they thoroughly understand at the time that they begin to be taught about multiplication is, in our view, genuinely multiplicative. One-to-many correspondence is a perfectly respectable way of solving some multiplication problems but, for the reasons that we gave in chapter 7, children need to understand other relations as well. Unless they understand and use functional relations, many multiplicative problems will be beyond them. The evidence demonstrates conclusively that, to start with, children find functional relations quite difficult: in fact one of the most important changes in children's multiplicative reasoning is their eventual mastery of functional relations. Of course, this is not the only development: children also have to learn how to deal with a new type of number, rational numbers, and that, as we saw in chapter 8, also causes them some difficulty.

These examples demonstrate that the starting-point in the development of any mathematical concepts is always the same. The first step that children take is to understand some of the basic relations that are part of the concept. The subsequent development varies a great deal from one concept to another, and depends on the nature of the concept, the situations in which children use it, and the conventional systems that they have to learn about. But children always start with simple relations and can reason about these relations logically and effectively.

2   Logical Invariants

We were actually saying something controversial when we argued just now that in some cases mathematical development takes the form of children learning about new relations. For, if true, this means that logical development plays an important part in the growth of children's mathematical knowledge. This is a familiar idea, but one that is heavily disputed nowadays.

It was, of course, a central idea of Piaget's that all the important changes in children's mathematical reasoning depend on logical changes: the child must acquire the necessary logical understanding in order to be able to count, measure, add, multiply and divide, and that, according to Piaget, is virtually all that the child needs to do to become mathematical. Piaget's view is an extreme one, and those who dispute it nowadays for the most part counter it with the opposite extreme – the claim that there is no such thing as logical development.

Our own position is different. Vergnaud's theory of three facets of mathematical concepts, which we have used here, means of course that we cannot agree that all of a child's mathematical development is paced by logical change. The weakness, as we see it, of Piaget's account of children's mathematics is that he had little interest in conventional systems, and that he had no coherent way of explaining why children often use their understanding of logical invariants in one situation and yet completely ignore these invariants in another situation where they are also central. However, we do agree with Piaget's general claim (though not with some of the details) that children's logical understanding changes radically between the ages of 5 and 15 years, and that some of these changes have a considerable effect on their mathematical understanding.

This puts us at odds with those who dispute the very phenomenon of logical development. We have not enough space in this chapter to review the evidence on which the claim against logical development is made, but anyway we think that we do not need to write this review. The claim against logical development rests on arguments about experimental tasks, such as the well-known conservation task, which are not part of the evidence that we have marshalled. On the other hand, we have presented data on children's performance in other tasks which seem to us to be directly related to mathematical reasoning, and we have argued that these data really do show considerable changes in children's abilities to think about and manipulate logical relations.

We will briefly remind you about some of our main examples without describing the actual evidence again. One clear example is the developmental changes in children's understanding of correspondence. Preschool children understand one-to-one correspondence quite well in the context of sharing, but for quite some time they fail to grasp its spatial equivalent – spatial one-to-one correspondence – as well. When they conquer one-to-one correspondence in its spatial form, there are still restrictions in the connections that they can establish between one-to-one correspondence and other logical relations. There are still some years to go before they can realize, for example, that, if three sets of flowers are each in one-to-one correspondence with one set of vases, then there is a three-to-one correspondence between flowers and vases. Of course, as we have already remarked in this chapter, this is not the end of the story, since there is still an appreciable gap between understanding one-to-many correspondence and the time when children eventually come to grips with functional relations.

The point that we want to make is that this is a sequence in which children's understanding of logical relations *per se* changes several times over with time. It is very difficult on the basis of the evidence that we have reviewed to think of any other explanation of the underlying changes here. There are, it seems, some logical relations which children understand quite easily and others which cause them more difficulty.

Much the same can be said about addition and subtraction. That adding to a quantity has the effect of increasing it and subtracting the effect of decreasing the quantity is something that young children easily understand. These relations might seem elementary but they are logical invariants of very great importance in mathematical reasoning, and it is impressive to find that they cause young children so little difficulty. But it is not enough just to understand these invariants. The child also has to realize that the two operations cancel each other out. Unless they grasp this inverse relationship they will be completely lost in any task which requires them to figure out the starting-point of a transformation, a point we examined in chapter 6. This understanding also develops, and it is another example of logical development which directly affects children's mathematical understanding.

It is, we should add, an aspect of logical development which played a central part in Piaget's own theory: he was the first to argue that children do not at first appreciate the relation between addition and subtraction, and he pointed out the consequences for the understanding of the additive composition of number. We saw in chapter 3 that there is a clear connection between addition and children's understanding of the decimal structure of the numeration system.

We conclude that logical development does influence the course of children's mathematical understanding. It is a significant influence, but not in our view the only one. There are other aspects to consider.

3 Using Logic in Different Situations: The Acquisition of New Number Meanings

Our book is full of examples of children using a particular logical relation to solve problems in one situation but not in another where the logical relation could be used. In fact much of the evidence that we have dealt with takes this form in one way or another. That is not surprising because this kind of evidence plays a very important role in research on mathematical development in general.

This sort of evidence is important because it can tell us one of two rather different things about children's mathematics. One reason for children succeeding in one task but not in the other is that, as far as the child is concerned, the situations are mathematically different and call on different logical invariants, despite the fact that on the surface they appear to most adults to be mathematically equivalent. By observing children in different situations we are reminded of distinctions that might seem superficial, but are not. For example, a quotative and a partitive problem might seem to us much the same thing but, as we have seen, to children they seem different: the actions they need to carry out when manipulating concrete representations of the objects in a problem situation are quite different when the problem is a partitive and when it is a quotative one. This difference in the manipulation of objects is indicative of a parallel difference in the operations of thought that are needed to connect the particular task with the logical relations that the child understands.

The other reason why children manage well in one task and poorly in a closely similar one is that the same logical relation might be connected to a new number meaning in a different situation. Let us return briefly to fact that children solve addition and subtraction problems which involve change quite easily. They also construct equal sets by one-to-one correspondence very early on. However, they have difficulty with comparison problems, which do not involve any other logical relations than the ones they already know. In comparison problems, children have to deal with a new meaning for number: number as a measure of static relations. But they do not grasp the connection between correspondence and measuring a static relation between sets: they do not take the number of elements without correspondence to be the value of the difference between the sets. That makes the problem 'Fred has 8 apples and Bob has 5. How many more apples does Fred have than Bob?' relatively hard. In contrast equalizing problems, which do not involve new number meanings, are relatively easy: 'Fred has 8 apples and Bob has 5. How many more do I have to give Bob so that he has the same as Fred?' only involves number meanings that children master when they first understand number as a measure of set size (through the logic of one-to-one correspondence) and as a measure of transformations (through the logic of addition/subtraction).

4 Logic and Conventional Systems

Much more attention has been given to the logic of mathematics than to conventional mathematical systems by people doing research on mathematical development. The relative neglect of conventional systems is a pity because what little we do know suggests that they play an important part in children's mathematical thinking. In particular, there is a rather subtle relationship between children's logical development and their knowledge of these conventional systems. This relationship is so important that it is actually impossible for us to understand the connection between logical and mathematical development without also knowing about children's acquaintance with conventional mathematical systems.

Children's logical skills are linked to their learning about conventional systems in three ways. One is, so to speak, a negative link. The state of a child's logical abilities sometimes holds back the learning of a conventional system: if the child has not developed an understanding of this or that logical relation, it is sometimes impossible for him or her to learn a particular conventional system. Our main example of this was about children's difficulties with the written numeration system. The mistakes that they make, we argued, are often caused by their not yet understanding the additive composition of number. It is easy to see that the hierarchy of units contained within tens, tens contained within hundreds, hundreds within thousands, and so on, demands an understanding of additive composition, and the data that we have presented show that children need to understand about additive composition in order to master the Hindu-Arabic system we use for writing numbers. If this particular link seems obvious to you, it is worth remembering that other researchers, such as Luria (1969), have suggested exactly the opposite: that we come to understand additive composition from learning to write numbers.

This so-called negative link can also take another form, one that Piaget drew attention to quite early on: it is possible to learn a conventional system but not know what it is for. This is his argument that children count at first without understanding what counting is for. Because they are incapable yet of making cardinal comparisons, they don't know when to use counting.

The second link that we make between children's logical development and their understanding of conventional systems is, on the other hand, inspired by the work of Vygotsky. It is that mastering a conventional system invariably makes it possible for children to be more effective and thus to put their logic to greater use. This is exactly what Vygotsky (1978) had in mind when he talked about cultural tools. There can be no doubt at all of the advantages which come with learning the decimal notation system, learning new measurement systems, and learning a notation for rational numbers – to stay with examples presented in this book. All of them depend on the child having a sufficient logical understanding, but all of them, too, allow the child to take greater advantage of his or her logic.

The third link between children's logical abilities and their experiences with conventional systems is the most speculative of the three. It seems likely to us that, in some cases, particular ways of using systems of signs can actually promote conceptual development by establishing a bridge between logical relations that the child understands and new ones, not yet mastered. Unfortunately, there is little work for us to draw on in order to make this point. We considered two examples in chapter 7. The first concerned children's understanding of area. The work by Nunes, Light and Mason (1993) that we reviewed indicated how children can come to structure logical relations in the parallelogram if they develop an understanding of area as 'number of bricks in a row times number of rows'. The parallelogram poses a difficult problem to children: they need to develop a new concept, that of height of a figure, which is distinct from the sides. The children who developed this particular formula for area, using this particular system of measurement, were much more likely to approach the parallelogram problem successfully.

The second example is from the work by Hoyles et al. (1991), and it involved constraining children's choice of representations of the relationships between numbers to multiplicative relations in a computer environment. The pupils engaged in this study have a previous understanding of multiplication but were not aware of some possibilities of multiplicative connections. They did not, for example, know how to make a number smaller by multiplication, and they did not seem to think of enlargement as a multiplicative relation; they enlarged figures by adding to the sides of the figure. When their expression of relations was constrained to multiplicative connections, many of the pupils seemed to adopt multiplicative relations preferentially afterwards. The representation through the computer language under the instruction conditions had helped them build a bridge between a sort of reasoning which they already knew (multiplicative reasoning) and a situation which they previously viewed as independent of this sort of reasoning. Conceptual development in both of these examples involves expanding the meaning of relations already known.

These studies indicate that systems of signs may have a much more influential role in development than has been acknowledged so far: they may offer a way of connecting situations that seem, at first glance, unrelated. But, as we pointed out above, much more research is needed on this third link between systems of signs and development.

5   Children's Concepts of Mathematics

The last aspect of our theory is the idea that, as children grow up, not only their mathematical concepts develop but also their concept of what mathematics is. Children's understanding of what mathematics is has a major effect on how they solve problems. There is now overwhelming evidence that the social definition of the situation in which a child is given a problem has a considerable effect on the way that he/she tries to solve it.

The phenomenon of 'street mathematics' (Nunes, Schliemann and Carraher, 1993) is the most powerful demonstration that we have of the strong effect of situations on children's approach to mathematical problems. The discovery of children who are capable of sophisticated and flexible solutions in commercial transactions, and yet stick rigidly and quite unsuccessfully to the taught algorithms when they are given school problems, establishes the importance of the social environment.

We should be disturbed at the phenomenon because of the clear demonstration that there are children who are being dismissed as failures quite wrongly. Many of the mistakes that they make in the classroom are due to the limiting effects of the classroom itself. These mistakes can no longer be attributed just to gaps and deficiencies in the children's mathematical reasoning. The classroom environment pushes them towards a definition of mathematics where the ways in which solutions are obtained takes precedence over their understanding. This social representation of mathematics as involving particular ways of solving problems is sometimes referred to in the literature as the 'didactic contract' (see Brousseau, 1987; and Douady, forthcoming). What a didactic contract involves is an agreement between teacher and pupils on what knowledge and learning of mathematics will be in their classroom. If mathematical problem-solving is always used in the classroom as a way of practising a procedure just taught by the teacher, the social definition of mathematics becomes the use of school-taught routines.

It could be argued that the 'street mathematics–school mathematics' phenomenon is a special case – that it only applies to a minority of children whose social circumstances ensure both that they take part in mathematical activities outside school and also that they are poor pupils at school. We do not agree with this and one of the main messages of our book is to make the case that social situations have a pervasive effect on mathematical reasoning. The youngsters in Pittsburgh who did not succeed with the school-learned representations of fractions (Mack, 1993) but succeeded when using their informal knowledge and the pupils in the study by Harel et al. (1994) on the conservation of taste all expressed the belief that, if you are given numbers in a mathematics assessment task, your job is to calculate with them.

This evidence establishes that children's mathematical successes and failures are not just a matter of their logical abilities. The children's understanding of logical invariants is important, as we acknowledged earlier, but so too is their social representation of mathematics, which sometimes leads children to put their logical knowledge to the side instead of using it. In some cases, when contrasted with the evidence of their own knowledge, pupils will claim that 'this is different, this isn't mathematics' – just like our darts player, who was convinced that he did not know how to multiply because he did not use the school-taught algorithm.

6 Final Comments

We hope that we have presented you with enough evidence to convince you that children are more than just logic machines and more than just recipients of teaching. They reason about mathematics and their reasoning improves as they grow older. They inherit the power of cultural mathematical tools partly as a result of being taught about them and partly because of informal experiences outside of school. The variety of mathematical experiences that affects them in almost every part of their lives can at first cause them difficulties, for one of their greatest problems is to understand that mathematical relations and symbols are not bound to particular situations. But the value of their informal experiences and the genuineness of their mathematical learning outside school should be recognized by parents, teachers and researchers alike. We should help children to recognize the power of their reasoning and we must help them to form a new view, a new social representation, of mathematics that will make it easy for them to bring their understanding from everyday life into the classroom. To do this we will have to build new social representations of mathematics which will allow numeracy to be viewed as a value for all in a new way. This need for a new representation of mathematics is the main concern of our book and, when it is generally shared at home and in school, the value of *numeracy for all* will at last be properly recognized.

References

Aidinis, A., and Desli, D. (1993), Children's ideas about heat and temperature. Unpublished undergraduate thesis. Thessaloniki: Aristotelian University of Thessaloniki.

Ball, D. L. (1993), Halves, pieces and twoths: constructing and using representational contexts in teaching fractions. In T. P. Carpenter, E. Fennema and T. A. Romberg (eds): *Rational Numbers: An integration of Research*, pp. 157–96. Hillsdale, New Jersey: Lawrence Erlbaum Associates.

Behr, J. J., Harel, G., Post, T., and Lesh, R. (1993), Rational numbers: toward a semantic analysis – emphasis on the operator construct. In T. P. Carpenter, E. Fennema and T. A. Romberg (eds): *Rational Numbers: An Integration of Research*, pp. 13–48. Hillsdale, New Jersey: Lawrence Erlbaum Associates.

Bell, A., Greer, B., Grimson, L., and Mangan, C. (1989), Children's performance on multiplicative word problems. *Journal for Research in Mathematics Education*, 20, 434–49.

Briars, D. J., and Siegler, R. S. (1984), A featural analysis of preschoolers' counting knowledge. *Developmental Psychology*, 20, 607–18.

Brousseau, G. (1987), Fondements et méthodes de la didactique. *Recherches en didactique des mathématiques*, 7, 33–115.

Brown, M. (1981), Number operations. In K. Hart (ed.): *Children's Understanding of Mathematics: 11–16*, pp. 23–47. Windsor: NFER-Nelson.

Bryant, P. E. (1974), *Perception and Understanding in Young Children*. London: Methuen.

Bryant, P. E., and Kopytynska, H. (1976), Spontaneous measurement by young children. *Nature*, 260, 773.

Bryant, P. E., Morgado, L., and Nunes, T. (1992), Children's understanding of multiplication. *Proceedings of the Annual Conference of the Psychology of Mathematics Education, Tokio*, August.

Bryant, P. E., and Nunes, T. (1994), *Children's Inferences and Measurement*. Paper presented at the annual meeting of the Developmental Section of the British Psychological Society, Portsmouth, September.

Campos, T., Jahn, A. P., Leme da Silva, M. C., and Ferreira da Silva, M. J. (1995), Lógica das Equivalências. PUC, São Paulo: Relatório de Pesquisa não publicado.

Carpenter, T. P., Fennema, E., and Romberg, T. A. (1993), Toward a unified discipline of scientific inquiry. In T. P. Carpenter, E. Fennema and T. A. Romberg (eds): *Rational Numbers: An Integration of Research*, pp. 1–12. Hillsdale, New Jersey: Lawrence Erlbaum Associates.

Carpenter, T. P., Hiebert, J., and Moser, J. M. (1981), Problem structure and first grade children's initial solution processes for simple addition and subtraction problems. *Journal for Research in Mathematics Education*, 12, 27–39.

Carpenter, T. P., and Moser, J. M. (1982), The development of addition and subtraction problem solving. In T. P. Carpenter, J. M. Moser and T. A. Romberg (eds): *Addition and Subtraction: A Cognitive Perspective*, pp. 10–24. Hillsdale, New Jersey: Lawrence Erlbaum Associates.

Carraher, T. N. (1982), O desenvolvimento mental e o sistema numérico decimal. In T. N. Carraher (ed.): *Aprender Pensando: Contribuicções da Psicologia Cognitiva para a Educação*, pp. 51–68. Petrópolis, Brazil: Editora Vozes.

Carraher, T. N. (1985), The decimal system: understanding and notation. In L. Streefland (ed.): *Proceedings of the 9th International Conference for the Psychology of Mathematics Education*, vol. 1, pp. 288–303. Utrecht, Netherlands: Research Group on Mathematics Education and Educational Computer Centre, State University of Utrecht.

Carraher, T. N., Carraher, D. W., and Schliemann, A. D. (1985), Mathematics in the streets and in school. *British Journal of Developmental Psychology*, 3, 21–9.

Carraher, T. N. and Bryant, P. E. (1987) Children's understanding of arithmetic operations. *Proceedings of the Satellite ISSBD Meeting, Beijing*, August.

Carraher, T. N., and Schliemann, A. D. (1983), Fracasso escolar: uma questão social (School failure: a social problem). *Cadernos de Pesquisa*, 45, 3–19.

Carraher, T. N., and Schliemann, A. D. (1985), Computation routines prescribed by schools: help or hindrance? *Journal for Research in Mathematics Education*, 16, 37–44.

Carraher, T. N., and Schliemann, A. D. (1990), Knowledge of the numeration system among pre-schoolers. In L. P. Steffe and T. Wood (eds): *Transforming Children's Mathematics Education*, pp. 135–41. Hillsdale, New Jersey: Lawrence Erlbaum Associates.

Ceci, S. J., and Liker, J. (1986), Academic and nonacademic intelligence: an experimental separation. In R. J. Sternberg and R. K. Wagner (eds): *Practical Intelligence*, pp. 119–42. Cambridge: Cambridge University Press.

Chapman, A., Kemp, M., and Kissane, B. (1990), Beyond the mathematics classroom: numeracy for learning. In S. Willis (ed.): *Being Numerate: What Counts?*, 91–118. Victoria, Australia: The Australian Council for Educational Research.

Cividanes-Lago, C. (1993), *Children's Understanding of Quantity and Their Ability to Use Graphical Information*. University of Oxford: unpublished D.Phil. thesis.

Cockcroft, W. H. (1982), *Mathematics Counts*. Report of the Committee of Inquiry into the Training of Mathematics in Schools. London: HMSO.

Confrey, J. (1994), Splitting, similarity and rate of change: a new approach to multiplication and exponential functions. In G. Harel and J. Confrey (eds): *The Development of Multiplicative Reasoning in the Learning of Mathematics*, pp. 293–332. Albany, New York: State University of New York Press.

Correa, J. (1995), *Young Children's Understanding of the Division Concept*. University of Oxford: unpublished D.Phil. thesis.

Correa, J., and Bryant, P. E. (1994), *Young Children's Understanding of the Division Concept*. Poster presented at the ISSBD, June–July 1994, Amsterdam.

Cowan, R. (1987), When do children trust counting as a basis for relative number judgements? *Journal of Experimental Child Psychology*, 43, 328–45.

Cowan, R., Foster, C. M., and Al-Zubaidi, A. S. (1993), Encouraging children to count. *British Journal of Developmental Psychology*, 11, 411–20.

Cunha, L. A. (1979), *Educação e desenvolvimento social no Brazil*. Rio de Janeiro: Francisco Alves.

Davydov, V. V. (1982), The psychological characteristics of the formation of elementary mathematics operations in children. In T. P. Carpenter, J. M. Moser and T. A. Romberg (eds): *Addition and Subtraction: A Cognitive Perspective*, pp. 224–38. Hillsdale, New Jersey: Lawrence Erlbaum Associates.

De Abreu, G. M. C. (1994), *The Relationship between Home and School Mathematics in a Farming Community in Rural Brazil*. University of Cambridge: unpublished PhD thesis.

De Abreu, G. M. C., Bishop, A., and Pompeu, G. (forthcoming), What children and teachers count as mathematics. In T. Nunes and P. E. Bryant (eds): *How Do Children Learn Mathematics?* Hove: Erlbaum. (in press)

De Abreu, G. M. C., and Carraher, D. W. (1989), The mathematics of Brazilian sugar cane farmers. In C. Keitel, P. Damerow, A. Bishop and P. Guerdes (eds): *Mathematics, Education and Society*, pp. 68–70. Paris: UNESCO (Science and Technology Education Document Series 35).

Desli, D. (1994), *Proportional Reasoning: The Concept of Half in Part–part and Part–whole Situations*. University of London: unpublished MSc thesis, Department of Child Development and Primary Education.

Douady, R. (forthcoming), Didactic engineering. In T. Nunes and P. Bryant (eds): *How Do Children Learn Mathematics?* Hove: Erlbaum.

Erickson, G. (1985), Heat and temperature: an overview of pupils' ideas. In R. Driver, E. Guesne and A. Tiberghien (eds): *Children's Ideas in Science*, pp. 55–66. Milton Keynes: Open University Press.

Erickson, G., and Tiberghien, A. (1985), Heat and temperature. In R. Driver, E. Guesne and A. Tiberghien (eds): *Children's Ideas in Science*, pp. 52–4. Milton Keynes: Open University Press.

Foyster, J. (1990), Beyond the mathematics classroom: numeracy for on the job. In S. Willis (ed.): *Being Numerate: What Counts*, pp. 119–37. Victoria, Australia: The Australian Council for Educational Research.

Frydman, O. (1990), *The Role of Correspondence in the Development of Number Based Strategies in Young Children*. University of Oxford: unpublished D.Phil. thesis.

Frydman, O., and Bryant, P. E. (1988), Sharing and understanding of number equivalence by young children. *Cognitive Development*, 3, 323–39.

Fuson, K. C. (1988), *Children's Counting and Concepts of Number*. New York: Springer Verlag.

Gay, J., and Cole, M. (1967), *The New Mathematics and an Old Culture*. New York: Holt, Rinehart and Winston.

Gelman, R., and Gallistel, C. R. (1978), *The Child's Understanding of Number*. Cambridge, Mass.: Harvard University Press.

Gelman, R., and Meck, E. (1983), Preschoolers' counting: principles before skill. *Cognition*, 13, 343–60.

Gelman, R., and Meck, E. (1986), The notion of principle: the case of counting. In J. Hiebert (ed.): *Conceptual and Precedural Knowledge: The Case of Mathematics*, pp. 29–57. Hillsdale, New Jersey: Erlbaum.

George, R. (1992), *A Study of Children's Understanding of Commutativity of Addition*. MSc dissertation, Department of Child Development and Primary Education, Institute of Education, University of London.

Goodnow, J. J. (1986), Some lifelong everyday forms of intelligent behaviour: organizing and reorganizing. In R. J. Sternberg and R. K. Wagner (eds): *Practical Intelligence*, pp. 142–82. Cambridge: Cambridge University Press.

Goodnow, J. J. (1990), The socialization of cognition: what's involved? In J. W. Stigler, R. A. Shweder and G. Herdt (eds): *Cultural Psychology: Essays on Comparative Human Development*, pp. 259–86. Cambridge: Cambridge University Press.

Gravemeijer, K. (1990), Context problems and realistic mathematics instruction. In K. Gravemeijer, M. van den Heuvel and L. Streefland (eds):

Context Free Production Tests and Geometry in Realistic Mathematics Education, pp. 10–32. Utrecht, Netherlands: Research Group for Mathematical Education and Educational Computer Centre, State University of Utrecht.

Gravemeijer, K. (forthcoming), Mediating between concrete and abstract. In T. Nunes and P. E. Bryant (eds): *How Do Children Learn Mathematics?* Hove: Erlbaum.

Gray, W. S. (1956), *The Teaching of Reading and Writing*. Paris: Unesco.

Greco, P. (1962), Quantité et quotité: nouvelles recherches sur la correspondance terme-à-terme et la conservation des ensembles. In P. Greco and A. Morf (eds): *Structures numériques laaelémentaires: Etudes d'épistémologie génétique*, vol. 13, pp. 35–52. Paris: Presses Universitaires de France.

Greer, B. (1992), Multiplication and division as models of situations. In D. Grouws (ed.): *Handbook of Research on Mathematics Teaching and Learning*, pp. 276–95. New York: Macmillan.

Greer, B. (1994), Extending the meaning of multiplication and division. In G. Harel and J. Confrey (eds): *The Development of Multiplicative Reasoning in the Learning of Mathematics*, pp. 61–88. Albany, New York: State University of New York Press.

Groen, G., and Resnick, L. (1977), Can pre-school children invent addition algorithms? *Journal of Educational Psychology*, 69, 645–52.

Hall, J. W., Fuson, K. F., and Willis, G. B. (1985), Teaching counting-on for addition and counting down for subtraction. In L. Streefland (ed.): *Proceedings of the 9th International Conference for the Psychology of Mathematics Education*, vol. 1, pp. 322–7. Utrecht, Netherlands: University of Utrecht.

Harel, G., Behr, M., Lesh, R., and Post, T. (1994), Invariance of ratio: the case for children's anticipatory scheme for constancy of taste. *Journal for Research in Mathematics Education*, 25, 324–45.

Harris, M. (1990), *Schools, Mathematics and Work*. London: Falmer Press.

Hart, K. (1984), *Ratio: Children's Strategies and Errors. A Report of the Strategies and Errors in Secondary Mathematics Project*. Windsor: NFER-Nelson.

Hart, K. (1986), *The Step to Formalisation*. Institute of Education, University of London: Proceedings of the 10th International Conference of the Psychology of Mathematics Education, pp. 159–64.

Hart, K. (1988), Ratio and proportion. In J. Hiebert and M. Behr (eds): *Number Concepts and Operations in the Middle Grades*, pp. 198–219. Hillsdale, New Jersey: Erlbaum.

Hatano, G. (forthcoming), Learning arithmetic with an abacus. In T. Nunes and P. E. Bryant (eds): *How Do Children Learn Mathematics?*, Hove: Erlbaum.

Heraud, B. (1989), A conceptual analysis of the notion of length and its measure. In G. Vergnaud, J. Rogalski and M. Artique (eds): *Proceedings of the 13th International Conference of the Psychology of Mathematics Education*, vol. 2, pp. 83–9. Paris: CNRS.

Herscovics, N., Bergeron, J. C., and Bergeron, A. (1986), The kindergartner's perception of the invariance of number under various transformations. In G. Lappen and R. Evan (eds): *Proceedings of the 8th Annual Meeting of the north American Chapter for the Psychology of Mathematics Education*, pp. 28–34. East Lansing, Mich.: PME.

Hoyles, C., and Noss, R. (1992), A pedagogy for mathematical microworlds. *Educational Studies in Mathematics*, 23, 31–57.

Hoyles, C., Noss, R., and Sutherland, R. (1991), *The Ratio and Proportion Microworld: Final Report of the Microworlds Project*, vol. III. London: Institute of Education, University of London.

Hudson, T. (1983), Correspondences and numerical differences between sets. *Child Development*, 54, 84–90.

Hughes, M. (1986), *Children and Number*. Oxford: Blackwell.

Inhelder, B., and Piaget, J. (1958), *The Growth of Logical Thinking from Childhood to Adolescence*. New York: Basic Books.

Kamii, M. (1980), *Children's Graphic Representation of Numerical Concepts. A Developmental Study*. Unpublished doctoral dissertation: Harvard University.

Kaput, J., and Maxwell-West, M. (1994), Missing-value proportional reasoning problems: factors affecting informal reasoning patterns. In G. Harel and J. Confrey (eds): *The Development of Multiplicative Reasoning in the Learning of Mathematics*, pp. 237–92. Albany, New York: State University of New York Press.

Karplus, R., Pulos, S., and Stage, E. K. (1983), Proportional reasoning of early adolescents. In R. Lesh and M. Landau (eds): *Acquisition of Mathematics Concepts and Processes*, pp. 45–90. London: Academic Press.

Kerslake, D. (1986), *Fractions: Children's Strategies and Errors: A Report of the Strategies and Errors in Secondary Mathematics Project*. Windsor: NFER-Nelson.

Kieren, T. E. (1988), Personal knowledge of rational numbers: its intuitive and formal development. In J. Hiebert and M. Behr (eds): *Number Concepts and Operations in the Middle Grades*, pp. 162–80. Hillsdale, New Jersey: Erlbaum.

Kieren, T. (1994), Multiple views of multiplicative structures. In G. Harel and J. Confrey (eds): *The Development of Multiplicative Reasoning in the Learning of Mathematics*, pp. 389–400. Albany, New York: State University of New York Press.

Kornilaki, E. (1994), *The Understanding of the Numeration System Among Preschool Children*. London: unpublished MSc. thesis, Department of Child Development and Primary Education, University of London.

Kornilaki, E. (forthcoming), Ordering series by one-to-many correspondence.

Lamon, S. J. (1993), Ratio and proportion: children's cognitive and metacognitive processes. In T. P. Carpenter, E. Fennema and T. A. Romberg (eds): *Rational Numbers: An Integration of Research*, pp. 131–56. Hillsdale, New Jersey: Lawrence Erlbaum Associates.

Lancy, D. F. (1983), *Cross-Cultural Studies in Cognition and Mathematics*. New York: Academic Press.

Lave, J. (1988), *Cognition in Practice*. Cambridge: Cambridge University Press.

Lave, J. (1990), The culture of acquisition and the practice of understanding. In J. W. Stigler, R. A. Shweder and G. Herdt (eds): *Cultural Psychology: Essays on Comparative Human Development*, pp. 309–27. Cambridge: Cambridge University Press.

Lima, M. F. (1982), Iniciação ao conceito de fração e o desenvolvimento de conservação de quantitades. In T. N. Carraher (ed.): *Aprender Pensando*, pp. 81–127. Petrópolis, Brazil: Editora Vozes.

Lines, S., and Bryant, P. (forthcoming), A cross cultural comparison of children's understanding of counting. (Paper in preparation.)

Luria, A. R. (1969), On the pathology of computational operations. In J. Kilpatrick and I. Wirszup (eds): *Soviet Studies in the Psychology of Learning and teaching Mathematics*, vol. I: *The Learning of Mathematical Concepts*, pp. 37–73. Chicago: University of Chicago Press.

Lybeck, L. (1985), *Research into Science and Mathematics Education in Gothenburg (Report No 85:03)*. Gothenburg: Department of Education and Educational Research, University of Gothenburg.

Mack, N. K. (1993), Learning rational numbers with understanding: the case of informal knowledge. In T. P. Carpenter, E. Fennema, and T. A. Romberg (eds): *Rational Numbers: An Integration of Research*, pp. 85–106. Hillsdale, New Jersey: Lawrence Erlbaum Associates.

Marton, F., and Neuman, D. (1990), Constructivism, phenomenology and the origin of arithmetic skills. In L. Steffe and T. Wood (eds): *Transferring Children's Mathematics Education: International Perspectives*, pp. 62–75. Hillsdale, New Jersey: Lawrence Erlbaum Associates.

Miller, K. F. (1989), Measurement as a tool for thought: the role of measuring procedures in children's understanding of quantitative invariance. *Developmental Psychology*, 25, 589–600.

Miller, K. F., and Paredes, D. R. (1990), Starting to add worse: effects of learning to multiply on children's addition. *Cognition*, 37, 213–42.

Miller, K. F., and Stigler, J. W. (1987), Counting in Chinese: cultural variation in a basic skill. *Cognitive Development*, 2, 279–305.

Miura, I. T., Okamoto, Y., Kim, C. C., Chang, C.–M., Steere, M., and Fayol, M. (1994), Comparisons of children's cognitive representation of number: China, France, Japan, Korea, Sweden and the United States. *International Journal of Behavioural Development*, 17, 401–11.

Muller, D. J. (1978), Children's concepts of proportion: an investigation into the claims of Bryant and Piaget. *British Journal of Educational Psychology*, 48, 29–35.

Nesher, P. (1988), Multiplicative school word problems: theoretical approaches and empirical findings. In J. Hiebert and M. Behr (eds): *Number Concepts and Operations in the Middle Grades*, pp. 19–40. Hillsdale, New Jersey: Lawrence Erlbaum Associates.

Noelting, G. (1980a), The development of proportional reasoning and the ratio concept. Part I – Differentiation of stages. *Educational Studies in mathematics*, 11, 217–53.

Noelting, G. (1980b), The development of proportional reasoning and the ratio concept. part II – Problem-structure at successive stages: problem-solving strategies and the mechanism of adaptive restructuring. *Educational Studies in Mathematics*, 11, 331–63.

Nunes, T., and Bryant, P. E. (1991), Correspondência: um esquema quantitativo básico (One-to-one correspondence as a basic quantitative scheme). *Psicologia: Teoria e Pesquisa*, 7, 273–84.

Nunes, T., Bryant, P., Falcão, J., and Lima, M. F. (forthcoming), Children analysing the structure of the numeration system: what helps?

Nunes, T., Light, P., and Mason, J. (1993), Tools for thought: the measurement of length and area. *Learning and Instruction*, 3, 39–54.

Nunes, T., Light, P., and Mason, J. (1994), Children's understanding of area. Paper presented at the annual meeting of the International Group for the Study of the Psychology of Mathematics Education, Lisbon, July.

Nunes, T., Light, P., and Mason J. (1995), What does a ruler look like? (Paper in preparation.)

Nunes, T., Schliemann, A.-L., and Caraher, D. (1993), *Street Mathematics and School Mathematics*. New York: Cambridge University Press.

Parrat-Dayan, S. (1985), A propos de la notion de moitié: rôle du contexte expérimental. *Archives de Psychologie*, 53, 433–8.

Parrat-Dayan, S., and Vonèche, J. (1992), Conservation and the notion of half. In J. Bideaud, C. Meljac and J.-P. Fischer (eds): *Pathways to Number*, pp. 67–82. Hillsdale, New Jersey: LEA.

Piaget, J. (1965), *The Child's Conception to Number*. New York: Norton.

Piaget, J., Grize, J., Szeminska, A., and Bangh, V. (1977), *Epistemology and the Psychology of Functions*. Dordrecht, Netherlands: D. Reidel.

Piaget, J., and Inhelder, B. (1975), *The Origin of the Idea of Chance in Children*. London: Routledge and Kegan Paul.

Piaget, J., Inhelder, B., and Szeminska, A. (1960), *The Child's Conception of Geometry*. London: Routledge and Kegan Paul.

Piaget, J., Kaufmann, J.-L., and Bourquin, J.-F. (1977), La construction des communs multiples. In J. Piaget (ed.): *Recherches sur l'abstraction réfléchissante*, vol. 1. L'abstraction des relations logico mathématiques. pp. 31–44. Paris: Presses Universitaires de France.

Power, R. D., and Dal Martello, M. F. (1990), The dictation of Italian numerals. *Language and Cognitive Processes*, 5, 237–54.

Resnick, D. P., and Resnick, L. B. (1977), The nature of literacy: an historical exploration. *Harvard Educational Review*, 47, 370–85.

Resnick, L. B. (1982), Syntax and semantics in learning to subtract. In T. P. Carpenter, J. M. Moser and T. A. Romberg (eds): *Addition and Subtraction: A Cognitive Perspective*, pp. 136–55. Hillsdale, New Jersey: Lawrence Erlbaum Associates.

Resnick, L. B. (1983), A developmental theory of number understanding. In H. P. Ginsburg (ed.): *The Development of Mathematical Thinking*, pp. 110–52. New York: Academic Press.

Resnick, L. B., and Singer, J. A. (1993), Protoquantitative origins of ratio reasoning. In T. P. Carpenter, E. Fennema, and T. A. Romberg (eds): *Rational Numbers: An Integration of Research*, pp. 107–30. Hillsdale, New Jersey: Lawrence Erlbaum Associates.

Riley, M., Greeno, J. G., and Heller, J. I. (1983), Development of children's problem solving ability in arithmetic. In H. Ginsburg (ed.): *The Development of Mathematical Thinking*, pp. 153–96. New York: Academic Press.

Rose, S., and Blank, M. (1974), The potency of context in children's cognition: an illustration through conservation. *Child Development*, 45, 499–502.

Samuel, J., and Bryant, P. E. (1984), Asking only one question in the conservation experiment. *Journal of Child Psychology and Psychiatry*, 25, 315–18.

Saxe, G. (1981), Body parts as numerals: a developmental analysis of numeration among the Oksapmin in Papua New Guinea. *Child Development*, 52, 306–16.

Saxe, G. B. (1991), *Culture and Cognitive Development: Studies in Mathematical Understanding*. Hillsdale, New Jersey: Lawrence Erlbaum Associates.

Saxe, G., Guberman, S. R., and Gearhart, M. (1987), Social and developmental processes in children's understanding of number. *Monographs of the Society for Research in Child Development*, 52, 100–200.

Saxe, G. B., and Moylan, T. (1982), The development of measurement operations among the Oksapmin of Papua New Guinea. *Child Development*, 53, 1242–8.

Schoenfeld, A. H. (1987), What's all the fuss about metacognition? In A. H. Schoenfeld (ed.): *Cognitive Science and Mathematics Education*. Hillsdale, New Jersey: Lawrence Erlbaum Associates.

Schoenfeld, A. H. (1988), When good teaching leads to bad results: the disasters of well-taught mathematics courses. *Educational Psychologist*, 23, 145–66.

Schonfeld, I. S. (1986), The Genevan and Cattell-Horn conceptions of intelligence compared. *Developmental Psychology*, 22, 204–12.

Schwartz, J. (1988), Intensive quantity and referent transforming arithmetic operations. In J. Hiebert and M. Behr (eds): *Number Concepts and Operations in the Middle Grades*, pp. 41–52. Hillsdale, New Jersey: Erlbaum.

Scribner, S. (1986), Thinking in action: some characteristics of practical thought. In R. J. Sternberg and R. K. Wagner (eds): *Practical Intelligence*, pp. 13–30. Cambridge: Cambridge University Press.

Seron, X., and Fayol, M. (1994), Number transcoding in children: a functional analysis. *British Journal of Developmental Psychology*, 12, 281–300.

Shweder, R. A. (1982), Beyond self-constructed knowledge: the study of culture and morality. *Merril-Palmer Quarterly*, 28, 41–69.

Silva, Z. M. H. (1993), A compreensão da escrita numérica pela crianca. Paper presented at the ISSBD Conference, Recife, Brazil, July.

Sinclair, A. (1988), La notation numérique chez l'enfant (avec la collaboration de d. Mello et F. Siegrist). In H. Sinclair (ed.): *La Production de notations chez le jeune enfant: langage, nombre, rythmes et mélodies*, pp. 71–98. Paris: Presses Universitaires de France.

Singer, J. A., Kohn, A. S., and Resnick, L. B. (forthcoming), Knowing about proportions in different contexts. In T. Nunes and P. E. Bryant (eds): *How Do Children Learn Mathematics?* Hove: Erlbaum.

Sophian, C. (1988), Limitations on preschool children's knowledge about counting: using counting to compare two sets. *Developmental Psychology*, 24, 634–40.

Spinillo, A. (1990), *The Development of the Concept of Proportion in Young Children*. University of Oxford: unpublished DPhil thesis.

Spinillo, A., and Bryant, P. (1991), Children's proportional judgements: the importance of 'half'. *Child Development*, 62, 427–40.

Starkey, P., and Cooper, R. (1980), Perception of numbers by human infants. *Science*, 210, 1033–4.

Starkey, P., Spelke, E., and Gelman, R. (1983), Detection of intermodal numerical correspondences by human infants. *Science*, 222, 179.

Starkey, P., Spelke, E. S., and Gelman, R. (1990), Numerical abstraction by human infants. *Cognition*, 36, 97–128.

Steffe, L. (1994), Children's multiplying schemes. In G. Harel and J. Confrey (eds): *The Development of Multiplicative Reasoning in the Learning of Mathematics* pp. 3–40. Albany, N.Y.: State University of New York Press.

Steffe, L. P., Thompson, P. W., and Richards, J. (1982), Children's counting in arithmetical problem solving. In T. P. Carpenter, J. M. Moser and T. A. Romberg (eds): *Addition and Subtraction: A Cognitive Perspective*, pp. 83–96. Hillsdale, New Jersey: Lawrence Erlbaum Associates.

Streefland, L. (1990a), Free productions in teaching and learning mathematics. In K. Gravemeijer, M. van den Heuvel and L. Streefland (eds): *Context*

Free Production Tests and Geometry in Realistic Mathematics Education, pp. 33–52. Utrecht, Netherlands: Research Group for Mathematical Education and Educational Computer Centre, State University of Utrecht.

Streefland, L. (1990b), Realistic mathematics education: what does it mean? In K. Gravemeijer, M. van den Heuvel and L. Streefland (eds): *Context Free Production Tests and Geometry in Realistic Mathematics Education*, pp. 79–90. Utrecht, Netherlands: Research Group for Mathematical Education and Educational Computer Centre, State University of Utrecht.

Streefland, L. (forthcoming), Charming fractions or fractions being charmed? In T. Nunes and P. E. Bryant (eds): *How Do Children Learn Mathematics?* Hove: Erlbaum.

Thompson, P. (1994), The development of the concept of speed and its relationship to concepts of rate. In G. Harel and J. Confrey (eds): *The Development of Multiplicative Reasoning in the Learning of Mathematics*, pp. 181–236. Albany, New York: State University of New York Press.

Van den Brink, J., and Streefland, L. (1978), *Ratio and Proportion in Young Children (6–8)*. Osnabrück: Paper presented at the annual conference of the International Group for the Study of the Psychology of Mathematics Education.

Van Lehn, K. (1983), On the representation of procedures in repair theory. In H. P. Ginsburg (ed.): *The Development of Mathematical Thinking*, pp. 201–54. New York: Academic Press.

Vergnaud, G. (1982), A classification of cognitive tasks and operations of thought involved in addition and subtraction problems. In T. P. Carpenter, J. M. Moser and T. A. Romberg (eds): *Addition and Subtraction: A Cognitive Perspective*, pp. 60–7. Hillsdale, New Jersey: Lawrence Erlbaum Associates.

Vergnaud, G. (1983), Multiplicative structures. In R. Lesh and M. Landau (eds): *Acquisition of Mathematics Concepts and Processes*, pp. 128–75. London: Academic Press.

Vernaud, G. (1985), Concepts et schèmes dans une théorie opératoire de la représentation. *Psychologie Française*, 30, 245–52.

Vergnaud, G. (1988), Multiplicative structures. In J. Hiebert and M. Behr (eds): *Number Concepts and Operations in the Middle Grades*, pp. 141–61. Hillsdale, New Jersey: Erlbaum.

Vygotsky, L. S. (1978), *Mind in Society*. Cambridge, Mass.: Harvard University Press.

Willis, P. (1977), *Learning to Labour: How Working-Class Kids Get Working Class Jobs*. Aldershot: Gower.

Willis, S. (1990), *Being Numerate: What Counts?* Victoria, Australia: The Australian Council for Educational Research.

Wright, R. (1994), *Commutativity in Word Problem Situations*. Portsmouth: paper presented at Developmental Section of the BPS, September 1994.

Wynn, K. (1992), Addition and subtraction by human infants. *Nature*, 358, 749–50.

Zweng, M. J. (1964), Division problems and the concept of rate. A study of the performance of second-grade children on four kinds of division problems. *The Arithmetic Teacher*, 1964, 11, 546–56.

Index

absolute values, 13, 81–3, 157, 161, 162, 167, 186, 206, 239, 240
academic intelligence, 108
addition, 6, 8, 9, 16, 18, 49, 52–60, 64, 66, 74, 75, 80, 94, 95, 102, 106, 107, 114–17, 119–29, 133–5, 137, 138, 140–2, 144, 150, 153, 160, 167, 186, 188–90, 195, 196, 199, 204, 205, 242–4, 250–3, 255, 257–60
  additive composition of number, 8, 9, 46–60, 62–9, 74, 75, 78, 81, 95, 141, 242, 244, 245
  additive composition tasks, 51, 59, 64, 68, 74, 81
  additive reasoning, 144, 145, 160, 161, 194, 195, 212
  change problems, 115, 116, 117, 124, 126–8, 130, 131, 134, 135, 140, 141
  comparison problems, 129, 131, 133–8, 141, 144, 186, 243
  composition of measures problems, 124, 125
  equalize problems, 130
  inversion, 117, 118
  invisible addend, 58–60
  missing addend problems, 116, 141
  start-unknown problems, 117, 118, 134, 135
  static relations, 129–31, 134, 135, 137, 138, 140, 141, 144, 243
  transformations, 124, 125, 127–9, 140, 141, 144
agreement between strategies, 38
Aidinis, A., 189, 249
Al-Zubaidi, A.S., 38, 251
analogy, 135, 183, 191
arbitrary units, 12
area, 2, 3, 17, 80, 110, 184, 187, 191–4, 245, 256
arithmetic, 2–4, 9, 33, 105, 107, 112, 116, 117, 119, 128, 129, 131, 134, 142, 151, 175, 176, 178–81, 183, 190, 198, 199, 253, 255–8
  arithmetic operations, 2, 3, 4, 9, 129, 131, 142, 199, 256, 258
arithmetic progression, 151
axioms, 10

babies, 21
balance scale, 169
Ball, D. L., 220, 249
Bangh, V., 142, 256
base ten systems see decades
Behr, J. J., 185, 205, 249, 253
Bell, A., 196, 249
Bergeron, A., 26, 254
Bergeron, J. C., 26, 254
best-profit problems, 179, 180
biology and biological phenomena, 10
Bishop, A., 110, 251
Blank, M., 29, 257
body parts, 12, 15, 16, 44, 257

Bourquin, J.-F., 160, 256
Briars, D. J., 28, 249
Brousseau, G., 247, 249
Brown, M., 163, 164, 249
Bryant, P., 29, 41, 53, 62, 63, 79, 81,
    116, 134, 135, 150, 153, 158,
    161, 163, 171, 172, 206, 215,
    216, 218, 249–53, 255–9
bugs, 107

calculators, 1, 3, 195
Campos, T., 202, 203, 250
cardinal number, 5, 7, 23, 24, 59, 60,
    245
Carpenter, T. P., 119, 121, 130, 205,
    232, 249–51, 255, 257–9
Carraher, D. W., 4, 104, 106, 107,
    109, 110, 176, 235, 246, 251
Carraher, T. N., 49, 50, 67, 105, 106,
    116, 119, 121, 250, 255, 256;
    see also T. Nunes
Ceci, S. J., 108, 250
Chang, A.-M., 66, 255
Chapman, A., 3, 251
Civadanes-Lago, C., 131, 251
Cockcroft, W. H., 3, 109, 251
Cockcroft Report, 3, 109, 251
Cole, M., 101–4, 108, 113, 252
commercial transactions, 246; *see also*
    vendors
commutativity, 117, 125–8, 141, 161,
    252
comparing sets, 35, 38–40, 42, 130,
    237
composite units *see* one-to-many
    correspondence
computers, 1, 19, 189, 190, 192, 195,
    196, 198, 200, 246, 250, 253,
    259
concatenation, 71
concrete and abstract reasoning, 124
Confrey, J., 10, 151, 154, 251, 253,
    254, 258, 259
conservation, 6, 7, 35, 36, 78, 184,
    185, 221, 222, 224, 241, 247,
    253, 256, 257
continuous quantity, 48, 124, 147,
    149, 205, 207–10, 215, 220,
    222–6, 228, 230, 232, 233
conventions, 3, 7, 10, 11, 13, 14, 17,
    41, 146

conversion of one measure into
    another *see* measurement
Cooper, R., 21, 258
Correa, J., 150, 153, 207–14, 251
counting, 5, 6, 8, 11, 12, 14–16, 19,
    20–49, 51–65, 74–6, 80, 86,
    87, 89, 92, 94–6, 102, 115,
    116, 121, 122, 125, 128, 131,
    132, 135, 140, 141, 161–4,
    167, 179, 193, 203, 204, 210,
    213, 215, 228, 231, 233, 237,
    245, 249, 251–3, 255, 258
  abstract counting, 22, 61
  count-all, 53, 54, 57, 58
  counting-all, 52–4
  counting discrete quantities, 48
  counting labels, 65, 94
  counting-on, 52–4, 56–8, 74, 253
  counting strategies, 40
  counting units, 11, 47, 48, 51
  double-counting, 162, 167, 203,
    204, 228, 233
  errors of omission and commission,
    25
  one-to-one correspondence
    counting, 57
  one-to-one errors, 28, 61
counting systems, 11, 12, 14–16, 22,
    30, 45, 47, 58, 63–5
  Chinese, 48, 61–3, 65, 66, 109, 255
  English, 11, 44, 45, 47, 49, 55,
    61–6, 69, 79
  French, 44, 45, 63–6, 73
  Japanese, 44, 45, 47, 48, 60, 61, 63,
    66
  Korean, 66
  Portuguese, 49
  regularity and irregularity, 61, 63,
    64–6, 88, 95
  Swedish, 66
co-variation *see* multiplication
Cowan, R., 38–40, 42, 251
culture, 2, 3, 7, 10, 11, 13, 14, 16, 66,
    77, 78, 101, 104, 108, 252,
    255, 257, 259
  cultural inventions, 13, 14
  cultural tools, 13, 245
  cultural transmissions, 13
Cunha, L. A., 178, 251
curriculum, 19, 20, 178, 179

Da Silva, L. M. C., 250
Da Silva, M. J. F., 250
Dal Martello, M.F., 73, 257
darts, 97, 98, 100, 101, 104, 107, 108,
    110, 247
Davydov, V. V., 80, 81, 84, 91, 251
De Abreu, G. M. C., 110, 111, 251
decades, 14, 15, 45, 47–9, 51–3, 61,
    63, 101, 188
  base ten systems, 14–16, 44, 46, 52
  decade structure, 15, 52, 53
  decade words, 15, 45, 63
  decimal structure, 14, 49, 55, 242
  tens, 11, 16, 45–7, 49, 67, 107, 244
decomposition, 107, 121
denominations, 44, 50, 51, 54, 62, 63,
    65, 68
denominator *see* fractions
density, 35, 187
Desli, D., 189, 209, 216, 218, 230,
    249, 252
detective game, 82
developmental stage, 61, 177
diagrams, 202, 203, 226, 229, 235
didactic contract, 247
directed numbers *see* numbers
discontinuous quantity, 147, 205,
    207–9, 212, 215, 220, 222–6,
    228, 229, 232
distance, 1, 77, 94, 187
distributivity *see* multiplication
division, 9, 11, 17, 102, 142–5,
    150–4, 199, 203, 205–10, 212,
    214, 215, 218, 220–3, 225–33,
    238–40, 251, 253, 255
  dividend, 206, 220
  division and fractions, 208
  divisor, 206–8, 210, 211, 220, 226,
    239
  long division, 11
  n-splits, 206, 209–12
  partitive problems, 210–13, 231,
    239, 243
  quota, 150, 153, 206, 208, 211, 213
  quotative problems, 210–14, 231,
    239, 243
  quotient, 206–8, 210, 211, 220,
    226, 238, 239
  splits, 145, 149–54, 205, 206, 208,
    210, 212, 220, 221, 223–6,
    230, 232, 251

successive divisions, 151, 153, 154
Douady, R., 247, 252

enlargement problems *see*
    multiplication
Erickson, G., 188, 189, 252
everyday mathematical activities, 1,
    170
extensive quantity, 104, 148, 184,
    188, 189, 205, 220–2, 225,
    226, 230, 232

Falcao, J., 53, 63, 69, 256
Fayol, M., 66, 73, 255, 258
Fennema, E., 205, 232, 250, 255, 257
Foyster, J., 3, 4, 252
fractions, 11, 20, 143, 147, 149, 150,
    154, 175, 176, 192, 202–5,
    208, 210, 215, 216, 218,
    220–2, 224–9, 233, 247, 249,
    254, 259
  denominator, 204
  equivalence of fractions, 202, 204,
    224, 226
  extensive aspects of fractions, 220,
    221, 225
  intensive aspect of fractions, 221
  ordering fractions, 226
Frydman, O., 41, 158, 160, 161, 206,
    252
functional factor, 199
functions, 9, 19, 168, 177, 182, 183,
    201
Fuson, K. C., 25–7, 32, 33, 36, 37, 39,
    42, 49, 252, 253

Gallistel, C. R., 23–5
Gay, J., 101–4, 108, 113, 252
Gearhart, M., 33, 257
Gelman, R., 21, 23–5, 27–9, 125, 252,
    258
geometrical progression, 152
geometry, 4, 253, 256, 259
George, R., 125, 126, 252; *see also* R.
    Wright
Goodnow, J. J., 108, 109, 112, 252
graphs, 3, 11, 19, 69, 235
Gravemeijer, K., 214, 229, 230, 252,
    253, 258, 259
Gray, W. S., 2, 253
Greco, P., 38, 253

Greeno, J. G., 115–17, 128, 133, 135, 257
Greer, B., 153, 196, 249, 253
Grimson, L., 196, 249
Grize, J., 142, 256
Groen, G., 60, 253
Guberman, S. R., 33, 257

Hall, J. W., 49, 253
Harel, G., 185, 205, 249, 253
Harris, M., 4, 253
Hart, K., 169, 170, 174, 175, 195, 226, 249, 253
Hatano, G., 46, 253
Heller, J. I., 115, 128, 133, 135, 257
Heraud, B., 14, 253
Herscovics, N., 26, 254
Hiebert, J., 130, 250
history, 5, 45
'how muchness' *see* rational number
how-to-count principles, 23
    cardinality principle, 23, 24
    constant order principle, 23
    one-to-one principle, 23–6, 28
Hoyles, C., 195, 245, 254
Hudson, T., 131–3, 254
Hughes, M., 122, 123, 254

illiteracy, 2
imperial system, 90
inflation, 4, 180–2, 192, 200
influence of teachers, 236
Inhelder, B., 86, 154, 186, 187, 215, 220, 221, 254, 256
intensive quantities, 148, 149, 153, 171, 173, 184–91, 199, 200, 205, 206, 221, 222, 225, 226, 230, 232, 258
    conservation of intensive quantities, 184
invariants, 10, 17–20, 41–3, 46, 47, 66, 75, 95, 114–17, 119, 121, 125, 144–6, 148, 162, 173, 175, 191, 199, 200, 206, 210, 235, 240–3, 247
inverse relationships, 116, 150, 238, 242
invisible economy, 105; *see also* street mathematics

Jahn, A. P., 250

Kamii, M., 67, 254
Kaput, J., 171, 177, 195, 254
Karplus, R., 169, 176, 254
Kaufmann, J.–L., 160, 256
Kemp, M., 3, 251
Kerslake, D., 202, 204, 226, 228, 254
Kieren, T. E., 145, 154, 205, 208, 220, 254
Kim, C. C., 66, 255
Kissane, B., 3, 251
Kohn, A. S., 171, 187, 258
Kopytynska, H., 79, 249
Kornilaki, E., 57–9, 157, 158, 254
Kpelle, 101–4, 113

Lamon, S. J., 220, 255
Lancy, D. F., 12, 255
language, 10, 155, 204, 224, 226, 228–30, 233, 246, 257
    linguistic cues, 55, 60, 63, 65, 117, 118
    linguistic hypothesis, 131
Lave, J., 108, 109, 112, 255
length, 35–8, 79, 83, 103, 124, 184, 191
Lesh, R., 185, 205, 249, 253
Light, P., 14, 86, 87, 91, 192, 245, 256
Liker, J., 108, 250
Lima, M. F., 53, 63, 69, 222–5, 255, 256
linear function, 182
Lines, S., 12, 25, 62, 89–92, 96, 102, 198, 255
logic, 4–14, 16, 17, 19, 20, 35, 36, 42, 45, 76–8, 86, 107, 108, 169, 177, 215, 226, 232, 237, 239–45, 247, 248, 254
    logic of measurement, 12, 78, 86
    logic of number, 42, 78
    logic of units, 13, 78
    logical development, 241–5
    logical inferences, 7, 36, 80
    logical principles, 5–7, 10, 14, 16, 108
    logical rules, 5, 8, 11, 77
logicians, 5
LOGO, 195, 196
Luria, A. R., 49, 74, 245, 255
Lybeck, L., 177, 255

Mack, N. K., 227–9, 235, 247, 255
Mangan, C., 196, 249
Marton, F., 116, 255
Mason, J., 14, 86, 87, 91, 192, 245, 256
mathematical procedures, 8, 11, 17–20, 33, 92, 95, 102, 109–12, 114, 119, 121, 128, 158, 161, 181, 196, 198, 215, 229, 230, 255, 259
mathematical symbols, 18, 201
mathematical techniques, 17
mathematical tools, 18, 248
mathematicians, 5, 101, 112
Maxwell-West, M., 171, 177, 195, 254
measurement, 3, 10–14, 20, 32, 34–6, 40, 41, 48, 51, 53, 61, 75–95, 102–4, 124, 125, 127, 129, 133, 140, 144, 149, 169, 191–3, 200, 206, 210, 215, 231, 237, 239, 245, 249, 250, 255–7
conversion of one measure into another, 84, 103, 169
measurement scales, 13
measurement systems, 3, 10, 12, 13, 48, 75, 76, 78, 94, 95, 237, 245
measuring operation, 14
rulers, 12–14, 76, 77, 79, 80, 82, 84, 86, 87, 89–95, 92, 94, 95, 193, 194, 237
units of measurement, 10, 13, 77, 79, 91, 92, 95, 102, 149, 192, 239
zero as the starting point, 86, 87, 89–91, 93, 97
Meck, E., 24, 28, 29, 252
memory, 15, 27, 45, 46, 54, 56, 62, 71, 80, 87, 94, 98, 211
memory strategy, 56
using rote memory, 15, 45, 112
metric system, 13, 79, 90
Miller, K. F., 61–3, 79, 106, 255
Miura, I. T., 66, 255
monetary systems, 48–52, 58
Morgado, L., 163, 249
mortality, 4
Moser, J. M., 119, 121, 130, 250, 251, 257–9
Moylan, T., 78, 257
Muller, D. J., 171, 255

multiplication, 9, 98–100, 102, 106–8, 142–201, 238, 240, 246, 249, 251, 253
Cartesian product problems, 163, 164, 168, 183
co-variation, 146, 148, 149, 151, 153, 168–70, 172, 173, 178, 183
distributivity, 99, 100, 107
enlargement problems, 170, 171, 195, 198
product of measures, 184, 192, 194
zero as the starting point, 144
multiplicative reasoning, 13, 20, 142–51, 153, 154, 157, 158, 161, 162, 168, 175, 180, 183, 188, 191, 192, 194, 195, 199–201, 205, 238, 240, 246, 251, 253, 254, 258, 259
multi-digit numbers, 50, 51, 68

Nesher, P., 162, 256
Neuman, D., 116, 255
Noelting, G., 169, 186, 187, 256
non-conventional units, 87
Noss, R., 195, 245, 254
numbers, 3–5, 7, 8, 13, 15–17, 21–3, 25, 30, 31, 33, 35, 41, 44–6, 48–52, 59–62, 64–71, 73–5, 80, 83, 86–92, 98, 102, 106, 107, 114–16, 119–22, 124–9, 131, 140, 141, 145–7, 150, 151, 153, 160, 167, 171, 173–5, 184–6, 188, 189, 196, 198–200, 202, 205–9, 220, 221, 225–32, 235, 239, 240, 244–7, 249, 250, 254, 255, 257, 258
directed numbers, 141
natural numbers, 141
negative numbers, 17, 141
number facts, 52, 121
number labels, 11, 71, 94
number meanings, 94, 122, 124, 125, 127, 128, 142–6, 148, 154, 199, 243, 244
number size, 126, 127
number systems *see* numeration systems
two-digit numbers, 69, 71, 80

understanding of numbers, 5, 7, 8,
  20, 21, 95, 140, 252, 257
written numbers, 49, 66, 67, 69,
  121
number words, 5, 7, 11, 12, 15, 22–4,
  30, 33, 42, 45–7, 49, 59–63, 95
oral numbers, 16, 17, 52, 59, 121
teen words, 15, 45
numeracy, 1–5, 10–13, 17, 19, 248,
  251, 242
numeration systems, 7, 11, 15, 16, 20,
  44–9, 52, 54, 55, 57, 60, 63–7,
  69, 74, 75, 94, 95, 242, 244,
  250, 254, 256
  Hindu-Arabic system, 46, 67, 244
  Roman numbers, 46
  written numeration systems, 49, 67,
    69, 244
  zero as a place holder, 67
numerosity, 32, 33, 36
Nunes, T., 4, 14, 49, 50, 53, 63, 67,
  69, 81, 86, 87, 91, 104, 107,
  109, 116, 119, 121, 134, 135,
  163, 176, 192, 235, 245, 246,
  249–53, 256, 258, 259; *see also*
  T. N. Carraher
n-splits *see* division

Okamoto, Y., 66, 255
Oksapmin, 12, 15, 44, 66, 78, 255,
  257
one-to-many correspondence, 144–51,
  153–7, 160–4, 166–8, 171,
  173–5, 177–81, 183, 189, 192,
  199, 206, 211, 212, 238, 240,
  242, 254
  composite units, 145, 162
one-to-one correspondence, 23, 26, 27,
  31, 35, 52, 54, 57, 59, 61, 70,
  74, 75, 87, 89, 94, 131, 134,
  135, 136, 138, 140, 141, 155,
  156, 158, 162, 206, 210, 236,
  241–4, 256
  spatial one-to-one correspondence,
    137, 242
  temporal one-to-one
    correspondence, 137
ordinal number, 5, 8, 46

Papua Nua Guinea, 12, 44, 257; *see
  also* Oksapmin

Paredes, D. R., 106, 255
Parrat-Dayan, S., 215, 256
partitive *see* division
part–part relations, 216, 218, 220,
  221, 225, 226, 232, 252
part–whole relations, 116, 119, 125,
  127, 128, 134, 141, 150, 153,
  203, 205, 215–18, 220, 221,
  225, 228, 232, 233, 252
Piaget, J., 5, 6, 8–10, 12, 30–2, 35, 36,
  86, 41, 142, 154–7, 160, 168,
  169, 177, 186, 187, 215,
  220–2, 224, 234, 241, 242,
  245, 254, 256
Piagetian, 9, 33, 37, 40, 221, 225
place values, 46, 67, 68
Pompeu, G., 110, 251
Post, T., 185, 205, 249, 253
Power, R. D., 73, 257
practical intelligence, 108, 251, 252,
  258
primitives, 10
principles before skills hypothesis, 24,
  25; *see also* how-to-count
  principles
probability, 17, 169, 186, 187, 189
product of measure *see* multiplication
proportion, 9, 89, 149, 154, 169, 170,
  172, 176, 179, 182–4, 195,
  196, 253–5, 258, 259
  half boundary, 172, 215, 216, 218
  orange juice problem, 169
  proportionality, 9, 154, 179
  proportional judgement, 172, 199,
    258
  proportional size, 171
protractor, 19
Pulos, S., 169, 177, 254
puppet studies, 24, 28, 29, 33, 40, 41

quota *see* division
quotative *see* division
quotient *see* division

ratio, 4, 77, 145, 146, 148, 150, 151,
  153, 157, 158, 160, 161, 186,
  187, 195, 198, 199, 253–7, 259
  corresponding units in ratios, 145
  ratio invariants, 145
  successive replications, 145–7, 151,
    153, 162, 167, 174–6, 181, 192

rational number, 202, 205–9, 220,
    221, 226–30, 232, 235, 240,
    245, 249, 250, 254, 255, 257
extensive and intensive aspects of
    rational number, 221, 232
how muchness, 220, 232
knowledge of rational numbers
    developed in and out of school,
    227
symbolic representations of rational
    numbers, 229
reading and writing, 2, 68, 69, 253
relations in mathematics, 3, 5, 7, 9, 10,
    18, 76, 77, 85, 102, 127, 129,
    130, 140, 144, 146, 148, 150,
    153, 154, 157, 158, 160–2,
    167–9, 171–4, 177, 178,
    182–4, 189, 190, 195,
    198–201, 203, 206–7, 209,
    211, 212, 215–18, 220, 221,
    225, 226, 232, 237–43, 245,
    246, 248, 256
relative values, 25, 51–4, 57, 67, 71,
    80–3, 85, 86, 111, 179, 244,
    251
repeated addition, 144, 153
repeated division, 153
repeated subtraction, 153
representation, 13, 16, 18–20, 58–60,
    68, 69, 75, 107, 114–16, 121,
    130, 140, 168, 194, 195, 206,
    210, 214, 227, 229–33, 235,
    243, 245–8, 254, 255, 25
Resnick, D. P., 2, 257
Resnick, L. B., 2, 49, 60, 114, 171,
    187, 206, 253, 257, 258
Riley, M., 115–17, 127, 133, 135, 257
Roman numbers *see* numeration
    systems, 46
Romberg, T. A., 205, 232, 249–51,
    255, 257–9
Rose, S., 29, 257

Samuel, J., 29, 257
Saxe, G., 12, 33, 78, 178–83, 192,
    257
scalar factor, 146, 147, 151, 153, 175,
    176, 181, 199, 200
Schliemann, A.-L., 4, 67, 104–7, 109,
    119, 121, 176, 235, 246, 250,
    256

Schoenfeld, A. H., 112, 257
Schonfeld, I.S., 38, 257
school mathematics, 104, 105, 108,
    111, 112, 182, 247, 251, 256
school type problems, 105
Schwartz, J., 148, 258
scientific concepts, 169
    understanding of equilibrium, 159
Scribner, S., 108, 258
second-order operations, 9
Seron, X., 73, 258
sharing, 1, 9, 41, 135, 145, 149–54,
    159, 160, 206–8, 213, 215,
    221, 228, 230, 237, 239, 242,
    252
shop task, 51, 53–5, 62, 63, 65, 66,
    68, 81
Shweder, R. A., 109, 259
Siegler, R. S., 28, 249
Silva, Z. M. H., 73, 250, 258
Sinclair, A., 67, 258
Singer, J. A., 171, 187, 206, 257, 258
social factors, 96
    social definition of mathematics,
        100, 101, 112, 235, 246, 247
    social environment, 246
    social representations, 235, 236, 248
social studies, 3
Sophian, C., 40, 258
specific situations in mathematics, 17,
    104
speed, 1, 98, 171, 189, 190, 259
Spelke, E., 21, 258
Spinillo, A., 172, 215, 216, 218, 258
splits *see* division
spreadsheets, 19
Stage, E. K., 169, 177, 254
Starkey, P., 21, 258
static measures, 124–31
statistical terms, 19
Steere, M., 66, 255
Steffe, L. P., 58, 162, 250, 255, 258
Stigler, J. W., 61, 63, 252, 255
Streefland, L., 2, 3, 171, 229, 230,
    252, 253, 258, 259
street mathematics, 104, 105–8, 111,
    178–80, 235, 246, 247, 250,
    256
street vendors, 105, 108, 178–80, 235
subtraction, 6, 8, 9, 17, 18, 49, 102,
    114–26, 128, 129, 133–5, 137,

138, 140–2, 144, 150, 153,
        199, 242–4, 250, 251, 253,
        257–60
successive replications *see*
        ratio
sugar-cane farmers, 110–12, 251
Sutherland, R., 195, 245, 254
systems of representation, 13, 19, 230
systems of signs, 17, 20, 94, 95, 104,
        107, 108, 119, 121, 140, 142,
        162, 191–4, 198–200, 227,
        235, 245, 246
Szeminska, A., 142, 215, 256

teachers, 1–3, 6, 17, 21, 48, 60, 87,
        96, 108, 110, 111, 178, 179,
        188, 236, 248, 251
teaching mathematics, 3, 4, 10, 19, 43,
        48, 49, 96, 101, 111, 114, 133,
        138, 168, 179, 182, 189,
        199–202, 229, 238, 248, 249,
        251, 253, 255, 257, 258
temperature, 7, 12, 188, 189, 249, 252
thinking tool *see* tools for thought
Thompson, P., 58, 189, 190, 258, 259
Tiberghien, A., 188, 252
tools for thought, 16, 43, 119, 140, 256
transitivity, 7, 8, 12, 13, 41, 42, 76–9,

81,154–6,157,161,215,237,239
trigonometry, 11

UNESCO, 2, 251, 253
units of measurement *see* measurement

Van den Brink, J., 171, 259
Van Lehn, K., 114, 259
vendors, 105, 108, 178–82, 200, 235
Vergnaud, G., 4, 10, 75, 116, 124,
        149, 177, 184, 205, 235, 253, 259
volume, 3, 80, 103, 104, 184
Voneche, J., 214, 256
Vygotsky, L. S., 245, 259

weight, 7, 12, 80, 103, 110, 146, 148,
        176
Willis, G. B., 49, 253
Willis, P., 110, 259
Willis, S., 2, 259
word problems, 104, 201, 249, 256
Wright, R., 125, 126, 128, 259; *see
        also* R. George
written numbers *see* numbers
Wynn, K., 21, 260

zero as the starting point *see*
        measurement *and* multiplication
Zweng, M. J., 231, 259